Silent Invasion

The Pennsylvania
UFO-Bigfoot Casebook

By Stan Gordon
Edited by Roger Marsh

SILENT INVASION
The Pennsylvania UFO-Bigfoot Casebook

By Stan Gordon
Edited by Roger Marsh

©2010 Stan Gordon

Interested parties may contact Stan Gordon at:
P.O. Box 936, Greensburg, PA 15601
724-838-7768
paufo@comcast.net

Up to date information can be found at:
www.stangordon.info

ISBN: 978-0-9666108-3-3

Library of Congress Control Number: 2010907424

First Edition

Printed in the United States of America

Typesetting & Design by Michael Coe of Bulldog Design
www.bulldogdesign.us

Cover illustration by Keith Bastianini
www.heavensshadow.com

10   9   8   7   6   5   4   3   2   1

Preface

A series of strange events was reported in 1973 from widespread locations across the state of Pennsylvania. Sightings of Unidentified Flying Objects (UFOs) were becoming common. Then, during the summer of that year, residents also began to report frequent close encounters with huge hair covered Bigfoot-like creatures as well as other mysterious events. For many weeks, police departments and newspaper offices received calls from frightened citizens as these strange encounters continued into 1974.

Researcher Stan Gordon led a team of volunteer investigators who responded to many of the Bigfoot and UFO sighting locations, and he documented other reports as they came to his attention. This anomalous outbreak involved multitudes of witnesses and brought many strange details to the attention of the investigators. Gordon's findings suggest that this was indeed a "silent invasion."

SILENT INVASION

Dedication

This book is dedicated to my wife, Debbie, and to my two step-children, Frank and Elizabeth. Without Debbie's love, spirit, and support, this book would never have been completed. Debbie stood by me as I pursued my quest to search for answers to the ongoing reports of UFO sightings and other oddities that continually came to my attention. Debbie endured the phone reports that came in at all hours of the night and day, and even accompanied me on some investigations. I am thankful to God that I have been blessed with such a partner in life. I am thankful to Debbie for sharing her family with me and making my life complete.

SILENT INVASION

Acknowledgments

During the years since 1959, when I first became interested in the UFO subject and other topics that dealt with the unusual, I have come in contact with thousands of interesting individuals. Some joined me in the search for answers to these unusual happenings. There are far too many people to acknowledge, but I am glad to have crossed paths with all of them. I want to thank all of the former members of the Westmoreland County UFO Study Group (WCUFOSG) and MUFON for their input and knowledge as we dealt with the events of that time period.

There are some individuals who deserve a special mention. One such person, who has worked by my side and accompanied me on numerous investigations since the early 1970's, is George E. Lutz. George's background includes having been an Air Force pilot and officer, and he has been a great asset over the years. George and I investigated many strange events together and we became close associates over the years. I consider George a dear friend. The two of us spent countless days and nights since 1972 pursuing reports of UFO sightings and mysterious creatures through the woods and valleys of Pennsylvania.

Robert McCurry was a member of WCUFOSG who participated in the investigation of some of the incidents during the

SILENT INVASION

1973 UFO and Bigfoot wave. Bob utilized his artistic talents to depict some of the events that were being reported at the time and some of his works are included in this book. Keith Bastianini, Charles Hanna, and Wayne Willis also provided illustrations for inclusion here.

Long before I had founded the WCUFOSG, I had met a great fellow named Arthur Haisley. The late Arthur Haisley of Greensburg was the Graphic Arts Supervisor for West Penn Power Company in the late 1960's. Haisley, as myself, had a great interest in the UFO mystery. Back then, we presented free illustrated lectures on the subject to community groups so we could educate them about this phenomena in our skies. I also spoke about the latest UFO sightings reported in our local area. Haisley was a great influence on me, and he encouraged me to continue to educate the public on these controversial subjects, as well as to continue my search for answers about these ongoing mysteries.

Brian and Terrie Seech, and Eric Altman of the PA Bigfoot Society, provided historical newspaper articles. I also want to thank The Latrobe Bulletin for permission to reproduce some of their news stories. I also want to thank John H. Reed, M.D., who has given me permission to use articles from SITU's periodical Pursuit.

I want to thank all of my friends and associates, as well as the public, who have encouraged me to continue to investigate the oddities that are reported, and to publish my findings so that all will have an opportunity to learn about the strange events that occasionally intrude into our normal lives.

Stan Gordon

Contents

SILENT INVASION

Introduction

It was on my tenth birthday in 1959 when my interest in strange and unusual happenings was sparked after receiving a radio as a gift from my parents. It was October 30, Halloween Eve, and the AM radio waves were buzzing with topics about things that go bump in the night. There were discussions about ghosts, monsters, and flying saucers. I became curious to learn more about these controversial mysteries. Were these stories just fabricated, a product of someone's imagination, or was there indeed some truth to these strange accounts?

I was an inquisitive young man reading science related books and experimenting with my chemistry set. Some of my relatives were involved in law enforcement, and I seemed to have an investigative trait that heightened my curiosity in learning more about these matters. I began to make frequent trips to the Greensburg city library and read all the books that they had on UFO's, ghosts and strange animals. Over time, I closely scrutinized the monthly periodicals and kept a close eye on local newspapers for any information concerning these anomalies.

Whenever I came across a local news story about a UFO sighting, I would contact the witness and obtain their first hand details about what reportedly occurred. Word of my interest in such unusual matters began to spread around the area and many unusual accounts came to my attention. The more people that I interviewed, the more I became convinced that many of the oddities that people were experiencing were explainable.

Many UFO sightings were indeed man-made or natural objects which looked strange under certain conditions. Many flying saucer or UFO reports were just bright meteors, planets, stars, satellites, and sometimes just lights reflecting off of meandering birds and insects. Other strange events quite often could be explained as well.

IFO. Not UFO
Conjunction of the Planets Venus and Jupiter
© Stan Gordon

Many of the stories that I was hearing originated from ordinary people from all walks of life. Some of these people I knew to be very reputable in the community and they were very reluctant to even discuss their mysterious event. Some people appeared very disturbed and concerned by their odd experiences. Many of these people found themselves in an odd situation, having to discuss these sensitive matters with someone that was much younger in years. Most indicated, however, that they were glad that someone was taking them seriously, and was at least taking the time to listen to what they had experienced without being ridiculed.

As more UFO reports came to my attention, it became apparent that some detailed UFO encounters could not be easily dismissed. Some of the UFO encounters that I began hearing about were very close range observations of large, solid structured metallic objects which performed maneuvers unlike conventional aircraft – including any known current technology. I became more intrigued, as there appeared to be more questions than answers concerning some of these strange aerial confrontations.

In 1965, a UFO incident occurred only a few miles away from my hometown of Greensburg. That was the UFO crash incident which took place near Kecksburg. That local unsolved mystery made local and national news at that time. The incident involved a fiery object which moved across the sky over a widespread area and was reported by multitudes of observers. That object, whatever it was, was said to have moved slowly and to have made turns before descending in a controlled-like manner into a wooded area just outside of Kecksburg, Pennsylvania.

Numerous eyewitnesses, including reporters who were on the scene that evening after hearing reports of the fallen object, confirmed a military response to that location. The next day officials stated that nothing was found in the woods, that their search turned up nothing. The official line was that witnesses had seen a brilliant meteor in the sky but nothing had fallen to the ground. Within days after the occurrence, there was much talk around the area that witnesses had seen a large military flat bed tractor trailer truck hauling a large tarpaulin-covered object away from the scene that night at a high rate of speed.

It was the Kecksburg incident that led me into a life long pursuit to try to find answers to the UFO phenomena and other mysteries. Today, many years after the Kecksburg event, I am still gathering information on that case. The evidence is overwhelming that an object of unknown origin did fall in 1965 and was apparently recovered by the military. Even now, so many years later, I continue to receive new information on this case which has yet to be resolved.

As local UFO reports came to my attention, I would conduct first hand interviews with those who reported such encounters, and quite often go to the scene of the event to investigate further. In the late 1960's, I became involved with the UFO Research Institute of Pittsburgh. The institute had among its membership some very professional individuals, including scientists and engineers associated with Westinghouse. Later, I became their UFO sighting telephone investigation coordinator. I stayed with the institute until its demise.

In 1969, I established a UFO Hotline in my home so the public could call in current UFO sightings. I also began to introduce myself to local newspaper reporters and police officials to make them aware of my interest in cases of an unusual nature. There I was, sitting down with experienced police officers providing them with details of incidents that I had accumulated about some very strange happenings. Surprisingly, I do not recall any serious ridicule and some officers showed an interest.

In order to obtain current information, I asked the police for their cooperation in passing on any reported UFO sightings or other strange events. In the months to follow, my phone line began to increasingly ring with reports of an unusual nature. Phone calls were coming in at all hours of the day and night.

While my interest focused on the UFO phenomena, I was curious about all of the other mysteries that were being reported on my UFO Hotline. Those calling in were reporting not only UFO sightings, but also claims of haunted houses, sightings of strange animals, unusual footprints, mysterious sounds and a variety of other mysteries. People from all walks of life and age groups who had seen something odd in the sky, or experienced a mysterious event of some kind, were now calling in. These people wanted answers for what they experienced, and I was determined to find out what was going on.

It soon became apparent that there was a lot more odd activity going on than I could handle on my own. I also realized that to properly evaluate these reported anomalies, I needed the assistance of people with training and experience from scientific and technical fields. It became my goal to organize a volunteer group of such people who could quickly respond to the scene of a reported phenomena and hopefully to get there while the activity was still taking place.

In 1970, I established the Westmoreland County UFO Study Group (WCUFOSG), the first of three volunteer research groups that I would organize which would investigate various phenomena in the county and elsewhere in the state. By 1975, we were receiving an increasing number of strange incident reports from throughout the state, so I made a name change to the Pennsylvania Center For UFO Research.

In 1981, I founded another group called the Pennsylvania Association For The Study Of The Unexplained (PASU) which remained active until November 1993. For many years I also was the State Director of Pennsylvania for the Mutual UFO Network (MUFON), which is the largest national UFO investigating organization. I currently continue to investigate and document these ongoing interesting events as an independent researcher.

During the years that these groups were active, I was joined in the field by many volunteers, including many professionals. Some were scientists, engineers and technicians. Others were educators, pilots, law enforcement officers, medical professionals and former military specialists. Some individuals had other backgrounds that provided useful input into this venture. Regardless of their talents, these people all had one thing in common with myself: to find the answers to these ongoing mysteries.

Some of the people who were associated with these investigative units requested to remain anonymous due to their professional positions. The ridicule factor associated with the UFO subject and other strange events, while not as apparent today, was much more of a concern in the years gone by.

I was trained as an electronics technician, so when I established WCUFOSG, I set up an elaborate radio communications center in my home. I also developed a two-way radio system where some of the investigators could quickly be dispatched to the scene of a reported mysterious occurrence. This provided a means of communication while out in the field conducting investigations. Also, a number of WCUFOSG members were trained by the Westmoreland County Civil Defense as radiological monitors.

WCUFOSG utilized the knowledge and expertise of the members, and in time became experienced in interviewing witnesses and gathering and documenting evidence obtained while conducting investigations. We were not out to prove that UFO sightings were evidence of alien visitors or that Bigfoot was an unknown primate. We were following the path of what the evidence and information revealed.

The team members were becoming familiar with incidents that could simulate a UFO sighting, or perhaps a ghostly apparition, or even an unusual animal in the woods. Over time it became apparent to the investigators that quite a number of the cases that would come to our attention could be explained. We also became aware that there were some incidents which did not have any rational explanation and that some of them had a highly unusual aspect to them.

The group obtained equipment and instrumentation that would be useful during our field investigations, some of which included radiation monitors, magnetic field detectors, metal detectors, cameras, and kits for gathering physical samples from the scene of a strange occurrence. I established contacts with some major Pittsburgh area companies which maintained analytical laboratories.

Some of these facilities offered to examine any odd materials that might be discovered during our investigations as a professional courtesy. In most cases, the labs asked to remain anonymous. While we had some field equipment and access to some analytical sources, we were still quite limited in our resources, as these were volunteer groups. We all conducted our investigations and did our research during the times that we were not working at our full time jobs.

SILENT INVASION

By the time 1973 rolled around, WCUFOSG had been very active and had investigated many UFO sightings as well as other unusual incidents around Westmoreland County, and other areas. The group had become well known and had received a level of respectability from law enforcement agencies around the commonwealth, as well as from the news media.

WCUFOSG quite often had strange incidents referred to them by the police or news media to investigate. UFO sightings were being steadily reported during 1973 across the Keystone state. WCUFOSG was constantly pursuing these reports of unusual aerial encounters, but none of us were prepared for the strange events that were about to unfold that summer.

Dozens of Bigfoot encounters were reported over a multi-county area. UFOs and huge hair covered creatures observed at the same time and location, mystery men, the destruction of physical evidence, and the apparent government interest of these events are just some of the experiences that we dealt with during that period.

It was during this chain of weird events that incidents occurred which had a decided impact on my life and the lives of some of the other investigators as well. It became apparent that there was more to the UFO and Bigfoot phenomena then we had ever imagined. These events were documented at the time of the occurrence and now many details concerning this unprecedented mysterious wave are being revealed for the first time.

Along with my team of investigators, I spent many days and nights searching the woods and mountains of Pennsylvania during the 1973-1974 events. We attempted to quickly respond to the location of many of these anomalies as the reports came to our attention. Frantic residents were calling police and newspaper offices to report their unsettling visits from huge hairy mystery monsters. Others reported strange objects in the sky, or in some cases, close to the ground.

Witnesses originated from many age groups, which ranged from children to adults. Numerous witnesses were very concerned about the strange events that crossed their paths, and quite often contacted law enforcement agencies or other resources to report their encounters in an effort to find answers for what had taken place. Many of the strange incidents discussed in this book were investigated and documented at the time of the occurrence. There were certainly some incidents that were obvious hoaxes and other instances where a misidentification of a natural object or known animal was found to be at the origin of the report.

Many of the witnesses were individuals who never believed that Bigfoot or UFOs could ever exist. That was until they had their own personal experiences. In many cases, their lives were drastically changed by these experiences. Many people were converted from doubters to true believers after experiencing first hand some truly mysterious events that were very real and un-nerving. Many of the interesting incidents which occurred during this time period are detailed in this book.

Encounters with huge hair covered and generally man-like creatures commonly known as Bigfoot have been reported throughout much of the United States and from many other parts of the world. Except for some alleged films, videos, and photographs, an assortment of footprints, and some other possible physical evidence, no substantial proof has surfaced that would prove once and for all to the scientific community that such elusive creatures really do exist. I have interviewed multitudes of Bigfoot witnesses, and I have observed fresh physical evidence at locations where such encounters reportedly took place. One of the most convincing types of evidence that something odd had taken place were the recurring cases where domestic and farm animals were behaviorally affected by the presence of these unknown creatures.

The questions remain, however, that if such beasts really exist, then why don't we have more physical proof, or indeed why is there no body of such a creature to examine? Some of the strange events that were reported and investigated during the 1973-1974 Pennsylvania wave discussed in this book may provide us with some clues to those questions. Some of the accounts reported in this book were also investigated at the time of the occurrences by the Pennsylvania State Police or other local law enforcement agencies. Some of these agencies filed reports on their investigations as they did with any other type of incident to which they responded. The state police generally filed these cases under a miscellaneous incident report. I was permitted to read some of these incident reports at the time.

Stan Gordon
Greensburg

The Ridicule Factor

In recent years, the UFO subject, and in fact various topics that deal with the strange and unusual such as ghosts and strange creatures, are being featured on many television networks. It is apparent that the public has a strong interest in such controversial matters and that the media has responded to the public demand to obtain more information. The aura of ridicule which surrounded the UFO subject for so many years appears to be dwindling. The public in general now appears to be much more open-minded concerning the UFO subject and other mysteries.

That was not the case back in 1959 when I began to seek answers to these strange reports. It was understandable why some witnesses asked to remain anonymous. This was also the same situation with some of the individuals who participated with me in the investigations of these unusual occurrences. Some of my associates held high positions in major corporations, education, law enforcement and the scientific community and were concerned over how their peers might judge them. However, there were some witnesses and associates who stood up publicly to any controversy or ridicule. These people felt that acknowledging the reality of the events gave the case and the subject in general more credibility. As time went on, when word of such incidents reached the news media, the incident that was reported was viewed as being more credible when an actual witness could be acknowledged and sometimes interviewed.

The odd events of 1973-1974 that this book focuses on were highly unusual. There was quite a lot of news media coverage as these events were unfolding at the time. While some of the cases that I will detail in this book were mentioned by the media, most of the events which you will read about are not widely known and many are being reported on for the first time. Most of the names that are associated with the cases I will discuss are pseudonyms.

What you are about to read is not a science fiction story.

(The creature and UFO incidents described occurred in Westmoreland County unless otherwise indicated.)

Part 1: Bigfoot

A history of mysterious creature encounters in Pennsylvania

We have all heard stories about Bigfoot, Sasquatch and the Yeti. Sightings of rather large hair covered man-like beasts, or in some cases, more ape-like specimens, have been reported throughout our country and from many other parts of the world. In the United States such creature encounters have been commonly reported in the Pacific Northwest. Many people seem unaware that sightings of similar hairy critters have originated from along the east coast as well, including many encounters in Pennsylvania and neighboring states.

Newspaper accounts describing observations in Pennsylvania of these hairy unknown beasts of the woods can be traced back to the 1800's. Historically, such creature accounts have been recorded for many years. In 1931, a dark hairy bipedal creature was said to have made some repeat visits to a farm in Fayette County near Indianhead. In July of 1954, a seven-foot-tall hairy beast was seen walking by a wooded area near Latrobe. At that location, rows of corn were found broken and odd footprints were seen nearby.

In the 1960's a number of Bigfoot observations were said to have occurred near West Newton and Lowber. One sighting in that area reportedly involved a close encounter with a white hairy creature. There are many even earlier accounts of such encounters with the hairy behemoths on record. During the late 1960's, when I was a student at Greensburg Salem High School I began to hear accounts of alleged Bigfoot sightings in Pennsylvania. There were rumors back then of strange incidents allegedly occurring near the Livermore Cemetery. Some stories originated from local teenagers who went parking with their dates in that scary remote location where they claim to have seen a gorilla emerge from the woods and then throw rocks at their vehicles. During later years, that general area became an active area for reported Bigfoot encounters. Since that time, I have had contact with numerous people who swear that they have encountered such mysterious hairy monsters from various locations in the Keystone state.

Part 2: 1972

Strange creature visitations and UFO sightings

During 1972, there were numerous UFO sightings reported in the state. Among those UFO events was a period of strange activity reported in southeast of Pittsburgh in Westmoreland County. During April and May, residents from widespread communities were reporting to authorities their observations of glowing spheres of light meandering in the sky. In some cases, formations of glowing objects were observed by many witnesses. It was during this local flap that on occasion, observers would also report some type of metallic material falling from the strange light sources.

Our WCUFOSG field investigators responded to the scene of some of these incidents and obtained samples of an odd metallic substance which looked somewhat like clumps of thinly shredded tin foil. Near Baggaley, on the Chestnut Ridge outside of Latrobe, several samples of the material were found in trees and interwoven in the grass. Near West Point, outside of Greensburg, the same type of metallic droppings was found near high tension power lines. The clumps of residue were comprised of hundreds of thin silver strands of various lengths of metallic material.

These samples were analyzed by various laboratories and were determined to be comprised primarily of aluminum, along with other known elements. While this material was somewhat similar to radar chaff that our military used to cause interference to enemy radar systems, these clumps of residue were apparently not designed to accomplish what radar chaff was manufactured for. The origin of this substance still remains unknown.

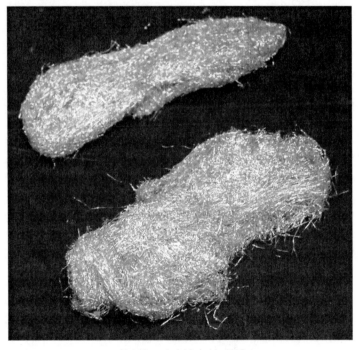

Metallic material found in 1972
© Stan Gordon

Besides the UFO activity, other rather strange events occurred during the spring and summer months of 1972, attracting the interest of the WCUFOSG. Residents who lived along Humphrey Road outside of Greensburg bordering a large wooded area began reporting strange high pitched screaming sounds bellowing from the woods. Other neighbors were reporting the sound of something heavy moving through the area as well. These people were unaware that residents who lived on the opposite side of the woods bordering a cemetery were also experiencing the same activity.

Two people in that same area were taking an early morning walk in May when they observed a very broad shouldered creature, dark in color and about five feet tall chasing after two dogs. As the creature continued to pursue the canines, the two adult observers walked over to the area where the creature was first seen to see if there was any evidence of its presence. At that location, they found several piles of fresh dung.

It may be an interesting coincidence that a security guard some weeks prior to that incident reported coming across a similar mound of huge odoriferous droppings off the Mount Pleasant Road near the University of Pittsburgh at Greensburg campus. The officer indicated that the droppings were much too large for a horse and was unable to offer an explanation as to what kind of an animal could have produced such a massive pile. To add to the mystery, just weeks before, the guard had found some strange large footprints not far from the same location.

Other reports of a strange creature and odd sounds continued to be reported in July along the woods on Humphrey Road. On the night of July 4, while hundreds watched a fireworks display at the Gee Bee department store on Route 30 east of Greensburg, something of greater interest was observed by many of the onlookers. A strange glowing object appeared in the sky and then shot off toward the city, passing over the cemetery near the area where the strange sounds and creature had been reported. The UFO made a ninety degree turn and moved off in the distance.

During the early morning hours of July 18, a couple living opposite of Humphrey Road, also in close proximity to the same cemetery, noticed two orange lights only about eight feet above the ground in some tree branches. The tree was only about twenty feet away from the witnesses and the lights were said to have been the size of a golf ball. To the witnesses, they looked similar to giant fire flies, but they did not blink on and off.

In the fall, passengers traveling near Latrobe reported seeing an animal similar to a chimpanzee and jet black in color. According to the startled observers, the creature was observed standing upright on two legs and later crawled over a guard rail. On the evening of October 1, people traveling on Route 30 east near Kingston Dam, located between Latrobe and Ligonier, reported to State Police at Greensburg that they had seen what they thought was a gorilla. The large creature reportedly walked out onto the highway and crossed in front of their vehicles. Also in early October, once again at a residence close to the cemetery mentioned earlier, a family reported that they heard movement and a scratching sound on their porch during the night. The next morning, a strange footprint was found on the steps going up to the porch. A color photograph was taken of the odd impression.

One very interesting series of Bigfoot occurrences also began about October of 1972, but did not come to our attention until sometime after the events. These events occurred up in the mountains near Champion and involved what appeared to be the repeat visits of a large hairy creature to a rural family and their property. The family had only lived at this location for about two months when a series of strange occurrences began. They did not know who to report these strange visitations to at the time, so a call was placed to the area Pennsylvania Game Commission office. There were no officers in at the time and they were reluctant to tell the secretary that there was a monster on their property, so they never called back.

At first they thought the dark, hairy visitor was a bear since in the dark they were unable to get a good look at it. When the creature approached the area, the family members said that they could actually feel the ground vibrate. With each step there was a thump. The family kept their gun handy in the event that the animal might go after their dogs. One of the fellows shot at the creature one evening as it walked down the road. They discovered large footprints in the area upon investigation. At night the creature would occasionally show up and walk around the yard, seeming to frequent a certain area of trees.

It was about three o'clock one morning when one of the family members and her friend pulled into their driveway. It was very dark and there was a heavy rain at the time. They turned out the car lights and the driver reached down to get her house keys. While still in their vehicle, the two people suddenly found themselves being thrown to and fro. Something was lifting and shaking the small car, causing the passengers to be thrown about. This frightening situation lasted for several minutes, then ended as suddenly as it began. The car had been moved a distance from where they had parked.

On another evening, their Saint Bernard seemed nervous and was very disturbed. The family heard their pet moaning some time later. Upon investigating, the dog was found with a large area of its skin missing from the hip area. Other large sections of skin were pulled back. The dog was bleeding profusely and there were long scratch marks on its thighs. Unfortunately, the dog died from its wounds.

When the creature returned one night, three family members along with a friend decided to investigate themselves in order to find out once and for all what the creature actually was. They grabbed a weapon and began to walk toward the yard where they could see the dark man-like shape standing there motionless. The witnesses say that they approached as close as about six feet from the creature. There was no doubt now in their minds that this was no bear. The creature looked like a hefty built man and stood about six and-a-half feet tall. The beast was covered with black hair and was very broad shouldered. Its long arms were stretched outward. It walked upright, just like a man.

The moon was reflecting off the creature's shiny face. Upon seeing the creature, a young boy in the group suddenly began to cry and became hysterical. Covering his face, he exclaimed, "Oh my God." The group hurried back to the house. The boy was still hysterical and a young female witness was also in tears. The family peered out the window and watched as the creature moved off in the distance. There would be other encounters with the creature at this location.

Another account had reportedly taken place a short distance down the road. The parents of a young girl had found it unusual that their daughter was not up and ready to go to school. When they went to her room, they found the child hiding under the covers. She did not want the covers removed and the parents had trouble taking them away. Once uncovered, the child appeared to be in shock and is said to have been taken to a doctor. The child later revealed that she had gotten up during the night and looked outside through a window. She said that she saw a big dark hairy man with pointed ears standing nearby.

There was a final incident with the unknown beast. Several friends were visiting their house during a party. While some of the group were drinking, one guest who was not intoxicated took a walk into the woods. It was a short time later that this man was found unconscious, the front of his face swollen, and had to be taken to the hospital. The man said he did not fall, but that something had hit him. Apparently, some of the group soon after saw a hairy creature and shots were fired at it. Supposedly, they followed a blood trail for a distance as it proceeded deeper into the dense woods. At some point, the men decided not to go any further. The creature was never seen again.

There was another very odd Bigfoot encounter which was believed to have occurred in 1972 near Penn Hills in Allegheny County. Once again, I did not learn of this occurrence until a while after the event when I had the opportunity to conduct an interview. That witness was twelve years old at the time this happened. She was a passenger in a car that was being driven by a relative. The girl was sitting in the back seat of the vehicle with a cousin. They were traveling down a dark road when suddenly the driver slammed on the brakes. Something dark was covering the windshield.

Whatever it was, it rolled over the top of the car, and ended up standing behind the vehicle. The kids crawled up toward the front of the car. What they hit was now standing behind them in the middle of the road. The witness said "It actually looked like a very large hairy man with no clothes on." The creature stood about eight feet tall and appeared slightly hunched. It kept watching the vehicle as the family sped away. The family never made an official report. The witness said that she would never forget what she had seen that night.

One of the strangest reports, however, occurred near Charleroi in Washington County in early October of 1972. It was sometime after this event that I received this report. The incident happened at about 8 pm in one of the small river town communities. The area where this occurred is surrounded by woods and old coal mines. Two teenaged boys were driving down a road heading for a friend's house when the driver of the car noticed a very tall figure running in their direction. Anthony (pseudonym) assumed that this was a tall prankster dressed up to scare some of the local kids, since in a few weeks it would be Halloween.

This very tall figure moved in front of his car, and Anthony drove his vehicle slowly up to the large form, making contact with its legs and actually pinned it against another parked car. The incident had taken place under some street lights, so the form could be seen quite well. As Anthony and his passenger looked up at the very tall figure, it became shockingly evident that this was not a human dressed up in a costume, but was indeed a huge unknown being. Anthony became alarmed as the creature put its arms on the hood of his car. The driver pulled his car back, which released the creature. The hairy beast continued to move down the street.

Anthony and his companion hurried down to his friends' house about two-and-a-half blocks away. About eight or nine teenage girls were outside the house on the porch at the time. Anthony was trying to tell the mother of one girl about what had happened, when they all noticed the huge beast approaching quickly in their direction. Anthony was now among the group of frightened onlookers trying to get away from the hairy hulk. The group began to panic, trying to get into the house, and some went through the glass window of the front door. Anthony was cut by the broken glass and began to bleed profusely. The creature ran off into the nearby woods.

Anthony was taken to an area hospital. When his mother arrived, he told her about what had happened and the creature they had seen. When George Lutz and I interviewed his mother, she said that when she arrived at the hospital her son was hysterical and crying. The woman told us that at first she did not believe her son's story of seeing the huge hairy creature, telling him that it had to be a big man in a costume. The teenager said, "I don't care if you believe me or not." The local police were called. The other kids were all reportedly quite frightened.

When George Lutz and I interviewed Anthony, he described the creature as standing at least seven feet tall. It walked upright and fast and was slightly stooped. It had a raggedy covering of dark brown hair, an ugly non-human face, and arms which hung down to the knees.

Several months after the creature encounter, Anthony began to experience another type of phenomena. With reluctance, the teen described his experiences. He had begun to see a floating grayish-glowing figure like that of a man but was not a complete form, as the legs were not visible. This figure was observed on more than one occasion and would just suddenly appear out of nowhere and would even go through a wall. The boy would scream out loud and yell at the being to "get away."

The story gets more fascinating, however. Anthony's mother, an educated woman, confirmed to us that she also had one experience in the same house that was quite similar. She was certain that the entity encounter had occurred in October of 1973. She was sleeping in her room and was awakened about 3 am by a brilliant light that came into her room. Then she saw a "silvery thing by the bed." The woman screamed and was now wide awake as she looked at the being. She described what she saw as a silvery, metallic, broad shouldered near human-like form. It had no hands, but what looked like claws. It had no feet and no lower body area visible. The being floated by the bed and somehow vanished. Then just days later, she was watching the news when a story came on the television about two fisherman in Mississippi who saw a UFO and floating beings. The woman told her husband that she had seen the same type of being. Her encounter only happened once. These experiences all occurred after the initial creature encounter was experienced by Anthony.

Toward the end of the 1972, there was another UFO incident of interest. This account, which involved a reported UFO landing, occurred about 6:45 am on November 7. The witness was driving to work on Route 993 near Harrison City when he saw something odd. It was just getting light out and visibility was good that morning. As the man continued to travel down the road, he noticed a strange object resting on an uncut grass field.

The witness traveled this road regularly and had never seen anything like that before. He stopped his car to take a better look. His first impression was that this was some type of float that was being built for a parade. As he sat there and studied the object, he realized that the object was not a float. The strange object was about forty to sixty feet in length and was described as an oblong triangular shaped object

Photo of George Lutz (left) and Stan taken in about 2008
Stan Gordon Archives

with a pyramid shaped dome at the top. From the base of the object to where the bottom of the dome structure began to form was about five feet. The dome structure itself was about six to eight feet high.

The whole object was brightly illuminated, but strangely did not reflect any light on the ground. The object itself was a florescent orange color, while the triangular area appeared not to be as bright. The pyramid domed structure was divided in half, and there may have been windows or possibly an opening. The right side half was a very bright orange color, while the left side was not as bright and reddish-orange in color. After watching this unusual sight for a short time, the witness became distressed and hurriedly left that location.

WCUFOSG went to the location of the sighting and searched the area for any physical evidence. We also interviewed other local residents who were unable to identify what the object might have been. From the position that the object was observed, it is possible that the object in question was hovering just above the ground. The general area near where this incident took place has been active for years with UFO sighting reports.

The members of WCUFOSG discussed the inexplicable nature of some of the cases that had come to our attention. We were aware of Bigfoot sightings reportedly taking place in past years in various state locations. We had considered the possibility that these creatures may indeed be a species of animal that science had yet to confirm.

We really did not know just what to make of those reports of strange lights and other paranormal events that were brought up by some witnesses who were reporting Bigfoot encounters. In the months to follow, we would be hearing of some really strange encounters.

Part 3: 1973

The Year of the UFO

If you were around during the fall of 1973, you might recall the numerous television news broadcasts and newspaper stories detailing the rash of UFO sightings taking place
throughout the country. It was a period of time when UFOs
were a major news item for weeks and the public began to
look skyward. My UFO Hotline here in Pennsylvania had
been active with sighting reports from the first day of 1973,
and the reports of strange aerial observations continued
throughout the year. There were, in fact, hundreds of UFO
sightings reported statewide and many of the most interesting sightings are included in this book.

On January 1, a UFO sighting was reported near Delmont.
At about 9 pm, a bright star-like object with various colored lights was observed stationary high above a barn.
The object suddenly took off with a burst of speed toward
the northwest, then slowed down, then once again gained
speed as it moved off into the distance. On January 16, near
Greensburg, a bright orange oval shaped object was seen
moving across the sky from the northwest to southeast until
it moved out of sight.

The next evening, there were numerous UFO sightings in parts of Westmoreland County. At about 6:20 pm, the UFO Hotline phones began ringing with reports of a spherical object, pinkish-orange in color, with a long white tail following behind it. The object was moving from the northwest to southeast, and moved very quickly and silently. The sightings appeared confined to an area between Latrobe and Ligonier. The Latrobe police station received numerous calls about the mysterious sky object, and a police radio message was broadcast to the area police cars to watch for the object. Both Latrobe Airport and WHJB radio in Greensburg received reports as well.

At 7:42 pm, other UFO reports came in from the Latrobe area where witnesses reported seeing two red spheres of light flying side by side in a formation that was moving in the direction of Greensburg. WCUFOSG investigators who responded to the report did not see anything unusual when they reached the area. Later, at 10:03 pm, there were additional UFO reports from the Ligonier and Waterford areas reporting a brilliant orange colored egg shaped object moving on a straight line course toward Johnstown. This object, which was observed through binoculars for over five minutes, did not make any sound.

At 10:30 pm, a UFO report was received from rural Hempfield Township. The witness, an airplane mechanic who was very familiar with conventional aircraft, observed a high altitude luminous object with two strobe lights, which did not conform with the navigational lighting standards. The object also had an unusually extra wide contrail behind it, which was unlike the other jet contrails in the sky at that time. Finally, that night at 11:20 pm at another location not far from the previous observation, two people reported seeing a glowing orange spherical object with a very long contrail moving towards the south.

Additional UFO reports continued throughout January. On the evening of January 25, a major UFO event occurred which even caught the eye of the local news media. It was a nice evening and the skies were clear. Some calls came in around 7 pm of a bright light in the sky, which was determined to be a star. Some other early evening reports were apparently just lights on high flying aircraft.

But just after 9 pm, the sighting reports became more interesting. Simultaneous reports were received from numerous residents from the Irwin and Jeannette areas reporting five orange round objects in formation moving across the sky. According to reports, this group of strange lights was observed for over ten minutes. One larger light separated from the others and hovered, while the other four lights broke into groups of two and moved off into the distance.

Other Irwin area residents who called in were very upset and certain that they were not watching conventional aircraft that over fly that area on a regular basis. Witnesses were also reporting a huge cigar shaped object hovering low in the sky. One witness I interviewed was very upset and stated, "What I saw next left me in fear- like seeing God. It appeared as low as the largest plane would fly. It appeared quite large and it's shape was like a cigar in appearance." There appeared to be hundreds of white lights on the object and there was a red light emitting from the back section. An odd smooth humming sound was heard until the object departed from the area.

The UFO Hotline in my home was being deluged with sighting reports. Area residents were also calling their local police and WHJB radio in Greensburg. Radio station personnel told me that some callers were frantic and almost hysterical. Some who called into the UFO Hotline were also very upset about what they were seeing. WCUFOSG investigators were being radio dispatched to various areas as the calls were received although it was apparent that witnesses had called in after the objects had departed those locations.

The next day, January 26, as the calls dwindled, we began to evaluate the events of the night before. There was no doubt that some of the observations were just lights from aircraft passing over the area. However, some of the observations were very detailed and interesting. We learned, in addition to the reports previously mentioned, that a formation of five lights reportedly hovered over the Crabtree area about 9:15 pm and were observed by residents from around Latrobe as well as in other areas.

About 10:15 pm, a man driving in his car near Derry just a few miles away from the town of Latrobe reported seeing a very large solid wingless cigar shaped object through the windshield of his car. The driver stopped his vehicle and got out to look directly at the strange object, which was low and motionless in the sky. What amazed the witness even more was that while under observation, the object reversed direction in mid air, then passed over the man's car and continued to move out of sight.

There had also been UFO sightings coming in from various other locations from throughout Westmoreland County and into the suburbs of Pittsburgh in Allegheny County. There were numerous reports of three amber colored lights separating, then joining back in a formation. They were under observation for approximately thirty minutes from some areas. An unconfirmed report was received of a strange light low in a field near Pleasant Unity. Additionally, some callers to a late-night KDKA radio talk show in Pittsburgh in Allegheny County reported seeing a large cigar shaped object with numerous blue and white lights over the Forest Hills area.

The next day the incident was a topic of discussion on Pittsburgh area radio talk shows. Several people were calling in reporting what they had observed. The story also appeared in local newspapers as well. What made the event even more interesting and more controversial was the fact that there was a malfunction in the radar control system at the Greater Pittsburgh International Airport that same evening. Apparently aircraft were being held in holding patterns over a large area until they could safely land.

There is no doubt that some witnesses misidentified some of the aircraft in the holding pattern over the area. Some witnesses, however, reported seeing the aircraft at the same time they were watching the UFO activity and were able to distinguish between the two. Various witnesses reported that as the conventional aircraft approached toward the UFOs, the unknowns would suddenly just vanish, then suddenly reappear when the aircraft moved off. In other instances, the UFOs would suddenly make a turn and speed off as the airplane approached. I also received verification from the PA State Police Aviation Patrol unit stationed in Washington, PA, that none of their helicopters were airborne that night for any night search missions.

SILENT INVASION

Part 4: UFO Reports Continue through 1973

Many of the UFO sightings reported appeared to be just misidentifications of natural or manmade objects. Quite a number of UFO sightings reported around the Westmoreland County area were determined to be a lighted night flying advertising aircraft that operated out of Latrobe Airport. The following are additional UFO reports (or reports of other oddities) from my records or newspaper accounts of that time period that are of interest.

February 10, 1973
Manor, 2am
Strange object hovers near railroad tracks
Witness reported a strange object hovering over the railroad tracks, while another object hovered in the sky.

February 11, 1973
West Point, 1:30am
Red spherical object reported in sky
A woman reported observing a red spherical object that had a depression at the top of it. The object moved through the sky and made a "bumping sound."

March 1, 1973
Reading, Berks County, evening
Strange flashing lights over Sailors Lake

In an Associated Press story published in the March 2, 1973 edition of the Reading, PA Eagle, State Police at Stroudsburg confirmed reports of UFOs with flashing lights over the Sailors Lake area. A state trooper sent to the scene said he saw four objects move over that location. Local residents said they spotted thirty nine objects during the evening on that Thursday night.

March 2, 1973
Hunker, 11:45 pm
Luminous domed object near ground

Two people traveling on a rural road claimed to have seen a luminous, domed-shaped object near the ground. The object was making a whining noise. The lights on the object, which flashed on and off, appeared to coincide with the sound of the car radio, which was going on and off.

March 8, 1973
Delmont, about 8:30 pm
Star-like object moves across sky

A man was driving home after a Boy Scout meeting when he observed an orange and red star-like object moving across the sky. The car was stopped and the witness exited the vehicle to look at the object, which was still moving. The object suddenly shot up into the sky, moved at an angle, and continued on until it was out of sight.

March 8, 1973
Hamburg, Berks County, 10:30 pm
Capsule-shaped object low in sky

The witness was returning home with her three-and-a-half year old son when the boy pointed out something odd in the sky. The woman shut off the car radio and lowered her window to observe a strange object, which was low in the sky. She heard no engine noise. The woman described a somewhat capsule-shaped object to me, saying it appeared to be a solid device with a rounded front section and "fire engine" red lights in that area.

The object appeared narrower in the back section with white lights that were alternating on and off, in a slow constant pattern. When first observed, the object was hovering about fifty to one hundred feet off the ground and about twenty five feet ahead in a field. After about five minutes, the object slowly moved off through the field until it was no longer visible.

March 11, 1973
Delmont, 2:45 am
Cylindrical shaped objects reported

A man reported observing three nearly cylindrical shaped objects, that while under observation, became brighter and dimmer.

March 11, 1973
Jeannette, 11:50 pm
Lights seen over radio tower

Witnesses reported seeing two solid white lights which appeared to be side-by-side hovering over the WHJB radio tower site along Route 30. While over the towers, there appeared to be bright flashes of light, similar to lightning, directly under the lights. The flashes would change colors at times, sometimes orange or blue. When the flashes occurred, the area under the two lights became illuminated.

March 13, 1973
Murrysville, 7:45 am
Transparent object observed in sky

The witness observed a UFO while looking out of a window as her husband was pulling out of the driveway. Her attention was drawn to a very strange shaped object moving across the sky that resembled an elongated arrowhead. The large device was transparent with a thin black outline. The front and rear of the object was more prominent. The object moved steadily across the sky in a straight line and was observed for about a minute. There were no lights on the object and no sound was heard.

March 15, 1973
Stahlstown, 7:20 pm
Elongated object seen 500 feet off the ground

Two people were in their vehicle near Cook Township on their way to church. The sky was cloudy at the time and there was a low cloud layer. They observed an elongated object about five hundred feet off the ground that was moving steadily across the sky toward the north. The object was solid and dark and there were a number of flashing lights at the bottom of the object which appeared to reflect off of the low clouds. They stopped the car and turned the motor off and said they heard no sound while the object was being observed.

March 15, 1973
Milton, Northumberland County, 8 pm
Odor, then strange objects reported

The Standard newspaper of Milton, PA, reported in their March 16, 1973 edition, that residents reported a strange smell in the area as the daylight was ending. Then area residents began reporting strange objects in the sky. Some witnesses reported one object, while others saw two or three. Some of the objects had flashing lights.

March 16, 1973
Mifflinburg, Union County
5:30 am Domed-shaped objects hovering motionless

The witness was up early and went to his car to look for something that he had left behind. When he went outside, he smelled a terrible odor unlike anything he had smelled before. He looked up toward the woods and saw something very unusual. Approximately eight hundred feet in the distance, he observed five domed-shaped objects, each estimated to be about fifty feet in diameter.

The silent objects were hovering motionless about eighty feet off the ground. The objects were luminous, and they appeared to have windows as well. There was a light emitted from the windows which was not as bright as the luminous devices. While under observation, the five objects began to move slowly from west to east in a straight line pattern. The four objects appeared to follow in the pattern of whatever the lead object did. The objects then tilted upward, rose skyward slowly, and went out of sight as they traveled towards the north-north east.

March 20, 1973
Bangor, Northampton County, 7:30 pm
UFOs reported to Blue Mountain Control Center

The March 21, 1973, edition of the Bangor, PA, Daily News, reported numerous UFO sightings being called into the Blue Mountain Control Center. One witness observed two orange lights passing over the quarry dumps.

March 20, 1973
Sunbury, Northumberland County, evening
Police officers sight object over housing project

The March 21, 1973, edition of the Bloomsburg, PA Morning Press, reported that two Sunbury police officers were dispatched to a location where a UFO was reported to be flying over a housing project. The two police officers confirmed sighting an object with various colored lights hovering over the structure. According to the story, the officers watched as the object rose vertically into the sky and disappeared.

March 20, 1973
Greensburg, 9:07 pm
Cigar-shaped object reported in sky

While driving north of Greensburg, a witness observed a bright silver colored cigar-shaped object moving across the sky from south to north. There were no lights observed on the object, which was estimated to be between thirty to forty feet in length. That same night, I received a similar report from Penn, near Jeannette. In this instance, witnesses reported seeing two cigar-shaped objects with three luminous portholes. A V-shaped glow was emitted from underneath. The objects followed along one behind the other as they moved through the sky.

March 28, 1973
Robesonia, Berks County, 1:30 am
Couple reports object on ground

A very strange UFO account was reported in the March 28, 1973, edition of the Reading, PA Eagle. According to the story, a Robesonia resident was awakened during the early morning by an unusual sound. He also awakened his wife as he went to look for the source of the odd noise. They reported seeing a strange object near the ground in a distant field. The object seemed to change shape, possibly caused by the lights of the object, which were also changing to different colors.

The couple, as well as their eight year old son, continued to observe the object and noticed that there appeared to be movement from within. The witnesses say they saw what looked like a black stick figure that moved around and bent over at times.

The family decided to call the local police to investigate. Apparently just before the police arrived at the scene, the lights of the object suddenly faded out and the object was gone.

April 2, 1973
Kutztown, Berks County, 10 pm
25 people, police report motionless object

It was reported in the April 3, 1973, edition of the Easton Express, that a UFO had been observed over the area by twenty five area residents as well as three police officers. One officer reported seeing a multi-colored object which was motionless, and then vanished.

April 3, 1973
Greensburg, 7:30 pm
Amber colored lights reported in sky

There were several independent reports from the downtown Greensburg area as well as in the vicinity of Westmoreland Hospital of strange amber colored lights in the sky. One family had just gotten out of the car at the hospital. The husband related to me that his wife was the first to notice the amber light in the sky above. Their first thought was that it was an aircraft in trouble. As they watched, they realized that the light was hovering.

About ten to fifteen seconds later, a smaller amber object dropped from the bottom of the main object and moved off on a horizontal flight path. Then a second smaller object also dropped from the bottom of the larger object and also sped off into the sky. The two smaller objects continued to be visible for about five seconds as they appeared to fly in and out of the clouds. As the couple walked toward the hospital, they lost sight of the main object. The witnesses compared the size of the main object as similar to a street light observed from about a block away. The two smaller objects were about one-eighth or smaller in size compared to the larger light.

April 15, 1973
Between Penn and Manor, 8:30 pm
Multiple witnesses report low flying object

During this evening, UFO sightings were reported by over a dozen witnesses from approximately a one mile radius near the communities of Penn and Manor, located near Jeannette. Between 8:30 and 9 pm, two people were traveling toward Penn when they observed a bright round object moving across the sky at the altitude of a small aircraft.

There appeared to be four separated square windows on the object from which light was emitted in various colors. On the top of the object there appeared to be a domed structure with a white light within it. Suddenly, an aircraft began to move in the direction of the UFO. The lights on the strange object suddenly went out and it suddenly hovered in place. When the aircraft departed the area, the UFO slowly moved off out of sight.

About 9:15 pm, two carloads of people were following each other on the Penn-Wegeley Road when they observed a strange object at a very low in altitude. The vehicles were traveling toward Manor and were about a mile outside of Penn when they first observed the object. Both cars pulled off the road and exited the vehicles to have a clear view of the strange sight.

The object was estimated to be about one city block away and only about two hundred feet off the ground. The partially elongated object was estimated to be about sixty five feet in length. The front vertical section was wider and approximately thirty feet in width. From the front, the object tapered back into the elongated configuration. The width at the rear of the object was estimated to be about twenty feet.

There were two round lights in the front vertical area which were separated about ten to fifteen feet apart. The lights were as bright as a street lamp. Three similar lights were evenly spaced in the horizontal section of the object. The lights would dim at times, then become brighter. There was a gray haze surrounding the entire object, making it difficult to determine an exact shape. Moving very slowly and steadily, it seemed as though it was just drifting. Because of its slow speed, the object was observed for over five minutes. Although it was silent, the local dogs became very upset by its presence. The location of the sighting was very close to the power transmission line and the Manor West Penn power substation.

Later that same evening about 10:55 pm, a man was traveling alone in his vehicle and had just passed the Manor West Penn power substation and was going around a bend and approaching the Wegeley stretch. Suddenly, his attention was drawn to a very large glowing motionless object just ahead across the railroad tracks about ten feet above the trees. The surrounding area was illuminated from the glow of the object. The man pulled off the road and stopped, then rolled down his window. Still curious, the man got out of his car to have an unobstructed view of the UFO. The glowing object was about seventy to one hundred yards from the witness, and about four hundred yards east of the power substation.

The witness described the shape of the object to me as similar to a glowing spinning top. It's size was estimated to be approximately thirty six feet in diameter. The object was spinning while in this hovering position, and lit up the area with a "burning white glow." The object itself appeared to be a solid structure and gave the witness the impression that "it was white hot like molten steel." The bright glow of the object was described as similar to a "morning snow." At the top of the spinning object was a dome shaped structure which was the same color as the object. Around the center of the object were two or three rows of square windows which emitted various colors of light.

Seeing the UFO was strange enough, but there was even more to this sighting. The man explained that there was "something that was coming out from it." The witness related how he saw what appeared to be a beam of light, or possibly some type of rope, which extended out about twenty yards from the left center side of the object. The beam or rope was attached to some type of form. The witness was reluctant to say that the form was human-like, only that it appeared to be a hulk or a torso, about eight to ten feet tall and had a color to it.

As he continued to watch, the attachment line and the unknown form suddenly just vanished. He described this as like a string of lights on one circuit all going out when the switch is turned off. Moments after that happened, the spinning object suddenly took off at high speed toward the Harrison City area. He was able to hear not only a high pitched sound as the object took off, but also the wind blowing through the trees as the object moved above them.

The driver had kept his engine running and headlights on when exiting the car. While watching the UFO, the car suddenly shut off and the headlights became as dim as a weak flashlight. As the object departed the area, the man noticed that his headlights became very bright. Shaken by his experience, he drove down the road to find a telephone where he called the state police. The state police referred the witness to call my UFO Hotline.

April 24, 1973
Spring Mills, Centre County, 7:45 pm
Oval shaped object approached observers

The April 25, 1973, edition of the State College, PA Pennsylvania Mirror reported that three people observed a white luminous object that was oval in shape. The object approached from the north and hovered over the home of one of the observers. The police were told by the witnesses that at one point, the outer section of the object changed to various colors.

April 29, 1973
Belle Vernon, 10 pm
Huge white ball observed 50 feet off ground

Driving toward Belle Vernon, a witness observed what he described as a huge white ball that dropped down a short distance away in front of his vehicle. The object hovered about fifty feet off the ground, then flashed white, red and blue lights. After about twenty to thirty seconds, the object flew off. Just minutes later, there was another UFO sighting reported from the Penn area of an object with red lights that stopped in flight, reversed direction, and then moved off in the distance.

May 5, 1973
Erie, Erie County, 9:10 pm
BB-shaped object crosses sky

The witnesses were in the backyard when they observed a golden BB-shaped object crossing the sky at a high altitude. The object moved steadily and too fast for a conventional aircraft, yet too slow for a meteor. The object, which was non-blinking, moved from north to south and faded out in the distant clear sky. About ten seconds later, an second identical object followed behind in the same path as the first object.

May 11, 1973
Greensburg, 10 pm
Disc-shaped object hovers 100 feet over lake

Reports were received that several cars on Route 30 east of Greensburg just below the Greengate Mall stopped to observe a disc-shaped object reportedly hovering over the nearby fishing lake. The object was said to be hovering about one hundred feet above the water surface, and windows could be seen on the object.

June 13, 1973
Irwin, 1 pm
Blimp-shaped object hovers 500 feet off ground

Several residents reported observing a large blimp-like object about forty feet in length hover approximately five hundred feet off the ground for several minutes before ascending almost straight up into the sky and was lost in the clouds. A check was made with the Pittsburgh airport, which confirmed that there were no blimps traveling through the local area at that time.

June 26, 1973
Between Greensburg and Latrobe, evening
Low flying spherical object moves across sky

There were several witnesses from the Mountain View (East High Acres) area reporting that they observed a yellow-orange spherical object that moved slowly over that area toward Route 30. The object was observed once at close range and twice much higher in the sky. Here is an account written by eyewitness Roger Marsh.

It was Tuesday, June 26, 1973. Elvis Presley was appearing in concert in Uniondale, NY. The Watergate Hearings were well underway. President Nixon met this evening at the Western White House in San Clemente, CA with Russian leader Leonid Breshnev. I was 16 years old and enjoying the summer days between my junior and senior year of high school. An aunt and uncle and their five children lived several blocks from my home in Mountain View (East High

Acres) outside of Greensburg, and I had driven there this one evening, parked in front of their home, and was standing along Seminary Drive with several of my cousins and friends just after dark.

As we were standing there talking, we looked up into the sky and noticed a very peculiar sight. An object the color of the moon, oval shaped, and at just above the tree tops, was silently gliding above the street in the distance. I recall at first that it appeared in the distance to be about the size of a full moon. We looked and we watched, and personally, I could not fit what I was seeing into the long list of mental pictures of what I knew was built to fly. There was a strange awe as the lighted shape drifted immediately overhead and then disappeared as it passed over the gates of what was then St. Joseph's Seminary.

The moment that I tend to lock into when recalling this sighting is that point when the object was directly above me. I would guess the size to be about 30 feet across and the entire object roughly the color of the full moon, and about 30 feet in the air. There was an eerie feeling as it moved – it was silent, but there was a whispy sound one might hear when a weighted object is moving through the air. This definitely appeared to be a solid object moving in a controlled manner. It had followed the path of Seminary Drive – coming from the direction of Mt. View Drive. At the point where Seminary Drive makes a 90-degree turn at the seminary gates, it continued in a straight line over the gates. The land within St. Joseph's Seminary slopes down to Route 30, and the object appeared to remain at this stationary 30 feet off the ground as it moved away from us and toward Route 30 until it fell out of sight.

After the light passed, I remember looking the opposite direction, down Seminary Drive behind me, and seeing four or five homeowners and their families, those who just happened to be out in their yards, standing in awe and staring in the direction of the seminary.

I immediately went to my uncle's home and telephoned my father, and then I drove to my home to talk with him about what I had just seen. As I pulled into our driveway, friends of my parents and their children pulled into the driveway as well. They got out of their car and told my father how they had just seen the strange light passing over their home on the other end of the neighborhood and they were convinced that it was a UFO.

After we all talked for several minutes, it was decided that the best sky viewing spot was from the front yard of our friend's home and we all drove there to watch. After an hour of sky gazing, my father went home, but I stayed with the neighborhood group that had grown to about 25 people.

About an hour later, a series of two more strange phenomena occurred. In the distant sky above, a much smaller light appeared. It was the same color, like the color of the moon, but appeared much smaller and much farther out in the sky. The object streaked across the sky at a very fast rate and then came to a sudden stop. It stayed in this stationary position for several minutes, and then made a sudden move downward and stopped again. Then it moved to the right a short distance and stopped again. And then it moved upward at a tremendous speed, stopping at about the altitude it had been at originally. It stayed in this spot momentarily, and then moved to the right a short distance, and then speeded downward again to the lower stopping altitude. It stayed at this position for several minutes, and then it whisked itself upward and off to the right at a very quick speed and finally disappeared from sight.

Within just several minutes of its disappearance, two jets moved into the same sky area and did formation-like movements in the sky, and then moved off into the same area that the UFO moved to. Now again several minutes passed, and two small planes came in, also in a formation-like move, circling the area, and they too moved off into the sky in the same direction.

We watched and the sky was silent for possibly another hour. And then the entire scene replayed itself exactly as it had the previous hour. The strange light appeared again in the sky, streaking across the horizon and stopping in the same spot, then moving downward rapidly, then moving to the right, then up again, then to the right, then down again, and then flying up and off to our right and disappearing. Again the two jets came flying close together, circling the area, and flying off in the same direction. The two light aircraft came as well, making the same formation circles, and again flying off in the same direction.

Our evening vigil went on for several more hours, but in vain. We saw nothing more.

These incidents that night were not reported to the authorities by anyone that I knew of—although my father called our sighting into ufologist Stan Gordon. Interestingly, I read about a sighting from that same day – from Phoenix, Arizona – where the description of the craft seemed very similar. A woman reported seeing a craft as a "large, illuminated spherical object, hovering in a spot just above some trees beyond her patio." (David F. Webb, Proceedings of the CUFOS Conference: 1976, p. 270). And in another case on the same date, "from a cabin on the Rothwell Ranch in Piedmont, Missouri, two men watched as a bright light that had a ring around it rose from low on the ESE horizon, moved up-down, then left-right, for a distance of 15 degrees over a 30 minute period beginning at 10:30 pm" (MUFON database of field investigations, case file dated July 9, 1973, field investigator Dan A. Rothwell).

June 27, 1973
Apollo, 12:15 am
Domed-shaped object emits red-green flames
A witness reported observing a dome-shaped object with red and green flames emitting from the center section moving across the sky.

June 28, 1973
North Charleroi, Washington County, 12:15 am
Fishermen engulfed in bright light
Several men decided to do some early morning fishing from the boat docks along the river when suddenly they were engulfed in a bright light from above. They looked skyward and saw that a bright round light was hovering low above them. The light stayed overhead, but moved in a slight rocking motion. An unusual humming sound emitted from the luminous source. A flashlight beam was directed toward the light in an on-and-off pattern. A similar light pattern was returned from the unknown light. This exchange of signaling occurred several times. The light stayed above for an extended period of time before it departed the area.

July 2, 1973
Irwin, 10:30 pm
Officer and wife watch object in the sky

A law enforcement officer and his wife observed a spherical gold colored object with what appeared to be two yellow headlights moving toward the west about five hundred feet above the ground.

July 5, 1973
Bethel Park, Allegheny County, dusk
Bright red ball in sky seen by witnesses

Several people witnessed a bright red ball of light making darting motions above their house. While under observation, the silent object would change colors from a glowing red, to pink, and then to a deep purple before it moved off in the distance.

July 6, 1973
Erie, Erie County, 1:39 am
Officer sees lights drop into lake

A police officer observed strange lights in the sky which appeared to have dropped into the lake. The officer observed two lights which appeared side-by-side for about five seconds. The left light was white, while the right light was red. The lights remained steady as they moved downward from the sky at a continuous pace. There was no sound detected while the lights were under observation. The officer called the report into his station and both the FAA and Coast Guard were notified. Apparently there were no reports of any missing aircraft.

July 8, 1973
Fayette City, Fayette County, 2 am
Witness observes ball in sky

The witness was sitting out on his porch when he saw a burnt orange colored ball in the sky that appeared to hover in the same location for about forty five minutes. The solid sphere made no sound and appeared to be spinning before it departed. The witness called the State Police at Belle Vernon, who told him to call the UFO Hotline.

July 14, 1973
Between Greensburg and Latrobe, 12:26 am
Man watches dome-shaped object in sky

The witness was driving on Route 30 heading west when he observed a dim orange-yellow object moving slowly across the sky in his direction. At first the man thought it was a small aircraft about to land at the airport, but as the object passed in the light of the moon, a solid domed-shaped object could clearly be seen. There appeared to be two amber colored lights close to each other at the bottom of the object. Once the object passed the moon, only the lights could be seen.

Suddenly from the top of the right side of the object, what looked similar to a bright reddish-orange flare, one which left a long thin trail of light, fell downwards. There were bright orange sparks, even brighter than the main object also seen at that time. The main object traveled about another eight seconds, when another similar flare and sparks were emitted. Suddenly the main light just went out. The witness speculated that either it turned off its lights, or it just suddenly vanished.

July 18, 1973
Jeannette, 8:50 pm
Man photographs BB-shaped object in sky

An odd golden BB-shaped object was observed and photographed by a witness with an extensive scientific background, who is also an amateur astronomer. The man noticed a bright light in the daylight sky, where no star or planet was known to be positioned.

The man quickly ran for his camera and telescope. Through the telescope, the object looked like a BB, with the sun reflecting off of the two corners.) He was able to obtain three color pictures before the object suddenly disappeared and could no longer be seen.

July 18, 1973-Object Photographed over Jeannette
Used with permission of the photographer

July 18, 1973
Latrobe, 10:15 pm
Football-shaped object seen low in sky

As a witness was watching the lighted advertising airplane flying over the area, a second object appeared in the distant sky. It appeared to be an aircraft with no landing gear and was moving in the direction of the witness. No sound could be heard from what was thought to be an aircraft about to crash land. When almost directly above the witness, he saw a glowing-football shaped object. The wings were not conventional in appearance, but long and thin. The wingtips had several cuts or points at the ends. There were no lights, landing gear, fuselage, nor tail or nose section. The object also had sharply defined edges. The object appeared similar in size to that of a Piper Cub aircraft. The object was silvery white in color, and was only about two hundred feet off the ground. It ascended until it was about five hundred feet high when it made a change in direction. The object dropped back down to about a two hundred feet altitude until it moved out of sight at an unbelievable speed, according to the witness.

July 21, 1973
Turtle Creek, Allegheny County, 10 pm
Single object in sky separates into three objects

While staring out of a window toward the west, a man observed a steady yellow-orange object that appeared stationary for several minutes. After about five minutes, the object moved off toward the south and then stopped. The witness called his wife who watched as the light began to move toward them. The object began to rise in altitude and rose straight up into the sky. As it moved upward, the object separated into three cone-shaped objects that suddenly vanished.

July 23, 1973
Pittsburgh, Allegheny County, 7:30 pm
Man observes transparent spherical object in sky

The witness was watching several fellows golfing near the South Park area. Looking toward the north, he noticed a small transparent spherical object, like a soap bubble, floating in his direction. The object was about fifteen to eighteen inches in diameter. The object when first seen appeared to be about sixty to seventy feet off the ground and about three hundred feet away. The sphere was moving in a descending straight line at about fifteen miles per hour.

As the sphere approached to a distance of about ten feet and about twenty feet overhead, the man reached to grab it, but it was still too far away. It appeared that at the same moment the witness stood up to attempt to grab the object, the sphere stopped and was motionless for just seconds. It then moved quickly off toward the west, gaining altitude and speed. As it moved away, it also appeared to change shape and became cylindrical. The sighting lasted about two to three minutes.

July 29, 1973
Irwin, 9:30 pm
Two women watch while yard illuminated by object

Two women observed two green lights in the distance behind this home. They assumed the lights were part of an airplane. As the object approached closer, it appeared to get larger in size and was round in shape. The object, which was now solid and luminous green, dropped lower to the ground and appeared to stop only a few feet above the backyard. The entire yard and window were illuminated by the object.

One woman hurried over to another location to get a better look only to find that the object was gone. The woman, after seeing the lights, felt cold and chilled all over. She went outside to look around and found her dog, which was tied behind the house, shaking and shivering and trying to get as close to the house as possible. At one point, the object hovered over some evergreen trees, which were only about eighteen feet high.

SILENT INVASION

Part 5: The Incredible Bigfoot Wave of 1973

July, 31, 1973
The prowler with glowing eyes

I was 24 years old in 1973, living in a quiet neighborhood in the City of Greensburg, which is also the county seat of Westmoreland County. Greensburg is a peaceful, family oriented community. As the summer of 1973 approached, I was spending more time in my 1969 Dodge Charger. My friends and I would frequently visit the Greengate Mall on Route 30 and stop in at some of the local fast food restaurants for burgers and shakes. One of our favorite haunts was the Winky's Drive In, where they served some really great fried chicken.

As I recall, the summer of 1973 seemed rather warm and humid. It was the time of the year which I looked forward to for some fun and relaxation. My summer jaunts were soon to be interrupted as I was about to embark on a trip into the mysterious- an adventure that one would have to experience first hand to consider the legitimacy of such events.

It began on August 7 when I received a phone call from a member of a family who wanted to make me aware of a strange incident which happened recently to another close relative. I could never imagine what an impact that phone call would have on my life. I also had no idea that this call would start me on an investigative journey into a bizarre series of strange events that still defies explanation years later.

The caller told me that the incident had taken place on July 31 in a rural location close to what was then the Greengate Mall complex located on Route 30 west of Greensburg. I immediately made a phone call and made arrangements to meet with the witness and I proceeded to that location. When I arrived, I met the man of the house who was the primary witness, as well as other family members. We sat down and before I had the chance to begin the interview, the witness asked me a startling question. "Do you see that before you're sick or before you die?" The "that" was what he was about to describe to me.

The witness continued on as he described what had taken place that evening as he was cleaning up in the bathroom. "I washed and I shaved and combed my hair and put some gunk on after shaving. I had some ice tea in a little jar. I'm putting on my slippers, and I started sniffling to beat hell. I said, 'what the hell could that be?' It smelled like something...a foul odor of some kind of cucumber or something."

The witness mentioned that the bathroom window was open and there was a screen on the window. "When I put the towel up against my face I saw two shiny eyes right in front of the screen. I sort of got scared, put the window down and here I had my tea on the window sill. It fell down, hit the commode, and fell on the floor." The witness indicated that the eyes appeared large and glowed red in the dark. The eyes appeared near the center of the window. Upon investigation,

July 31, 1973-Window where glowing eyes were seen staring at man
© Stan Gordon

the bathroom window was found to be over eight feet off the ground.

The family dogs were tied outside at the time. The family members thought that it was odd that the dogs, who frequently barked, were silent when this event was taking place. Other people in the house also smelled the foul odor that night. One boy said that it smelled like sulfur to him. The day after the incident, the witness had trouble breathing and was taken by ambulance for medical treatment. The man felt that the uncanny episode the night before may have triggered this medical condition.

May or June encounter with a Bigfoot in the Greengate area

During the interview with the family, another surprising detail came to my attention which had not been previously mentioned. A young boy in the room recounted a fairly recent occurrence, one which his mother verified. It seems that another teenaged son and some neighborhood boys had come to the house one day and told the others about their encounter with a strange giant hairy creature. This incident had occurred in late May or June, which was prior to the event with his father in the bathroom. The boys were walking on Greengate Road and were heading toward the mall around dusk on that particular day.

As the story unfolded, the mother of the boy suddenly stood up and demonstrated the movements of the tall hairy beast as described by the boys. The woman commented, "It was walking like this, big and furry." Then she went on to describe another more recent occurrence with her teenaged son. The woman stated, "Then the other day they were burning some brush up there. He and another boy heard something like sniffing up there, breathing heavy, like a horse, the boy said. That same night something threw a stick at his feet, and boy did they run. They came in the house."

Just then, the teenage son who was involved with those incidents entered the house. His mother asked him about the sound he had heard recently. The young man stated," It was almost dark. We heard like a snort, something like a horse, but it was real, real loud." I interviewed the boy at this time and later interviewed some of the other fellows concerning their previous encounter with the creature. They indicated that they had taken a short cut to go to the mall and they heard some noise in the bushes. The guys began to throw rocks in that direction thinking a deer was hiding in there.

As they started moving ahead, they suddenly saw a creature emerge from the bushes that was unlike anything the boys had ever seen. The bipedal hairy humanoid was walking quickly across the road and continued through the field. It was apparently heading up the hill behind their house. The boys described the creature as walking upright like a man, with pointy ears and long arms that did not swing as it walked. The beast was very tall and the boys estimated that it stood between eight and nine feet tall. The torso was relatively thin and the body was black and furry. The witnesses estimated that the creature weighed between two and three hundred pounds.

As we discussed the odd events that had been reported in this small local community, the family members brought up the fact that a neighbor's dog had recently turned up missing. They also mentioned that their relative who lived only a few miles away had their large police dog attacked violently by something. I would soon discover that similar stories about dog attacks and missing animals would become commonplace in the months ahead.

August 7, 1973
A strange three-toed discovery

After I had completed my interview with the group, I asked permission to walk up the hill behind the house to look around the area where the creature was observed. A few of the local boys decided to tag along and walk up the incline with me. As we moved up the hill, we carefully were looking over the terrain for any disturbances. We spent some time on the embankment and saw nothing out of the ordinary. Just as we were about to depart the area, I looked ahead and was startled to see the strangest footprint that I had ever come across.

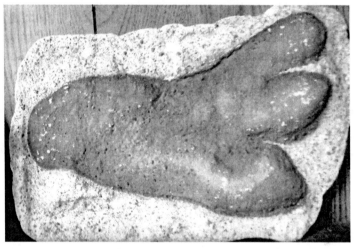

August 7, 1973-Cast of 3 toed footprint found near Greensburg
© Stan Gordon

The group of young men was also quite amazed at the strange impression that lay on the ground before us. The ground conditions in that area were not conducive for good tracks. Only one complete footprint was discernable. I measured the imprint, which was thirteen inches in length, and eight inches in width, but oddly, it had only three large toes. I radioed from the scene to the UFO control communications center in my home and another member of the WCUFOSG soon arrived at the scene. Photographs and measurements were taken of the track. We then mixed up some plaster of paris and made a detailed casting of the impression.

August 7, 1973
Beaver County
Creature with glowing eyes looks into mobile home

The odd details that had been revealed during the interview were indeed interesting. That- along with the discovery of the three-toed footprint made this quite a thought provoking day. The unusual events of that day were still not complete. While still at the scene of the footprint find, I received a radio alert from the UFO control center that one of our WCUFOSG investigators in Beaver County, located northwest of Pittsburgh, had called in to report that he was following up on a strange incident which had occurred about 1:40 am, also on August 7.

Reportedly, a man who resided in a mobile home community in New Sewickley Township had told police that he had been frightened by a tall hair covered creature. The witness described the creature as looking something like a gorilla, but with glowing red eyes. The creature was estimated to be about eight feet tall, was covered with hair, and was apparently looking through a window into the residence.

The WCUFOSG investigator said that he had obtained information from the investigating police officer that he had found an odd footprint at the scene of the incident. Another investigator and I discussed these two cases and found it interesting that while many miles apart, both incidents had similar details.

More Creature Sightings
Bigfoot reports continue throughout the area

In the days and weeks to follow, more information was coming to our attention indicating that other sightings of these hairy beasts were being reported from various widespread locations. Word was spreading quickly around some of the communities in Westmoreland County that local residents were encountering these unknown creatures. As the stories continued to come in, we attempted to track down their origins and found that in many cases, the events were unfounded. Some of the encounters, however, seemed to have credibility, and some witnesses were concerned and frightened.

A report was received concerning an incident that occurred during the month of June. Two eight year old children near Monongahela, PA, in Washington County, had come across a large creature that was black in color, was very hairy, and was digging in some coal. The kids emphasized that the creature had red eyes and a bad smell. The frightened kids ran home to report their experience to a parent. One child even drew a detailed sketch of the creature's face.

Not far from Monongahela in Washington County in late July, a man also reported seeing a similar creature down in the Mon Valley area. The man claimed that he saw a very tall, dark, hair covered creature that he estimated to stand about ten feet tall near a creek. The man said that he had called the local police who did investigate his report. The witness said that afterwards, he also called the state police to inquire about the creature that he saw. The man said that the officer he spoke with was skeptical of the creature reports, but he did indicate that their barracks had been receiving other reports of alleged creature sightings.

It was later learned that a family that lived near Merrittstown in Fayette County had an unsettling experience around late July as well. The incident occurred during one early morning when the wife recalled that it seemed as though the normal outdoor nature sounds were unusually quiet. She was standing near an upstairs window when she heard the sound of movement along her steps that surround a section of her rural home. Looking out the window, she saw the shadow of something huge moving nearby.

Her husband saw something quite tall running past a window from another location in the house as it moved toward a nearby creek. The couple only saw their uninvited guest for a few seconds. It was a creature that appeared ape-like and huge, yet slightly stooped. The woman stated that she could not even scream out at the time, as she was overcome with a feeling of fear, and began to cry. Her husband stated that whatever it was, it was not human.

The family commented on how strange their dogs reacted during this nocturnal visit. The dogs, which generally obey their masters, never responded when called. The dogs were later found hiding inside the garage. But it was how they got inside the garage which is most interesting. Apparently, the dogs were so frightened by the strange intruder that they tore some of the bottom of the garage door off to gain entry. After this ordeal, the couple detected an odd odor in the air which they said smelled similar to rotten eggs. In the distance, the people heard something large moving through the water in the nearby creek, and then the sound like a baby crying rang out from that direction.

About that same time period, over in Jeannette in Westmoreland County, folks there were also reporting wailing sounds at night, like that of a crying baby. The reported sightings of hairy monsters were becoming more wide-spread. On July 25, outside of Jeannette just after dark, a young man went outside to do some chores when he heard some noise in the nearby brush. About fifteen away, a tall hairy creature with red eyes stepped into view. The witness ran into the house to tell other family members about what he had seen.

On August 3rd near Plum in Allegheny County, a woman was sitting outside enjoying the summer weather when she heard the sound of someone walking. As she turned around, she was startled to see a nine to ten foot creature covered in white hair. The creature was only about ten feet away from the witness and was staring in her direction. The woman's dog did not bark while the creature was nearby and it re-mained quiet during the entire episode. The witness went on to say that the creature appeared to be slightly stooped, was very broad shouldered, and had a pear shaped head.

Other unusual reports were coming to our attention which suggested that this strange activity was not only continu-ing but also increasing in intensity. People were reporting strange high pitched sounds, large unidentified footprints and tales of family pets and farm animals that appeared frightened. And then there were the increasing reports of missing dogs as well as other animals.

One incident possibly related to the current series of reports occurred during the early morning hours of August 8, when Greensburg Police responded to a burglar alarm at Mount Odin Park. The investigating officers reportedly saw a very tall figure running along a high fence in the distance as they approached. The unidentified subject had vanished before they could get their lights on the culprit. On August 13, the UFO Center received a phone call from a newspaper reporter who stated that he had received information from the state police concerning the sighting of a nine foot hairy creature reportedly seen near the village of Hecla.

It was during one evening in July or August when two men were walking by the railroad tracks near Grapeville and heard the sound of brush crackling in the woods. Suddenly, they observed a dark humanoid shape with red glowing eyes running ahead of them. To see this strange apparition was odd enough, but they also reluctantly described other unusual activity that occurred during this encounter. It seemed that at one point, the form that was on one side of them suddenly just seemed to vanish, then it quickly appeared on their opposite side.

While they were observing this activity, no sound of movement was detected. The location of this incident near Grapeville is only a short distance down the road from Radebaugh. It is in this general rural area where a number of Bigfoot encounters were occurring. In the weeks to follow, we would hear other accounts from witnesses who not only encountered the strange beasts, but also experienced other anomalies.

On May 11, 1973, there was a report that motorists traveling along Route 30 were stopping their cars to watch a disc shaped object with windows as it was hovering low over a fishing lake just down the road from the Greengate Mall. Did this UFO sighting have any bearing on the Bigfoot activity which was soon to become active in that general area? The areas near Greengate Mall, Radebaugh and Grapeville, would become a hotbed for Bigfoot encounters.

In time, a more remarkable series of encounters would be reported from widespread locations where a UFO and Bigfoot would be seen together at the same time and place. What type of direct relationship exists, if any, between these two anomalies, remains unclear. But as more cases would unfold, it brought forth many more questions for which we had no answers.

August 4, 1973
Harrison City, 9:25 pm
Hour glass-shaped object seen over power line

The witness was sitting on the porch listening to the radio when she observed an hour glass-shaped object which was very bright, hovering over a power line.

August 4, 1973
New Alexandria, 10:27 pm
Spherical object with fiery debris hovers over garage

A spherical object hovered in the sky over a garage. The object was dropping some fiery debris which fell toward the ground. Some small aircraft appeared to follow the object as it moved over the ridge.

August 10, 1973
Greensburg Country Club golf course, 9 pm
Circular object spotted with illuminated windows

A woman and her children were driving on Route 130 when they observed a solid circular object which appeared to be descending toward the golf course as if it was going to land. The object was described as being as large as a family size car and was flat on the bottom. The witnesses were only about one hundred fifty feet from the UFO. The woman told me that there were windows all around the craft which were illuminated from within. This location is very close to Radebaugh Road and the Greengate Mall area.

August 14, 1973
near New Stanton, 4:30 am
Police officer observes glowing eyes

It was about 4:30 am on August 14 when a police officer on patrol in a wooded area near New Stanton noticed what he thought at first were reflector lights on a trailer. When the officer stopped for a better look, he soon realized that these were not reflectors at all, but appeared to be two glowing eyes, each about the size of a fifty cent piece. The eyes were connected to a tall, dark shape which the officer estimated was about eight feet tall. I spoke with the officer, who was quite reluctant to discuss his experience, but he was sure that he had seen something quite out of the ordinary.

August 14, 1973
Greensburg, 1 pm
Creature seen near fishing pond

A man was fishing about 1 pm just a short distance down the road at a lake near the Greengate Mall outside of Greensburg. The fisherman reported seeing a hairy bipedal creature walking in the nearby woods. This is the same lake that the UFO was reported hovering over at low level on May 11.

August 14, 1973
Greensburg, 1:45 pm
Another daylight creature observation near Radebaugh

A short time later that same day, two men were walking along the railroad tracks near Radebaugh Road over the hill from the Greengate Mall. It was a nice afternoon about 1:45 pm, when the men heard some noise in the dense brush. They assumed that a deer was approaching. What they saw was no deer, as they were suddenly startled when a tall hairy ape-like creature ran quickly out of the brush and continued across the tracks.

One of the witnesses, Philip Maline, age twenty two, was later interviewed by Vic Ketchman Jr., a reporter for the Irwin, PA Standard-Observer newspaper in the August 17, 1973 edition. The article headline was, "Eyewitnesses Sight Creature In District."

Maline, in his submitted report, indicated that he and his friend heard the sound of something running in the weeds and expected to see a deer, not an eight to eight and-a-half feet tall ape-like creature covered from head to toe with hair. The bi-pedal creature walked in a somewhat stooped manner, and swung its arms as it moved off. The creature was about fifty yards ahead of them, and they could see that it was sort of hunched back as it moved ahead.

Also at the time of the observation, they detected a rotten smell in the air. At one point the creature dropped down on all fours after it crossed the tracks. The men cautiously moved ahead still trying to observe the creature.

When I interviewed Maline, the witness indicated that the creature, which never looked at the two men, moved very quickly into the woods. I decided to contact Greensburg Fire Chief Edward Hutchinson. The Greensburg Fire Department was well equipped and trained, and among their assets was their bloodhound team used for area search and rescue operations. I made a request to Chief "Hutch" to take the bloodhounds to the location on Radebaugh Road to see if they could pick up the trail where the creature was seen earlier that day.

The bloodhound team responded that evening. They searched the area around the railroad tracks and around the woods where the creature was seen. Unfortunately the search came to a quick halt, and ended up as inconclusive. The dog team had to be called out on an actual lost person search incident. As I recall, the report came in that a young boy had decided to go out and search for Bigfoot in the woods near his home and apparently had not returned. It was about dusk, and locating the young fellow was indeed a priority. I later learned that the boy was found in good condition.

Some of the investigators and I were walking back from the site at Radebaugh when we witnessed a frightful sight. Not far down the road we watched as a car drove onto the railroad tracks. The car got stuck just as a train was approaching the area at a high rate of speed. Our hearts were pounding as the car barely made it out of the way of the train at the last minute. The location at Radebaugh is just a small jaunt down the road from where the man had seen the glowing eyes looking in the bathroom window in July, near the same location where the group of boys had seen a hairy creature cross the road as they were walking to the mall.

Also on this same evening near Irwin, several men claimed to have seen a tall, hairy creature walking near a cemetery in the area around Brush Creek Road. The next day, another witness also reporting in from the Irwin area, claimed to have seen a hairy creature entering a cave by sliding in on its back.

Railroad tracks along Radebaugh Road as seen in 1973
© Stan Gordon

August 14, 1973
Monroeville, Allegheny County, 9:25 pm
Disc-shaped object low in the sky

The witness was traveling near Monroeville when he observed a disc shaped object very low in the sky. The object tilted sideways while under observation.

The Creature Accounts Make the News

The steady increase of reports and inquiries from the public concerning the creature sightings indicated that the public was seeking information. There were already a lot of rumors and exaggerated stories circulating in some communities, and a decision was made to inform the local newspaper media about what was reportedly occurring.

The Bigfoot story was a major news maker when it broke, especially around the local communities where the creature sightings were reportedly taking place. The Latrobe Bulletin, The Irwin Standard-Observer, and the Jeanette News-Dispatch were among the local news media that covered the story as it unfolded.

Soon after the initial press stories hit the news stands, the phone calls at the UFO Control Center began to dramatically increase. The newspapers and even local law enforcement agencies were also inundated with calls from the public about the strange creature accounts. What we were learning was that people in some communities had apparently been seeing these hairy monstrosities for weeks but were reluctant to come forward. Many people had concerns that they would only be ridiculed.

While some callers were reporting recent creature observations, others claimed to have seen such hairy beasts in past years as well. Some of the people calling in were just curious and wanted the latest information. Other folks were volunteering to join searches for the mystery animals, and some callers were very frightened. The phone lines and two-way radio system in my home were buzzing with activity day and night. Police radio transmissions were also active with incidents dealing with possible creature sightings.

August. 15, 1973
Hutchinson, evening
Huge strange footprints in Hutchinson

On the evening of August 15, the UFO Center received a call from the state police about a report of huge footprints being found near the small community of Hutchinson. A newspaper reporter assigned to the Bigfoot search happened to be following our investigations that day and joined some

WCUFOSG investigators and myself as we proceeded down Route 136 to examine the tracks at that location.

It was later that evening when we arrived at this very remote rural site near Hutchinson. It was a warm and foggy night and it seemed as though much of the populace of the village had been eagerly awaiting our arrival. There were many inquisitive people there of all ages, including children in their pajamas.

The glow of safety flares placed on the ground by the onlookers prior to our arrival produced an eerie reflection on a series of huge three-toed footprints, the likes of which I had never seen before. They were not in fact the same configuration as the three toed footprints found elsewhere. Rather than the foot being narrow at the heel and wider at the toes, on these footprints, the width of the entire foot was nearly as wide as the span of the toes. Additionally, the joints in the toes were clearly defined. The footprints were twenty inches long and seven inches wide. The tracks were well formed and impressed deeply into the ground.

The foggy conditions created a spooky atmosphere at that location while we photographed the area and the tracks. We then made a plaster casting of one of the better impressions. The locals wanted to know just what kind of animal could make such a track. If this was a hoax, someone had gone to a lot of trouble.

August 15, 1973-Local residents turn out to look at the odd footprints
© Stan Gordon

August 15, 1973-strange footprint found near Hutchinson
© Stan Gordon

August 15, 1973
Hutchinson, before midnight
Something strange in the cornfield

Upon seeing the tracks and after interviewing some of the onlookers, the reporter needed to find a telephone to call in his story. The closest phone was just down the road on Route 136 where an outdoor phone booth was located. It was approaching midnight and there was not much traffic along the rural route. We pulled off the road to the right where the phone booth was located. The reporter needed some time to talk on the phone. Our group gathered around our vehicles as we discussed the unusual nature of the huge footprints that we had just seen. To our left across the road was a cornfield that seemed to cover quite a large area and continued up a hill.

The normal background sounds penetrated the countryside as crickets chattered away. As we were talking, suddenly the sounds got quieter and the group detected a strange sound like someone gasping for air. The asthmatic-like sound seemed to be originating from the higher part of the cornfield. We all stood still and concentrated on the uncanny noise. We then realized that something heavy was moving very slowly down the hill in our direction. Apparently the gasping sound was originating from whatever it was that was moving toward us and it was getting louder and closer.

WCUFOSG investigators did not generally carry any firearms on investigations. One person who had accompanied us that night and who worked with law enforcement became alarmed over whatever was approaching and readied his firearm. Our hearts were pounding as the heavy thud of something walking through the cornfield was getting increasingly closer. We figured that in a matter of seconds, this unknown intruder would be coming out onto the roadway in front of us.

As we anxiously awaited the arrival of this unknown visitor, a car suddenly rushed down the road and broke the silence. The loud sound of the passing vehicle must have scared the intruder, since whatever it was now was moving back up the hill. Unfortunately we were not able to pursue. The reporter had to get back to his office and we needed to take him back into town since he was unfamiliar with the area.

In the weeks to follow, other strange incidents would be reported from this general area. One local farm reported that something had killed numerous chickens. During the next couple of days, more creature reports were coming in from around Westmoreland County. In particular, many creature reports were originating from around Derry Township, only a few miles from Latrobe.

August 16, 1973
Derry Township, evening
Creature lying in field

One incident on August 16 reportedly involved a man who was driving that evening through a rural section of Derry Township when he noticed a large, hairy creature on the ground apparently resting on a grassy area. It appeared as though the creature was eating. Upon later examination by the witness, a large depressed area was located at that site.

August 1973
Derry Township
Creature pursued near Newcomer plant

Another incident in August occurred in a wooded location behind the Newcomer plant in Derry Township. On that particular day, some witnesses had observed a Bigfoot-like creature running toward and entering those woods. The local authorities were notified and a pursuit of the creature is said to have taken place. According to accounts, the searchers came across a path of large footprints that went into the woods.

The sound of something large and moving fast was heard in the distance ahead of the posse. Once the searchers saw the remarkable tree damage in the area, they decided not to go any further. Some pine trees along the path were reportedly pulled out from the ground, as if they were in the way of the quick moving behemoth. Barry Clark, a WCUFOSG investigator, and an experienced woodsman, went to the scene after hearing about the occurrence. Barry was amazed at what he saw. The creature had apparently torn out small pine trees and had broken some limbs. Barry stated, "It would have been impossible for five men to uproot a tree like it did."

Barry recalled one particular tree, a six-and-a-half foot tall white pine. He hypothesized that the creature had grabbed a hold of it, tearing the bark and branches with its strength, and apparently pulling the tree right up out of the ground. Barry found no signs of any tractor tracks in the area. There were large flat footprints observed in the area.

Barry commented, "It was something to see." Bob McCurry also went to that location after learning of the incident and took some pictures of the uprooted trees. Other people in the area also took pictures at that location as well.

August, 1973-Uprooted tree near the Newcomer plant
Used with permission of Robert McCurry

August 17, 1973
Kingston/Route 30, evening
Creature carrying deer

According to information received from a news media source and other individuals, an incident reportedly took place during the evening along Route 30 near Kingston only a few miles from Latrobe. Reportedly, a man was driving down the highway when suddenly a large, hairy creature carrying a dead deer crossed the roadway and entered the woods. A search is said to have taken place for the creature, and some police cars were reported at the scene.

August 18, 1973
Wegeley, 3:18 am
Huge creature in yard

A man called in a report from the Wegeley area, near Manor at 3:18 a.m, reporting that he and his wife observed an eight-foot-tall dark creature standing in their front yard. The witnesses had called the state police, who sent a car to check around the area.

August 18, 1973
Slickville
Creature near a mine shaft.

The UFO Center received a call from the state police and 911 dispatch center concerning a possible creature sighting near Slickville. A woman walking in the area was said to have seen a creature running across a road in the vicinity of an old mine shaft.

As the frequency of creature reports intensified, so did the influx of phone calls being made to the local police departments or state police, and often to the news media. The police did respond to some of these incidents, but in many instances, the law enforcement agencies were commonly referring callers to contact the WCUFOSG.

As the creature activity increased, the volunteer members of the WCUFOSG began to staff the operations center in my home twenty four hours a day. I was managing a local electronics retail store at the time and I had the opportunity to take some vacation time to investigate these ongoing incidents. I devoted several weeks investigating these mysterious cases as they unfolded.

Code Red!
Public safety officials became concerned
One police source called the developing situation a "nightmare." Public safety officials became concerned. The Westmoreland County 911 radio system at that time was based at the Greensburg police station in City Hall. Radio calls for police and fire personnel were dispatched from that location. For a period of time, as these creature reports continued to escalate, a special "Code Red" signal was broadcast to me over the Westmoreland County Civil Defense and fire dispatch radio channel.

This would alert me to the fact that an unusual incident had just been reported, and that I was to call into the 911 center to obtain the information so that I could follow up with an investigation. I had a very high frequency radio receiver in my car, and I was continually monitoring for such calls. I also had a number of meetings with state police investigators at the Greensburg Troop A headquarters who wanted to be kept updated on the current status of our research. I had heard, but never verified, that some troopers who patrolled the roads in Westmoreland County during this episode, were carrying high powered weapons in their patrol cars.

August 19, 1973
Derry Township, 2 am
Creature in field

A couple was traveling down a rural road in Derry Township about 2 am on August 19, when they noticed something very large in a field. At first they thought it was a bear. It was at first bent over as though it was doing something. When it stood up, it began to walk upright and the witnesses could see it's arms. They could also see that this creature was very large. The creature was initially seen near a large tree, then it passed by some other trees and began to move in the direction of the witnesses' car. The two people became alarmed and hurried down the road. I went down to the site to look for evidence, but nothing tangible was found.

August 19, 1973
Herminie, 6:50 am
Woman chased by creature

Later that morning, a woman was walking down a rural road heading to her employer's home outside of Herminie. It was about 6:50 am when she became aware of a loud breathing sound, and also noticed a terrible smell in the air. She had just passed about twenty feet from the corner of the road when she also heard the sound of a car skidding. Turning around, she saw that the vehicle had almost hit a guard rail. Her attention was drawn to something else which frightened her much more than the near vehicle accident. A very large hair covered creature was running upright only short distance behind her and moving in her direction. The creature was emitting a rapid heavy breathing sound, and it's red eyes were clearly seen.

The woman was nearly hysterical at the sight, and her first thought was to take off her shoes so that she could run faster down the road. When she got to work she told her boss about the monster, but he did not believe her. She later told another local person about the frightening experience. That person went back to the location where the encounter reportedly occurred. At that exact location, the man found a strange footprint which was much larger than his size twelve shoe, and the grass was trampled down. Other footprints were found which indicated that the creature had turned and had gone into some bushes. It appeared that the creature had gone down in the direction of a ball field. No tracks, however, were found in that location.

I was called to the scene, and I interviewed the witness as well as some other local residents. Cathy (pseudonym) appeared very shaken as she described to me what had happened. She said she did not take a lot of time to study the physical traits of the creature once she saw it, as her only thought was to get away from it. She said the beast weighed several hundred pounds, and was large, broad shouldered and hairy.

We found skid marks on the road where the witness said the car had squealed. One could speculate that the driver of that car may have also seen the creature, and slammed on his brakes in response to this encounter. We also located some large footprints that were not detailed enough to cast. The tracks led into some brush and into a berry patch. It looked as though the berries at one location had all been eaten.

While I was looking along the edge of a back road near the ball field searching for evidence, a car suddenly came around the bend at a high rate of speed and just missed hitting me. I went over to the car and found the driver quite intoxicated. The other locals knew the driver, and were able to get him home safely, and off the road. I was unable to locate any additional evidence.

August 19, 1973
Buffalo Mills, Bedford County, 8 pm
Creature walks down street

We had been hearing reports concerning a strange being that had reportedly been seen strolling down the street of the small rural community of Buffalo Mills, quite a distance away in Bedford County. This strange account later appeared in various publications. At about 8 pm, some of the locals were startled to see a human-like being of gigantic proportion. The stranger stood around nine feet tall, and was wearing clothing which was made of some odd shiny fabric, and of unusual design. This bizarre visitor walked quietly down the street drawing much attention. Where he came from, and where he went to is another part of this mystery.

August 20, 1973
Donahue, 12:01 am
Creature seen by railroad tracks

It was just after midnight on August 20 when several people were sitting in a car near Donahue. Their attention was drawn to a large, dark, man-like creature in the distance. They could see the shape of the creature, which was illuminated by the headlight of an approaching train. The witnesses became alarmed and quickly left the area.

August 20, 1973
Saint Vincent Cemetery, Latrobe, 9:20 pm
Creature near car, engine stalls

About 9:20 pm, a man was driving his car near the Saint Vincent Cemetery near Latrobe when a large hair covered creature ran out in front of his car. The creature could easily be seen in the headlights of his vehicle. The driver also mentioned another peculiar event. It seems that moments after the creature passed by, his car engine suddenly stalled out. The driver had never had any engine problem prior to this occurrence.

August 20, 1973
Keystone area, Derry Township, 10 pm
Witness passed five feet from creature

Mr. Edwards (pseudonym) was driving up the Derry-Superior Road not far from Keystone Park around 10 pm The man had just gone over a hill when his attention was drawn to a tall creature a short distance ahead that was illuminated by his headlights. The creature was described as standing over six feet tall, hair covered, with long arms and big red eyes, and "it stunk like something fierce." The driver smelled the odd odor just before the creature came into sight. Upon observing the unusual beast, Edwards stopped his vehicle to take a better look. The creature also appeared to stop, and looked toward the vehicle.

Edwards soon continued down the road, and passed about five feet from the creature. The creature never approached the car. The driver looked into the rear view mirror and the creature was still walking along the road. The witness stated that he could see the arms of the creature moving, and they were a little longer than that of a human. The witness had seen a bear before and he knew that this was not what he had seen.

August 20, 1973
near Irwin
Numerous Bigfoot tracks discovered

On August 20, a number of large three-toed footprints were discovered in a wooded location outside of Irwin. Local police reportedly went to that location the next day and searched around the area. The WCUFOSG was notified about the footprints on August 22, and an investigating team responded to that location. At that rural site, a series of detailed right and left tracks with a long stride were found on solid ground. They led into a muddy area, continued into a creek, and then led up an embankment that led into some woods.

The tracks were thirteen inches long, and fifty nine inches apart, and were similar to other imprints that we had been seeing at various locations. We all agreed that if the tracks were fabricated, someone had gone to a lot of work to create such a scene. In the muddy area, it appeared that whatever made the tracks had slid at one point. A number of casts of the various imprints were taken. One track was very clear, and we actually dug up the footprint and ground around it, and removed it intact for study. Just as we were taking a picture of one very clear footprint, a dog walked onto the track. I guess the dog was also curious about all of the activity at that location.

August 20, 1973
Derry
Creature hit by car reportedly vanishes into thin air

The Derry police contacted me about a strange incident reported to their office by a passing motorist. The man told the officer that he and his wife were driving between Hillside and Millwood when a large ape-like creature suddenly ran out in front of their car. According to the officer, the man appeared upset, but quite sincere, and stated that he hit the creature with his vehicle. The man swore that upon impact, the creature just disappeared.

What Are We Dealing With?

The events of this day were eye opening. The numerous reports of the Bigfoot creatures were indeed strange enough. Since the outbreak of these creature encounters, I was under the impression that we may well be dealing with an unknown zoological specimen that had yet to be scientifically confirmed. Looking over the incidents of this day, as well as reflecting back on some of the odd details that had been revealed with some other creature encounters in the past, I began to wonder what indeed we were really dealing with. A creature walks in front of a car and the motor begins to stall. In another case, a creature reportedly is hit by a car and vanishes upon impact. What about the fellows who say they saw a creature near Grapeville, which appeared on their one side, then suddenly re-appeared at an opposite location? I had no idea what mysteries would lie ahead.

About this same time, reports were coming in from around Derry Township and Latrobe that farm animals were being spooked by something prowling around. Strange noises and odd footprints were being reported. In one case, a horse became so frightened that it tried to kick its way out of its trailer. The owner stated that the animal became so wild that they almost had to destroy it.

A three toed footprint preserved for study
© *Stan Gordon*

August 21, 1973
Greensburg, About 12 am
Three creatures on golf course

Joe Banks (pseudonym) and two other people were walking on the grounds of the Greensburg Country Club just after midnight. The country club is located between Greensburg and Jeannette and just down the road from Greengate Mall. The trio was looking for night crawlers to use for bait on their upcoming fishing trip. About twenty yards away, they observed two Bigfoot-like creatures on the green, which appeared to be stooped over, not perfectly erect.

The three people stopped to watch since the creatures were not making any moves in their direction. Two of the witnesses, after a short time, ran back to their car. Joe stood there for about two minutes studying the strange beasts. Both creatures seemed black in color. The first creature was about five to six feet tall, and the other was smaller, about four feet tall. The witness said they were both walking upright and they definitely were not bears. Joe was amazed at the very fast pace that the creatures could walk. It seemed to him that in the time you could snap your fingers, they had disappeared in the trees.

The man had a low powered flashlight which he shined on them. Joe then returned to the car and left the area. Being curious, Joe called some other acquaintances and told them what he and the others had seen. About thirty minutes later, four individuals returned to the green where they had seen the creatures initially. Joe described how they drove in from a different location, and from that angle they could light up the green with the headlights from the car. Interestingly, the two creatures were still there. As soon as the headlights struck them, the beasts ran behind some pine trees near the road.

The witnesses got out of the car to have a better look. Soon after the two creatures were lost from view, the witnesses heard a noise from behind them. A large dark figure was exiting the woods a distance away- and walking in their direction. This creature was much taller than the other two. It stood at least seven to eight feet tall. The appearance of this huge creature was strange enough, but one of its physical traits stood out. The eyes of the creature appeared to glow red, and oddly, the eyes did not appear to be at an even level. The witnesses had enough and jumped into their car and left the area.

August 21, 1973
Latrobe, 12:15 am
Red eyes looking in high window

It was about the same time that the incident was occurring between Greensburg and Jeannette, but at a location about eight miles away on Donohoe Road outside of Latrobe that a witness reportedly saw two large red eyes staring into a window of a house which was eight feet off the ground.

August 21, 1973
Kingston/Latrobe, am
Creature prowling near mobile home

During the early morning hours on this same date, a family living in a mobile home near Kingston (located between Latrobe and Derry) reported hearing loud horrifying screams, a sound like heavy breathing, and something knocking on the side of their home. This event and other encounters with a large hairy creature near their residence caused the family to pack up and leave that location for a short time. The family had reported these events to the state police.

August 21, 1973
Derry, 2:30 am
Woman has face-to-face creature encounter

About 2:30 am also on August 21, a very strange incident occurred near Derry. It was a very warm night, so Sue Mace (pseudonym) decided to leave her window partially open to get some air. The woman was suddenly awakened out of her sleep and was horrified to see a grotesque face looking at her through the window only three feet away. The window was nine feet off the ground. The drapes had been pulled back by the creature. The woman stated that the animal had to be taller than her window since it had to stoop down when looking around into the bedroom. The woman looked again, confirming to herself that she was awake and not dreaming.

When the woman moved, the creature got up and turned, and moved straight back away from the window in an awkward and slow manner. Sue saw the drapes draw back to a closed position. It was quiet outside. The witness thought it odd that she could not hear the thing moving away. Some outside lighting illuminated half of the face. Sue said that she would never forget that hideous sight. She described the shape of the face as round, and it had dark hair. She could only see from the nose up, since it was blocked by the bottom of the windowsill.

The nose was flat, and pushed back, and similar to a gorilla. The eyes were more round than oval, and seemed deep set in the cheek bones. The eyes were dark, with no whites, and no eye lids, eye lashes or eyebrows were seen. Underneath the eyes there were wrinkles or layers of skin which looked almost burnt. The skin around the eyes and nose appeared flesh colored. She said that the cheek bones were high, and the eye sockets were not like that of a human, but were flat, and the eyes were deeply embedded.

When the creature moved away, Sue, who was too frightened to close the window, ran into the bedroom of her teen-aged daughter, who in turn closed that window. A short time later, her daughter ran into her mother's bedroom to which her mother had returned. The girl told her mother that she had seen the biggest shadow she had ever seen. The girl was used to the shadows cast from the surrounding trees, but this was different. This shadow was huge. The sound of something large could be heard walking, and it sounded heavy. A strange smell then filled the house.

The odor was described like something dead, or old rotten meat that had been left out. The smell lingered in the house for several days. I learned of the incident when I received a call from the Derry police chief. The women had waited for a couple of days before reporting their experience. The only reason they even reported what happened was due to the fact that they had heard a rumor that the Derry Police had shot and killed the creature. That was indeed not the case.

The women had heard talk about the supposed Bigfoot sightings, and they knew it had been in the newspaper, but neither of the two believed the accounts until then. The police chief seemed impressed with the detailed description that Sue was able to provide. The officer said that the witness looked it square in the eyes, and it was only three feet from her. As soon as I received the information, I headed for Derry where I met the chief at his office. From there, he took me down to the house where the incident occurred, and I interviewed Sue and her daughter. Upon entering the house, I could smell that awful stench that was still lingering inside the dwelling. I would also have to describe the odor as something similar to rotten or decayed meat.

The women showed me their rooms and described in detail what they saw and experienced that morning. No footprints were found near the house when I arrived, but Sue said she saw odd footprints the next day when the grass was wet. There was a grassy area, however, stomped down by the daughter's bedroom window.

Bedroom window where creature looked in at woman
Used with permission of the photographer

The daughter had been out with friends the day before the incident. She got in very late at about 4 am She heard a strange noise up in the backyard which she described as a metallic or the rattling of tin sound. The dogs were also carrying on and barking ferociously and there was the sound of something large moving around. A similar metal on metal noise would be a common feature mentioned by various creature witnesses in the days ahead.

August 21, 1973
Greensburg, 5:30 pm
Girl sees creature near housing development

It was around 5:30 pm later that same day that another Bigfoot sighting was reported from a housing development on the Greensburg-Mount Pleasant Road. The weather was cloudy and overcast. The area is a rural location surrounded by woods.

The witness was a very intelligent young girl who was able to provide me with a detailed account of what happened and what she observed. Judy (pseudonym) was standing outside watching a young boy on his bicycle doing some tricks. About two hundred feet down the road, the witness saw a creature cross the road.

The creature was about three feet away from an approaching car, which squealed its brakes as it stopped. The unidentified driver stopped abruptly, then drove quickly down the road. According to the young lady, the creature had stopped and looked towards the vehicle. It then turned around and walked back in the direction from which it came.

The girl gave me a very detailed report describing the creature that she saw, along with a sketch. The bipedal man-like creature which the girl called "the monster," was described as "about six feet tall, husky, and very broad shouldered. He was the same color as a chestnut brown horse. His hair was about five inches long all over, and sort of "silky." The creature was at first standing in a sideways position to the witness. The front of the creature was facing the car, and it's back was toward the woods. The creature then turned it's back toward the witness.

Judy went on to explain that the arms of the creature stayed by it's side and did not swing as it moved. "The creature had taken two steps, then it walked faster, heavy and clumsy." The creature walked faster than a man normally would. There was little or no neck observed, and no ears were seen. The witness also indicated that the legs appeared to be stiff, and not bent like an ape.

I talked with Judy's parents, who considered her very reliable, and they mentioned that after the incident, she was a little excited and shook up. I also talked with other local residents who had some interesting recent accounts to relate. Strange three-toed footprints, lots of odd screams like howling coming from the woods, and unusual foul smells were discussed. One sound was described as a two-toned high-low pitch, like a man howling.

August 21, 1973
Trafford, 9:30 pm (UFO)

Two people were sitting outside on a porch near Trafford at about 9:30 pm when they noticed red, green, and white lights in the sky. The witnesses said the lights appeared similar to Christmas tree bulbs. The lights were not high in the sky and were darting around and changing positions. The odd lights were observed for about forty five minutes before they departed.

August 21, 1973
Norvelt, 10:15 pm
Creature runs out of woods

Just a few miles away from the location of the creature sighting on the Greensburg-Mount Pleasant Road, there was another incident reported at 10:15 pm That same night, several people riding in a car near the Westmoreland County fairgrounds near Norvelt watched as a large hair covered creature ran out of the woods and crossed the road in front of them.

August 22, 1973
Trafford, 12 am (UFO)

About midnight a woman who lived near Trafford reported that the power suddenly went out in her house. She also noticed the sudden silence outside around her residence, as the crickets stopped chirping. Also, her dog, appeared upset by something. The lady went upstairs to her bedroom, and a short time later, she heard strange sounds. First a beeping- then a strange whirling sound that seemed to be just outside her window.

Then a light suddenly flashed and lit up the area around the window for an instant. The witness was too afraid to look outside after seeing the light. The woman felt a chill go through her. Listening intently, she could hear the unusual noise as it suddenly began to fade in the distance. Still later, the sounds of crickets returned. A WCUFOSG investigator went to the scene to interview the witness and to look for any evidence, but nothing was found.

August 22, 1973
West Newton
Strange sounds, dogs disturbed, odd smell

Later that day, another family at a rural location near West Newton reported hearing a sound that at first was like a calf bawling. The sound seemed to be getting closer to their home. The family had numerous dogs which began to bark intensely. Then a loud growling sound, which was even louder than that of the dogs, could be heard. At least one dog began to whimper. Some men turned on lights outside and began to search, they heard something seemingly large running off into the dark.

The next day, marks were found on the ground where something appeared to have stepped. The family also found that the garbage had been strewn along with some odd scratches on the dog houses. Similar events occurred on this property for about a week. On one occasion, the smell of something rotten permeated the air. These people were familiar with the local animal sounds and were convinced that something unusual was stalking the woods nearby.

August 23, 1973
Apollo, Armstrong County, 9:10 pm (UFO)

A man reported observing a bright orange ball which appeared low in the sky over Apollo.

August 23, 1973
Yukon
Creature pursues car down the road

Fred and Mary Smith and their children (pseudonyms) were visiting some relatives near Yukon at about 9 pm The small group of people was standing outside having a friendly conversation when they were interrupted by a loud crying-moaning sound that seemed to be coming from the nearby woods. The Smiths pulled out of the driveway in their car and were slowly traveling down the road when suddenly a huge figure emerged from out of the bushes and staggered onto the roadway. The family stopped to look at the giant creature, which Mrs. Smith described as looking like an ape.

When they stopped, the creature began to move faster in their direction. The creature was walking upright, but it's legs seemed to be bowed. The witness said it actually was staggering like an intoxicated person. They also noticed that the creature, besides having long legs, also had long arms. The driver quickly picked up speed to get away from the unknown visitor.

August 23, 1973
Penn
Family sees creature near their home

That evening there was a report near Penn that a Bigfoot creature had been seen near a rural residence.

Local Businesses Utilize Creature Reports

Latrobe is well known for being the hometown of famed golfer, Arnold Palmer, and the late children's television host, Mister Fred Rogers, as well as the location where the banana split was created. However, in 1973 it also became a focal point for the Bigfoot activity that was reportedly taking place around that community. The local newspaper, The Latrobe Bulletin, was covering the current creature reports extensively. For many days, Bigfoot was making the front page. There was even talk that The Tonight Show starring Johnny Carson was going to mention the local monstrous happenings.

A local company based out of Latrobe airport that used a small aircraft with a lighted animated display drew attention to the current Bigfoot news by flying over the area at night. That aircraft was also identified as the source for some reported UFO sightings in the area as well. The local restaurants and retail stores were also using Bigfoot as a sales gimmick. Bigfoot Burgers were a specialty at the time.

The airwaves of the local radio stations around Latrobe were filled with calls and discussions about the hairy creatures that many people were claiming to see. Even a local electronics store, the Stereo Shack, used the local Bigfoot excitement to help promote the new police radio scanners that were becoming very popular.

August 23, 1973
Latrobe radio station receives tape of creature sound

On the night of August 23, a chilling wailing-crying sound is said to have been heard in the Third Ward section of Latrobe. An audio recording of this strange cry was recorded by an unknown man who contacted a disc jockey at radio station WQTW in Latrobe the following day. The station copied the tape, and the D.J. conducted a short interview with the unknown caller, who refused to provide his name or phone number.

A member of the WCUFOSG talked with the D.J. who provided what little information he had about the recording. He indicated that the sound was strange, and it sounded something like a baby crying. He was going to broadcast the mysterious sound over the air, as well as the interview with the caller. The D.J. suggested to our member that we should study the tape to see if we could discern additional details since he had limited information.

All that was learned is that the man who recorded the sound claimed to have seen something strange in the woods on August 22, but he recorded the sound from that same area the next day. He said that he also smelled an odor like rotten eggs. The caller never contacted the station again and his identity has never become known. A scientific analysis of this recording was later conducted by the Society For The Investigation Of The Unexplained (SITU) from New Jersey to try to determine the source of this sound.

There was a preliminary report on the sound analysis published in the VOL. 7 NO. 1, January, 1974, edition of "PURSUIT," the publication of SITU. The article was written by Robert E. Jones, who had traveled to the Westmoreland County area from New Jersey, to investigate the creature reports first hand. Jones wrote, "At present, an attempt is being made to analyze the recording through sonographic (voice print) analysis. In November 1973, a number of sonograms were made through the courtesy of Kay Elemetrics, a firm in New Jersey that specializes in the manufacture of Sonogram equipment.

The first sonogram was taken in the 80 Hz to 8000 Hz (hertz-a unit of frequency equal to one cycle per second) range using a wide band filter. The results indicated that the major portions of the sound were in the lower range, so the second sonogram was made in the 40 Hz to 4000 Hz range. Two other sonograms were made: one similar to the second, using a narrow band filter, and the other of my voice for purposes of comparison. In December, the sonograms were studied by a biologist who had some experience with sonogram analysis of primates.

Although his studies had been rather limited, his opinions were such as to justify further analysis of the tape. His conclusions were: "(1) that the frequencies fall within the usual animal range. (2) that the patterns appear not to be humanly or mechanically produced, and (3) that the sounds are not those of any primate with which he is familiar." I am unaware of any further tests results that were published by SITU on the audio tape.

As more sightings were being reported by friends and neighbors in the Latrobe area, the local citizenry became more interested and some people were alarmed. A group of locals with four wheel drive vehicles formed a group called "the Bigfoot Patrol" who began to conduct their own search to look for the elusive hairy creatures. In some instances, they were helpful in providing information to the WCUFOSG.

A Visit to Carnegie Museum
As the sightings continued and as we gathered some physical traces which had been recovered from the locations where a creature incident reportedly occurred, we began to seek out other resources that would have specialized knowledge relating to zoological matters. A Westmoreland County veterinarian was contacted. He was very cordial and met with us one day after his office hours were over. We discussed some of our findings with him and showed him some of our casts. He seemed very intrigued, but was quite limited to what he could do in regards to any sample analytical work.

A decision was made to contact the Department of Mammals at the Carnegie Museum in Pittsburgh to see if they would have an interest in the information we had gathered about the Bigfoot sightings reported in the area. I was hopeful that one of their experts would take a look at the physical materials we had obtained. Besides the casts, there were some other samples which could possibly be related to the mysterious animal reports.

I was able to reach Dr. Doutt, who was associated with the Department of Mammals. There was no doubt that Dr. Doutt seemed skeptical about the local creature sightings, but after hearing some of the details about what had been occurring, the scientist expressed some curiosity about our investigation and findings. Dr. Doutt also seemed interested in looking at the material and casts we had.

We set up a meeting at his office in the museum in Oakland. The scientist's eyes widened as he looked at the three-toed cast I had placed on the table before him. We talked for quite a while about the details that were unfolding concerning the creature observations and patterns. He brought to our attention that some of the local Bigfoot accounts sounded similar to the Native American tales of the legendary Wendigo, the mystical creature of the woods.

Dr. Doutt asked me if I could leave the materials so that he could have some time to study them, and I complied with his request. There were other conversations with the museum in the following days. There seemed to have been some interest in having some museum personnel travel out to Westmoreland County to look into the creature reports for themselves. I learned, however, that at that time, the people who would normally be involved in such a study were currently obtaining specimens in South America. I never heard if any museum personnel ever did conduct such a study.

August 24, 1973
Monongahela, Washington County, Early morning
Creature on roof of house

A very unusual report came in from Washington County that occurred during the early morning hours of August 24. What appeared to be a large hairy creature was said to have been walking on the roof of a house. The information on this case and some other events that occurred within days of each other in this small rural community outside of Monongahela is intriguing. As you read this account, you will understand why. According to Jill Novak (pseudonym), some strange activity had begun about three or four days earlier when the locals began to hear weird crying sounds coming from the woods near their homes.

Jill and some friends were taking a walk down the street when a very strong sulfur type odor filled the air. Jill said the smell was so strong that she could hardly breathe. Her eyes were watering and her nose seemed to become dry. They ran into the house and were still overwhelmed by the odor. Later that evening, the strange screaming sounds started again and then there was the sound of something heavy walking on the roof of her home. The house was built so that there was easy access to the roof.

Jill was by herself and very frightened. Jill called her friends, telling them about the sounds on the roof. It was later that night when the loud walking and thumping noises started again on the roof. This time a strange large shadow could be seen. Jill was familiar with the lighting around the house, and there had never been a shadow in that location before. All that could be made out was what appeared to be a long hair-covered arm with fingers.

While gardening the next day, Jill found some odd footprints. Jill was also aware that another family living close by had also been reporting strange activity. That family had been hearing something heavy running through some gravel up the road as well as hearing the sound of something walking across their porch for a couple of days. On one recent occasion, a boy was watching television in the house when he saw a strange creature looking into the window. The creature was bent over, as it had to crouch on the porch to look inside. The beast seemed to have a hump on its back. Once observed, the creature ran down the road.

On her neighbor's porch, what looked like claw marks or finger marks were seen on the window. Also, another discovery was made. On the porch were two black hairs that had a strong odor to them.

Another odd account from this small community was the report that a woman had just returned from the grocery store with a large meat order. She went into the house for a moment, leaving the packages of meat in the back seat of the car. The woman went outside to get her groceries only to find them gone. On the back seat were mud and odd prints, which suggested that some large creature had been in the car, and apparently had stolen the meat.

Ken R., a WCUFOSG investigator with an extensive technical background, responded to that area to interview witnesses and to obtain details of the events. Ken recalled that the first incident that he responded to in that area was late one evening. Ken arrived in the area soon after the incident had occurred, and he went to a home to find a man and his wife visibly shaken. The man had a shotgun in his hand. His wife was holding a Bible. Ken recalled that these folks had a large German Shepherd that appeared very frightened and would not come out of it's dog house.

The man told Ken that he saw the devil standing up in the nearby field. What the man saw was a tall figure with large glowing green eyes. What had drawn the man outside was that someone or something was throwing very heavy large rocks from the field toward the house. He could hear the thump of something heavy hitting the ground. It was the large rock that landed on the front of his vehicle that drew the most attention. The rocks were too heavy for him to lift.

Ken also obtained the two smelly hair samples for study. After returning home, Ken recalled watching his dog cower as it smelled the hair samples. Ken wrote up a report on these events to send to me to keep on file. He also packaged up one of the hair samples and sent that along in the same envelope. Ken had phoned to give me an update on the reports and told me that he had sent the report and a hair sample and had personally mailed it at the local post office.

A few days later, I still had not received the letter and the important enclosure. Becoming concerned, I called Ken back. He confirmed that he had sent the envelope to me, and did not know why I had not received it. Ken then mailed me his second copy of the report. It also never arrived. During one telephone conversation between Ken and myself discussing these events, our discussion was suddenly interrupted by a loud metallic electronic sound. The odd interference was drowning us out. We could barely hear each other.

Ken said my voice did not even sound familiar. In the weeks to follow, this electronic interference would become more common whenever I was discussing the creature matters with some individuals. Later, Ken personally hand delivered the hair sample to me. I could smell a very unpleasant odor on the hair. Since we now had to deal with the possibility that our mail was being intercepted by someone, we were very concerned over mailing out any physical evidence such as hair samples.

Another mysterious event occurred in Ken's home around the same time. Ken kept all of his reports and materials concerning the Bigfoot investigations that he was involved with in a filing cabinet. Ken went to get his reports one day only to find that all of this information had vanished. All of his files of family matters were in their proper locations in that cabinet. Only the materials on the creature cases were gone. I remember Ken being very upset at the time over this matter. Ken was a professional and good with keeping records and had never misplaced any files before. Why were only these files missing?

Ken had investigated some other creature reports. One incident was unfounded. Another case had occurred in Washington County near the airport. Ken remembers interviewing a law enforcement officer who had recorded some strange animal sounds for several nights in that area. That material was missing from his file as well.

August 24, 1973
Herminie, 9:55 pm
Bigfoot in backyard, dog frightened

It was just before 10 pm, also on August 24, that another creature incident occurred near Herminie. A WCUFOSG investigating team accompanied me to that area. This incident occurred in a neighborhood where there is a large wooded area surrounding this location. Property owner, Bob Thomas (pseudonym), had just cut the grass in the backyard. He went inside and left his dog tied to a chain in the backyard, which gave his pet a lot of room to move around.

Bob soon heard the dog barking excitedly and quickly ran to the backdoor to see what was disturbing his pet. The dog appeared very upset by something and was acting crazy, running quickly back and forth from the bottom to the top of the yard. Looking toward the garden, Bob saw a tall hairy man-like creature about thirty feet away. It was too big to be a human. He noticed a strong odor in the yard similar to rotten eggs. Next to the creature was a garden hose which it had apparently knocked over. A large tree limb from high in the tree was also now lying on the ground in the backyard on the freshly cut grass. Most interesting was what appeared to be a fresh huge footprint impressed in the newly cut grass. The track was eighteen inches long and over seven inches wide. Had the creature climbed up into the tree? On the tree trunk were what appeared to be claw marks and some large branches appeared to have been freshly broken.

A possible path that the creature took back into the woods was located. Some large specimens of dung were found in the backyard. Bob said that he had noticed the dung when he was cutting the grass. He said that the droppings were piled up like that from a horse, and it was too large to be from his dog.

August 24, 1973
Superior, 11:30 pm
Bigfoot pulls out electrical line from mobile home

While we were searching for evidence down in Herminie, a radio alert from the 911 dispatch center came across the VHF radio monitor in my car. I called in for my message to learn that another creature incident had just occurred near Superior, a location in Derry Township. The police were on the scene investigating, and they requested that we send an investigation team to that location, which was in the Superior Mobile Home Court. I obtained directions and contact information, then led the investigating team on our next adventure.

SILENT INVASION

When we arrived at the mobile home community, we were told that the police had just left the scene. The incident that we were investigating had occurred at about 11:30 pm and began when Beverly Burns (pseudonym) heard a sound like something scratching on the back end of her mobile home. She called her son, who also heard the odd noise. They walked into the back bedroom, and from there they could hear a sound coming from outside of the home, that sounded like a baby crying. They verified that their cat was inside the trailer in another room.

Suddenly, the electricity began to go on and off in the trailer. Mrs. Burns opened up the back door of the residence. It was dark. The woman's eyes quickly focused on a huge dark form which stood only a few feet away. The woman was overwhelmed with fear and only took a quick glimpse at her uninvited visitor. According to the witness, the creature was gigantic. It stood way over six feet tall, appeared black in color, and was sort of husky.

Upon seeing Mrs. Burns, the creature twisted around and then ran off between some of the other mobile homes. Mrs. Burns screamed. At the same time there was a very odd strong smell in the air that several people noticed. One neighbor stated that it was like sulfur. Once the creature ran off, the smell dissipated. Mrs. Burns called the police and her son grabbed his gun and went outside to look around. Mrs. Burns had her dog tied outside behind the dwelling and close to where the creature was observed. She found her dog whimpering, whining, and not barking. Mrs. Burns said it was like someone was covering the dog's mouth.

When the police arrived, they checked the property and searched for evidence. Some odd looking footprints were found. A police officer put a box over the tracks to protect them until our team arrived. The officer also noticed that the electrical line that ran from the outside meter box to the mobile home had been displaced.

When our team arrived at the Superior Mobile Home Court, we talked to Mrs. Burns, her son, and some neighbors. After hearing Mrs. Burn's scream, a next door neighbor looked outside and saw the creature running down through the court. The woman's son wanted to know if these creatures were dangerous. He was told that we did not have any cases where a creature had hurt anyone. Her son wondered why none of our investigators were armed.

We first searched the area behind the residence. Initially, the scratching sound gave the impression that the creature was near the mobile home. There had been some large blocks stacked in that area. Those blocks had been knocked down, apparently by the creature. As one team member was examining the electrical meter box, he noticed that the lead seal on the box had been broken. The electric line from the box to the trailer had been pulled right out of the ground. We advised Mrs. Burns to contact West Penn Power to come out and examine the damage to the electrical meter.

There were some unusual footprints around the mobile home as well. There were some possible scratch marks on the house as well. Some other residents of the mobile home court mentioned that about a week before they had heard strange crying sounds and the sound of something heavy walking. More strange events were soon to be reported from this same mobile home community.

August 24, 1973
Claridge, 11:30 pm
Bigfoot encounter

At the same time that a creature was reported at the Superior Mobile Home Court in Derry Township, another creature was reportedly seen about eighteen miles away to the west, near Claridge. The witness was Bill Barker (pseudonym), who had just recently returned to the area after an extended vacation. He was pulling up to his home when his headlights caught something on the side of the road, which then walked out onto the roadway. What Bill saw was a man-like creature that was gray in color with white spots on its body. The creature appeared to be over five foot tall, and weighed about one hundred eighty pounds. The witness said this creature was not real tall, and it was not fat, but bulky. The man stopped his car and shined his high beams toward the figure. It ran from one side of the road to the opposite side.

Bill turned his car around to position himself where he could get a better look at the strange sight. The creature was now standing next to a telephone pole near a wooded area. Bill was still curious and pulled up into the middle of the road and flashed his headlights on the beast. He watched as it ran into the woods. Bill had gotten to within ten feet of the animal. The man said it walked something like a gorilla, and at times it was almost running. He said it must have had its head tucked down, as he could never see the face.

Bill had been away from the area and was unaware of the local Bigfoot stories. He called the Penn Township Police who arrived on the scene, but the creature was no longer there. Bill told the police that he was not drunk and he did not take drugs. He was sure of what he had seen. Bill later learned that another neighbor about 3:30 am was awakened by a terrible foul odor.

A WCUFOSG investigating team went to the scene to interview the witness. They found Bill to be very credible, and he had not been influenced by the press reports since he had not been home. The team found some possible footprints while examining the area. The only clear impression, which had three toes, was found going up a steep hill. Nearby, the team found a pine tree with the top broken off. Further on down the path, four more small pine trees were found with their tops broken off and lying nearby. The investigators were unable to break off any of the pine tree tops with their hands, as the tree was too springy. They also noted that there were old coal mines in the vicinity.

August 24, 1973
Derry, 11:45 pm
Creature lying in field
The events of August 24 ended with a report at 11:45 pm outside of Derry that some men using a high beam light caught a glimpse of something large and dark lying in a field.

August 25, 1973
Hillside, 8 pm
Boy on mini-bike five feet from creature
The next day, August 25, a young fellow who lived near Hillside just a short distance from Derry reported a close encounter with a Bigfoot. It was around 8 pm when the boy was riding his mini-bike when suddenly his vehicle stalled out. He then heard a snorting sound coming from behind him. He turned and was startled to see a creature standing

there and looking at him from a distance of only about five feet away.

The witness described the creature as covered in black hair and about eight feet tall. There was just a small amount of brown-black hair on the face. The nose was large, and the eyes were about the size of a ping-pong ball, but bright red. The boy did not smell anything except the gas smell from his mini-bike. It was still light outside, so he was able see the creature clearly. The boy's dog was following behind him, but as it got close toward the creature, it dropped down to the ground and began to bark at it. The creature then ran off toward the woods. The boy was disturbed by the experience, and the next morning he called the local newspaper, The Latrobe Bulletin, who told him to call the WCUFOSG.

August 26, 1973
Luxor, 5 pm
Creature chases family from woods

It was a sunny and warm day, so the Barnes family (pseudonum) decided to take a ride out to Luxor to do some target shooting up by the slag dump. The family had some relatives who lived in that area and they knew the woods very well. Mr. and Mrs. Barnes and their eleven year old daughter, Olivia (pseudonym) were walking up to the location where they could safely practice shooting with a .22 rifle. The area is surrounded by woods, cliffs, and old mines and caves. Mr. Barnes and his daughter walked down into the dump area to get some old bottles to use for target practice. The man heard the sound of brush cracking and looked up to see a long hairy muscular arm breaking the brush.

The man yelled to his daughter and wife to run. His daughter had been told to keep an eye out for snakes, and thinking that was what her father was alerting her to, turned to look. Coming out of the brush only about twenty five feet away, was a huge hair-covered creature that growled when it saw them. The man realized that his .22 rifle would not protect his family from this giant creature. The girl became hysterical and started running as the creature approached. They all ran about one-half mile before stopping in what they considered a safe area.

The young girl was very upset and frightened. She was able to give her family, as well as myself, a detailed description of what the creature looked like. She said that it was tall and very muscular and it stood about seven to eight feet tall. It was covered in long black hair and the arms of the creature hung down to the knees. She could clearly see its two orange colored eyes, and the nose was like that of an ape. The girl also said the ears were kind of pointy and yet kind of round.

She also saw two sharp teeth "like that of a vampire." When she saw the creature coming out of the brush it was walking upright, but then dropped down to all fours and began to chase her. None of the family noticed any unusual odors. The girl refused to return to Luxor for quite a while. The next day the area was searched for evidence, but no tracks were found on the hard ground. The family said that there was definitely some type of creature lurking in the countryside.

(Note: While working on this book I coincidentally crossed paths with the Barnes family. Olivia remembered the event very well and still had difficulty talking about it. She stated that after all of the years since the incident, she hardly ever mentioned the incident to her friends fearing they wouldn't believe her. She recalled how for many years after the creature encounter, the first thing she did when visiting her relatives who lived near Luxor, was to immediately lock the doors so the creature couldn't get in.)

SILENT INVASION

Artist conception of creature which chased family near Luxor
Used with permission of Robert McCurry

August 26, 1973
Derry, 11:30 pm
Creature observed near ball field.

About 11:30 pm a man emptying some garbage reportedly saw a large hairy creature near a ball field near Derry.

August 27, 1973
Superior, 6:50 am
White creature seen near mobile home community

It was about 6:50 am on August 27, when a woman saw something unusual just before leaving to go to work. The lady who lived in the Superior Mobile Home Court in Derry Township had gone outside to check the temperature. Up in the woods behind a tree, the woman saw a large, dirty white hair-covered creature. The beast appeared to be reaching up into the tree for something, then it walked into the woods and was not seen again.

August 27, 1973
Blairsville, Indiana County, 8:20 pm
Strange activity at mobile home

Also on August 27, a family who lived near Blairsville was so frightened by some strange events that they called the state police, who referred them to the WCUFOSG. The family was traveling on a rural road near their property about 8:20 pm, when they heard loud screams coming from the woods around them. These sounds were unlike anything they had ever heard in the area.

They slowed down and listened to the piercing cries which bellowed about five to six times. When they arrived at their mobile home, their dogs were carrying on. Suddenly a bright rust colored flash of light illuminated outside in front of a window. The dogs suddenly got quiet. The flash was followed by the loud sound of something banging hard on the side of their trailer.

August 27, 1973
Kingston, 10 pm
Man shot at creature.

That evening back at Kingston, a small community between Derry and Latrobe, a man and his nephew were taking a walk down a country road, anticipating some target shooting with a .22 rifle. Some other boys came running over telling the two fellows that they had found some large footprints back in the woods. The man was skeptical, but said that they would go take a look. Later that evening, the man noticed something in the distance running across a field and told his nephew that he was going to see what it was.

He told his nephew to go to the house and get a flashlight, which the man took the flashlight and went into the field. He saw a tall black creature run among some trees. He shined the light around and then into the trees, where he could see shining eyes. The witness told me that the eyes were in between the trees, not up in the trees. As soon as the light would hit the eyes, it seemed that the creature would turn its head. At that time the witness noticed a faint smell like someone had broken some rotten eggs. The man admitted that he was scared.

Then his light caught the creature. The head of the animal touched the high limb of one of the trees. Suddenly the creature took two steps toward the man, and he fired several rounds from his .22 at the beast. He was unsure if he actually hit it. But after he fired, the creature went down on all fours for a second, then stood back up on two legs and ran back into the woods. The witness told me that the creature ran really fast and did not make any sound when it was shot at. The witness knew a local person who was involved with the "Bigfoot patrol." The group searched the area just after the incident, but nothing was found.

August 27, 1973
Donohoe, 10:20 pm
Creature on bridge

About 10:20 pm that same evening, a family was driving from Greensburg to Latrobe were approaching the bridge on Donohoe road, when according to a witness, an eight or nine foot tall dark hair-covered creature was standing in the middle of the high structure. The driver stopped the vehicle. They were unable to back up because another car was behind them. The witness I talked with said the family was scared to death. The witnesses watched as the creature ran off the bridge and into a nearby wooded area. The witness stated that now that she had seen the creature herself, she now believed that it did exist. The witness had called the Latrobe Police, who referred the caller to the WCUFOSG.

August 27, 1973
Irwin, 10:30 pm
Red eyes looking in window

It was around the same time that a person in the Irwin area reportedly saw something with red eyes looking in her window.

August 28, 1973
Beech Hills, 3 am
Woman looks into the face of a creature

Just a short distance down the road from Greengate Mall and up over the hill from the Greensburg Country Club, lies the rural housing community of Beech Hills. It was on August 28, when a very close range creature encounter occurred there. I talked with the witness just minutes after her very close observation of something she called "horrifying." The woman who reported the experience was visiting with friends at that location when this incident occurred. That house was built low to the ground, so the bathroom window was at eye level.

It was about 3 am when Tonya Lake (pseudonym) was awake in her home and noticed a hideous face through a window directly in front of her. It appeared only three feet away from behind the screen and was looking directly at her. Tonya was terrified and she was nearly hysterical when I interviewed her. Tonya told me that she was so shocked by the sight of the creature that she ran to another room.

Tonya was saying, "Oh my God, it just looked at me." Tonya surmised that the creature had seen the light go on in the room and saw her walk in. The creature seemed to be crouched down and was rising up when she saw it. Tonya described the extremely ugly face as dark and hair covered. The head was larger than that of a human male. She could see two pointed ears and a deeply set ape-like nose. There were other physical features that really scared Tonya, including the two large glowing eyes that were reddish-orange and just glaring. The woman also described two large fang-like teeth in its mouth.

Tonya had mentioned that a short time before her encounter, she heard a real funny noise outside, which sounded similar to the screech of an owl, but different. The witness was certain that it was not an owl sound. Tonya noticed no strange odor at the time, but recalled that a dog was chained outside near the house when the incident occurred. Strangely, the dog did not bark, which it normally did when strangers were around. Tonya told her friends about what had happened. Soon after gaining her composure that morning, Tonya called the state police to report what had happened. The woman told me that she was very concerned that this creature could hurt someone.

The state police told her to call my UFO Hotline number to report her experience. Tonya was feeling very fearful and decided to leave that location for the night. Her friends took her to her home outside of Jeannette. What makes the story even stranger, is that the same or a similar creature reportedly was seen at that woman's home a short time later. We would find out in time, that this was not a unique case where a witness would see a creature, then go to another location, only to have a Bigfoot creature appear a short time later.

The next day I drove out to the Beech Hills location to investigate. A state trooper had already responded to that location and had searched for evidence around that residence. The officer had found what appeared to be a three-toed footprint near the garbage dump by the woods behind the house. I took pictures of the impression and searched around the house and the nearby woods. After this incident, I met with state police detectives at Troop A Headquarters in Greensburg to discuss this case and the status of our current investigations.

August 28, 1973
West Mifflin, Allegheny County, 3 pm
Creature walking in backyard

The same afternoon as the Beech Hills incident, Investigator Ken R. received word from a contact that a police agency in the West Mifflin-Munhall area in Allegheny County had received information that a woman had seen a large hairy creature walking through her backyard in a relatively residential area. The police were contacted but did not want to discuss the incident.

August 28, 1973
Superior, 7:30 pm
Mystery man confiscates and destroys evidence

That evening, August 28, back in Derry Township at the Superior Mobile Home Court, another strange event was about to unfold. The UFO Hotline number in my home had been ringing constantly that day. I was in the middle of an ongoing conversation, when it was interrupted by a telephone operator with an emergency call.

The operator had broken in as a result of an emergency request from a witness who was concerned about an event that had taken place just a short time before. The woman had been trying to get through on my constantly busy phone lines with what she believed was important information. She also indicated that she had left a message before making this call, but we had never received her message.

The woman calling was Beverly Burns (pseudonym), who reported that a creature had pulled out her electrical wire at her trailer home on August 24. Beverly told me that she was afraid that she might have done something wrong. Beverly went on to explain that at about 7:30 pm, a stranger showed up at her mobile home. Beverly did not know the man's name. The man told her that he was an investigator from Ohio and had an identification badge with his photo on it. Beverly did not look it over very carefully, but she remembered seeing the words UFO and Ohio. Beverly described him as short and a little heavy set and wearing a gray work uniform. He had brown hair, no glasses, and was wearing a gray belt with some kind of face on it. The vehicle he was driving was a brown station wagon with a luggage rack that did have an Ohio license plate.

What Beverly thought that she might have done wrong was to give this mystery man some hair samples that she had found caught on the steps near where the creature had been seen. The woman told the man that she had been trying to contact me about finding the hair when the man said that he would take the samples and give them to me. He also informed her that he would be back in town in about three days with some other men to continue investigating the events in the area.

The man would not tell Beverly how he obtained her name, and she thought that the man was acting very fishy. Other neighbors had been coming over to the residence and looking at the odd footprints that had been found. One young fellow was taking Polaroid pictures of the foot impressions while the unknown visitor looked on. Suddenly the man approached the boy and ripped the photo from the boy's hand. The boy said, "I have just made a picture." The man said, "You have just made us a picture." The visitor then wrinkled up the photo in his hand and put it in his pocket. The boy was still there when she called me.

The man also wanted Beverly to describe to him the details about her encounter with the creature. He wanted to know if she was the lady who had the scratch marks on her trailer, and she replied that she was. He seemed very interested in the footprints that the locals were looking at. Beverly was quite upset as she told me what the man did next. This odd-acting investigator had put his foot down into the footprints, kept moving his foot back and forth, destroyed the impressions. The man then stated, "It has been destroyed." The man had written down the measurements of the footprints before doing away with them.

The neighbors were very upset with this man's actions and told him that they were calling the police. The man then reportedly jumped into his car and sped out of the area at a high rate of speed, nearly turning over sideways, never to return. Who this mystery man was has never been determined.

August 29, 1973
McChesneytown, Evening
Creature seen near residence

It was on the evening of August 29, that an incident occurred near McChesneytown, a community just outside of Latrobe. Mrs. Harris (pseudonym) was in bed reading and her children were asleep in their rooms. First she heard a tapping on her window, then a strange moaning sound. She then noticed a large, dark shadow near the house. She called a neighbor who told her that her young daughter, whose window faced the Harris home, was crying and pointing to the window.

The woman was so upset over the strange uncommon sound, that she called her husband, who was working at the time. After they hung up, Mrs. Harris heard scratching sounds outside, and a different sound which was more like that of a baby crying. Mr. Harris, concerned for his wife's safety, called the state police in Greensburg who patrolled their area.

Mr. Harris soon arrived at his home and he and another neighbor began to scout the area to see where the strange crying sound had originated. About three blocks from his residence, the two men observed two large eyes in a field. The eyes were deep red with an orange cast to them and they were staring in the direction of the two men. The eyes were about six inches apart. The men noticed that area of the field that they were traveling through had been trampled down by something heavy. They hurried back to Mr. Harris's home to obtain a camera and a gun. By the time they returned to that location, whatever it was had gone.

The next day, Mrs. Harris found what appeared to be a hand print with three curved fingers, like claws, on the side of her house. She also noticed that some of her plants on the porch appeared to have been chewed up, but the base stems were untouched. The dogs in the area that night were extremely upset and barking.

August 29, 1973
Greensburg, evening
Boomerang-shaped UFO seen;
Bigfoot shot at in same area

That same evening, August 29, only a few miles outside of Greensburg in a rural housing development, a highly unusual event occurred. The witness involved was the wife of a prominent doctor. The lady had observed a large, solid boomerang-shaped object with windows that had moved over her neighborhood and had hovered there for a short time before leaving. The lady also said that she noticed an odd sulfur smell at the time as well.

Later that evening, she heard the sound of nearby gunshots. She found out the next day that the gunfire had originated from another doctor's residence just a short distance away. Reportedly, that other doctor went outdoors to see what was disturbing his dog, that had been barking excessively. When he went outside, there was a huge, hairy creature like a big ape nearby. The doctor ran back inside the house for a rifle. He fired several rounds at the creature, then quickly ran back into the house as the beast ran off. The man refused to discuss the matter. Apparently the creature was not injured.

August 30, 1973
Superior, 6:30 am
Creature seen near mobile home court

A man who resides in the Superior Mobile Home Court woke up early at 6:30 am and heard a loud crying sound. The fellow was lying in a bunk bed and was high up where he had a good observation point to look out the window which faced the woods. The man watched as a large hairy ape-like creature about one hundred feet away walked through the woods behind the trailer.

August 30, 1973
Greensburg, Radebaugh Road, 6:45 pm
Creature seen near railroad tracks

It was that same evening, August 30, that a youngster was riding his bike on Radebaugh Road behind the Greengate Mall complex, when he saw a large, dark hairy creature walking across the railroad tracks. This is the same area where other creature sightings had been previously reported.

August 31, 1973
A strange coincidence. Witnesses from two cases observe creature again the same day

Kingston, 2:45 am A family who had previously seen a creature near their residence called the state police to report that a large, hairy creature had come back to their property.

A woman who was a passenger in a car traveling near Route 130 and Greengate Road observed a large, hairy brown-colored creature run across one of the golf courses and continue into the woods. This woman previously had a close encounter with a Bigfoot-like creature in recent weeks.

Late August 1973
near Cooperstown
Bigfoot lifts trailer

In late August, Barry Clark responded to a Bigfoot incident that occurred in the vicinity of Cooperstown, not far from Latrobe. The case involved a woman who lived in a mobile home with her small dog. On the evening of the incident, the dog became very upset and was barking very excitedly. The woman looked out of her window, which was about eight and-a-half to nine feet off the ground. She was alarmed to see a "big hairy beast" standing next to her home and taller than the window. The creature was banging and scratching on the side of the mobile home. It seemed that the more the dog barked, the more upset the creature became as it increased its annoying activities.

Then the woman became even more frightened as the creature actually lifted the corner of the mobile home off of one of the support blocks, then set it back down. The hysterical woman called the state police. By the time they arrived, the creature had departed. When Barry got to that location the next day, the woman told him that she was scared to death and could not take these types of events anymore. Barry searched for footprints, but the ground in the area was hard. He did notice, however, that the support pillar on the back right hand corner of the mobile home was out of place. It had been moved.

Westmoreland County map showing locations of Bigfoot activity
Used with permission of Wayne Willis

Part 6: Strange activity during August 1973

Reports of strange activity continued to be received from the area in the vicinity of the Greengate Mall, extending from along Greengate Road and over to Radebaugh Road. That area was quite rugged back then. There were rolling hills and cliffs surrounded by a large wooded area. There were also mine shafts and caves around the area. On a number of occasions, searches of this terrain were conducted by members of the WCUFOSG for any evidence of the mysterious hairy visitors.

There was an incident that an investigative team and myself responded to along Radebaugh Road heading towards Grapeville. We had been notified that some people taking a short cut through the woods had come across a series of large three-toed footprints. When we arrived, we found several clearly defined tracks, quite similar to the three-toed footprint that I had discovered just down the road on August 7. The location of these tracks was well off the main road and well hidden.

The footprints were clear enough to cast, so we mixed our plaster material and poured it into each impression. It would take a while for the mixture to harden. While waiting, a radio call came in informing us that we needed to respond to another possible incident. We decided to leave the castings to harden, anticipating that we would soon return to pick them up. As expected, we returned to the location of the tracks within an hour. To our surprise, all of the castings had been destroyed. Someone, for whatever reason, had smashed and kicked all of the drying molds. All of the evidence had been lost.

On a number of occasions while out in the field investigating the ongoing incidents, some of my associates and myself noticed and commented about the odd lightning that we had observed several times in the sky. We had noticed this phenomenon during the day and night at various times and locations. We all knew what heat lightning looked like, as we had all seen it during previous summers. I do not recall any reports of thunderstorm activity around the general area at those times. This seemed different, however. We saw large silent orange flashes of electrical energy in just one specific location in the sky. Somehow when we saw this, we had an ominous feeling that this was something other than a normal weather related event.

Near New Alexandria, unusual footprints were found twelve to fourteen inches long. Police were continuing to receive reports of creature sightings around Derry Township, and footprints were reportedly seen in the Third Ward area of Latrobe.

Near the small community of Keystone and around Kalamazoo Road, both near Herminie, local folks had been finding mysterious imprints on the ground. Near an old mine, strange sounds were being reported. Some of the locals had reportedly been shooting at a large, hairy creature running through the woods.

Just down the road from the Kingston Bridge between Derry and Latrobe, something odd was seen in the woods by a child who came home screaming. Armed family members who went into the woods found weeds tramped down in the area. In the days ahead, something was screaming in the woods which frightened the family. They smelled a strong sulfur-like odor. On another occasion, the screams were just outside their home, and the next morning they found the grass all tramped down along with a strange footprint in the vicinity from which they heard the sounds. The family had called the state police to report these events and the family said that they did respond to the scene.

A woman who lived near the village of Gray in Somerset County was interviewed by a radio personality of radio station WVSC in Somerset. The woman believed that a Bigfoot had recently been behind her mobile home. Something making loud, strange sounds like a baby crying was approaching closer as she and a friend talked. Neither woman had heard anything like it before.

A man was hiking in a wooded area of Crawford County and observed two unusual footprints in a creek bed. Whatever made them appeared flatfooted. The tracks were five-toed, and were about twelve inches long and five and-a-half inches wide. There was a right and left track. The left impression appeared to have more weight on it. Next to these two tracks, about a foot away, were two smaller versions of what appeared to be the same type of footprint. The smaller impressions were coming up out of the creek bed. The creek area where the footprints were located was muddy and there was a lot of debris there, such as pebbles and twigs. A human being standing there without shoes would surely have felt some pain. The witness did make a cast of one of the larger footprints. No other tracks, human or otherwise, were in the vicinity of where the footprints were found.

Near the village of Baggaley, (near Latrobe), in August or September, 1973, several local residents discovered a number of odd looking footprints near the garbage dump area. The largest of the tracks was about seventeen inches long. The night before, the man's daughter and some other individuals saw a UFO with two red lights on it moving toward the dump area.

Rumors of the mysterious continue

There were two very strange stories circulating around the area which were brought to our attention several times by various people. We attempted to follow up on these accounts, but never found any information which was verifiable. The first incident reportedly occurred during the week of August 31 near West Newton. A man living on a farm in that area heard a commotion in his barn. Something was apparently upsetting his farm animals.

Upon investigation, he came across a Bigfoot in the barn and reportedly shot and killed it. He notified authorities, and at one point government agents arrived at his farm and hauled the dead creature away. He was reportedly told not to talk about the incident. This account was never confirmed. The other report, which was somewhat even stranger, involved the alleged sighting of a giant man-like creature, which had huge wings. The creature reportedly flew over a road in the Donegal area. That story was similar to the famous Mothman sightings which had occurred in West Virginia in the late 1960's.

Did Bigfoot damage the air conditioner?

Roger Marsh had his own encounter with what may have been a Bigfoot. He tells his own story here.

The summer of 1973 I was 16 years old and frequently accompanied my father, Bill Marsh, when he would go out on Bigfoot investigations with Stan Gordon. Our family lived in the Mountain View, East High Acres subdivision between Greensburg and Latrobe. I was intrigued with the reports of UFOs and Bigfoot, but never imagined I could be involved in a Bigfoot sighting myself. What are the chances? I would ask myself. The reports are coming in from random people, but the idea that someone involved in the investigations could have a sighting was out of the question.

My bedroom was built over our home's two-car attached garage – and you entered from a private staircase in the first floor laundry room. The staircase hugged the outside wall and then opened up into my room. There was a railing in my room that outlined the staircase and a window near the top of the stairs.

The bedroom window was the double-hung type and sat a full story and-a-half above the ground outside. An air conditioner occupied the lower half of the window, and a set of heavy drapes covered both the top and bottom of the window.

Late one evening I was sitting in my bedroom when I heard the distinct sound of what sounded like a baby crying outside my window. I recall listening very intently and slowly moving toward the window. It was a sound that I had never heard before – a wailing sound, but with characteristics of a baby crying.

SILENT INVASION

The thought went through my mind that someone might be playing a joke on me. I was one of eight children, but probably the only kid in the family with a strong interest in both UFOs and Bigfoot. But with the late hour, I doubted that any family member or friend would actually be outside making this much noise. I was honestly scared and did not know what to do. I moved slowly toward the window and the sound continued. I got to the railing at the staircase and actually leaned over it and put my hand on the drapes. Whatever it was seemed to be just on the other side of the curtain.

I thought for just a moment later and reflected on whether or not there could be an actual Bigfoot creature outside my window and whether or not I wanted to have the experience of seeing one. I also wondered about being hurt by the creature if indeed it was there.

With my hand shaking as I held the drape, suddenly there was a loud bang on the air conditioner – something had just hit the air conditioner with a strong force. This caused me to let go of the drape and jump back into the room – and then I quickly dashed down the staircase into the first floor. I was panicked. With the later hour, I knew my parents would be asleep – so I ran down into the basement where an older brother had a bedroom and found him awake. I told him my story and the two of us cautiously went back to the first floor and to a side door not far from my bedroom window.

We first threw on the outside lights – three spotlights housed in the lawn that lit up this side yard area – and then we stepped outside. Nothing. No creature and no sounds. I soon went back to bed and tried to forget about what happened.

But the following morning over breakfast, I relayed to my father what had happened. He was a bit upset that I had not thought to wake him up – and quickly went outside to investigate on his own. One look at the air conditioner and he was off to the garage to get a ladder. With the ladder in place, he climbed up for a look. While my report of hearing strange wailing sounds could now not be proved, the banging sound on the air conditioner could. My father discovered that the metal grating on the outside of the air conditioner had a large dent in it as though someone with a large fist had taken a swing at it. But with the thickness of the metal, my father surmised that it would have taken an awful lot of muscle to do that much damage.

The only other detail to the incident is now as mystery as my father passed away. While reviewing the air conditioner damage, he saw what appeared to be hairs left behind. I remember my father quickly climbing down the ladder and going inside to get tweezers and an envelope – and then mounting the ladder again to carefully pull out the hairs. And then I recall looking at the hair sample in the envelope, but I cannot recall what ever became of the sample. No footprints were found near the scene.

Lancaster County Creature Reports

We had heard reports that creature sightings had been occurring in the Pennsylvania Dutch region in Lancaster County. The Vol. 7, No. 1, January, 1974, edition of SITU's publication PURSUIT, on page 17, talks about those creature encounters experienced by the local residents. Two brothers doing farm work reportedly saw the creature they described as gray in color and having a white mane. The creature also was said to have tiger-like fangs, curved horns, and long, grizzly claws, and moved on two legs. The farm horses were said to have been frightened by the approach of the beast, and the two fellows were thrown from their wagon.

According to the story, the next evening and a few miles down the road from where the first incident took place, another farmer who was clearing his field had a similar creature come after him. The farmer used his scythe and swung at the approaching strange beast. The creature was said to have ripped the scythe from the farmer's hands. The farmer escaped, and the next day the tool was found with the wooden sections eaten away.

Then on another area farm, a woman reported that a similar creature ran off with two geese. The woman reportedly ran after the strange beast, which then was said to have thrown one of the geese at her with such strength that the woman was knocked down. The creature ran off in the distance.

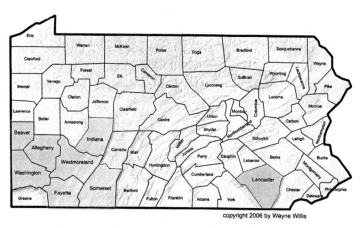

copyright 2006 by Wayne Willis

Pennsylvania map showing counties where Bigfoot sightings were reported
Used with permission of Wayne Willis

September 1, 1973
Penn Township, Early morning
Did Bigfoot creatures depart from a landed UFO?

Penn Township is a small rural community located just a short distance away from Jeannette. That area, located near Harrison City, has a long history of close UFO encounters. I received a very early morning call on September 1, from a male caller who had a strange story to relate to me. The man sounded very serious and thought that he should make me aware of this information. According to the caller, he knew three women who had a frightening experience. The women were reluctant to report the account, fearing ridicule, and they did not want to get involved.

The women told their friend that they were traveling on a country road near Penn when they observed a large UFO which was on the ground. The object was described as metallic and rectangular in shape. The witnesses slowed down to observe the object. While they looked on, a door-like structure suddenly appeared, along with steps that led from the doorway.

Then the most unusual aspect of the encounter reportedly occurred. The women said that exiting the doorway were two very tall, hairy Bigfoot-like creatures that ran down the steps and continued into the nearby woods. That was the last they saw of the creatures and UFO as the women sped away from the area.

September 1, 1973
Youngstown, 6:35 pm
Creature approaches baby at cemetery

That evening at about 6:35 on September 1, Mrs. Paul (pseudonym) and her baby were visiting her mother's grave site at the Youngstown Cemetery. While placing some fresh flowers on the grave, the young mother heard what she thought was the sound of a baby crying in the distance, but did not pay much attention to it thinking that it was coming from a house over the hill. She also noticed a strong annoying odor, like something that had been dead for a while. Mrs. Paul visited the cemetery daily and had never smelled this before. Her young child was walking around the area and approaching near the edge of the woods, about thirty feet away. At about the same time, the child began to cry. The mother looked toward the baby and was shocked to see a tall, hairy creature with large red eyes standing in the weeds, only a few feet from the child.

It seemed as though it was when the baby began to cry, the creature started to slowly walk toward the child. The woman ran without hesitation and grabbed her baby, then quickly got into her car. The woman said the creature was at least six feet tall and covered with long black hair. It had long arms and there was hair on its arms and down over its shoulders. The eyes were large and appeared like balls of fire. The nose was wide and it had pointed ears.

The face had features of an ape. She described the creature by saying, "It looked like a man, but it wasn't. And I didn't take time to look. It could pass for an ape." The woman rushed to her father's farm, which was located about five miles away, outside of Latrobe. Her father said that when she arrived at his home, she was very upset, and stated that his daughter is a very brave person.

September 1, 1973
Latrobe, 7:35 pm
Did a creature follow the mother and baby to a distant farm?

It was about one hour after Mrs. Paul and her baby had encountered a creature in the Youngstown Cemetery, that her relatives on the farm to which she fled had their own encounter with a Bigfoot creature. Whether it was the same creature that somehow followed the mother and child to the family farm or another similar creature, we will never know. The farm is located in a rural area outside of Latrobe. Some other family members noticed at the time that their farm animals were acting oddly. The dogs were lying down and growling. One dog was lying in it's dog house and just moving its eyes around, seemingly afraid to move it's head. A pony appeared very frightened as well.

One woman saw a huge, dark creature step out from the corner of the farmhouse. The creature was about six to seven feet tall and hair covered. It had very long arms and was standing erect. A foul odor was also in the air. Another man saw it running toward the woods. He shot at it, but missed. The family called the state police to report what had happened at the cemetery and at the farm. A state trooper later went to the farm to interview the witnesses. The trooper escorted Mrs. Paul and the baby back to their home a few miles away, since the woman was afraid to drive by herself after her scary encounter. A WCUFOSG team was sent to the cemetery to search the area.

During the search, the remains of a dead sheep were found. The carcass had apparently been there for a while. It appeared that something had eaten the animal. I went to the farm to interview some of the witnesses that night and upon speaking with Mrs. Paul, it was apparent that she was very disturbed over the experience. She felt that the creature had picked up the scent of the baby and had followed them to the farm.

Here indeed was another case where a person had seen a creature at one location, and a short time later a creature showed up at the second location where the witness had relocated.

September, 1973
Stroudsburg, Monroe County, 11 pm (UFO)

A very detailed observation of a UFO was reported by a man driving west on Route 80 heading towards the Pocono Raceway area. As the man began to travel uphill, he noticed about five cars had pulled off to the side of the road. The drivers of the cars were all standing around talking. As the man passed the group, he observed what he thought at first was some new revolving restaurant which appeared to be located off an exit ramp. As the man approached closer, what he was looking at seemed to be located just over the tree tops near the eastbound lane.

When he had a clearer view, he realized that nothing was holding up the structure. The witness was now becoming somewhat alarmed, but pulled his vehicle over until he was parallel with the object on the shoulder of the westbound lane. The witness stated that he sat there in disbelief for several minutes trying to figure out what he was observing. The man lowered his window to have a clear view of this object, which he said was so close that he could hit it with a stone.

The man cautiously opened his door and at the same time he kept his car running in neutral with the brake on. He then stepped out of the vehicle onto the roadway, where he looked over the details of what he now determined to be a strange craft. The object was a solid disc shape with white lights spaced a few feet apart around the center of the craft. One light appeared to be out of place or missing. There was also a red blinking light on the top of the object. The red light appeared to be attached to a pole-like structure. The object itself was estimated to be about fifty to seventy five yards in diameter. The object, which was completely silent, hovered about one hundred feet off the ground and revolved slowly and continuously. As the witness continued to watch the object for several more minutes, the disc suddenly made an altitude adjustment, from a level position to 45 degrees downward, as if the craft was observing the observer.

The witness then jumped into the car, took off the brake, but still remained there and continued to watch in amazement. As the witness gathered more courage, he got out of the car again completely fascinated by what he was seeing. A few minutes later, a tractor-trailer came up the road. The witness said he looked at the truck driver, who looked at him, then looked at the object, then sped off down the road.

The object once again made another altitude change, from 45 degrees, back to a level position. In a few more minutes the object then began to move over the wooded area and the eastbound lane of the highway. In a matter of seconds the object shot off into the distance and became just a dot of light. It then made what the witness described as an incredible left turn.

September, 1973
Greensburg, 8:30 pm (UFO)
Several people had just left the Greengate Mall area and were traveling down a back road. One of the passengers noticed

a strange object in the sky to her left and brought it to the attention of the others. At the same time, they noticed that another car was pulled off the road, and the passengers were also watching at the object. The object appeared to be about the size of a passenger car, was ball shaped, and had red and white blinking lights around the center area. There was also a beam of light emitting from the object which seemed to be searching the ground.

The object was descending and gave the impression that it was going to land. The witnesses were frightened by what they saw and located a telephone where they called the state police to report their UFO sighting. The state police referred the witnesses to my UFO Hotline. I learned that the witnesses had also observed a night flying advertising aircraft and they said that what they saw that evening was much different.

September 2, 1973
Adamsburg, 4 am
Creature scares couple in mobile home park

Jerry Forbes (pseudonym) was a resident of the Placid Manor mobile home court near Adamsburg. It was about 4 am on September 2, when Jerry and his girlfriend decided to turn off the television in the living room and retire for the night. It was a warm night and the bedroom window was open, as well as the curtain. Shortly after retiring, they heard a loud growling sound, more like a moan, that broke the silence from within the home. The couple became alarmed and listened quietly. They soon heard the sound of something moving through the weeds and the sound of something large approaching closer to the dwelling increasingly frightened them. Jerry looked up and saw the outline of a dark head at the window which was more than eight feet off the ground.

Jerry jumped out of the bed. The large prowler ran around the side of the structure. The sound of something heavy walking off into the distance could easily be heard in the quiet of the night. The WCUFOSG was notified. Our team went to the area and found some three-toed impressions in the area.

September 2, 1973
Indiana, Indiana County, 5:30 am
Creature standing near a garage

A resident who lives in a mobile home in a rural area outside of the city of Indiana was out in his yard when he observed a large hairy bipedal creature standing down by his garage at about 5:30 am The creature stood about eight feet tall, was covered with hair, and had an ape-like face which seemed somewhat sunken. The creature had one arm up on the side of the building and the hair just hung down from the appendage. To the witness, it appeared that the beast was trying to stabilize its balance. The man did not notice any odd smell or sounds at the time. The creature stood and looked at the man, then suddenly took one step toward the witness. The man ran away and the creature apparently left as well.

September 2, 1973
Alverton, 10 pm
Red eyes and strange footprints

Alverton is a small rural community located between Scottdale and Ruffsdale. About 10 pm two local residents were talking outside when their attention was drawn in the dark to two large red eyes staring toward them. The men went back to the house to get a gun. When they returned, the creature with the red eyes was gone. More strange incidents would occur at this location during the next couple of weeks. A WCUFOSG investigator went to the scene to obtain more details. The next day was to be another very active period for strange events.

September 3, 1973
Erie area, Erie County, early morning, (UFO)

I received information on the UFO Hotline that police officers from around the Erie area were observing a UFO hovering in the sky.

September 3, 1973
Alverton, 2 am
Tall figure observed, footprint found

About 2 am near Alverton, a woman saw an unusually large figure standing by the house. The next morning, family members went outside to look around the living room window area where the figure had been seen. They found a large footprint about twenty inches long. One witness stated that the footprint was too big for that of a human.

September 3, 1973
Glassport, Allegheny County, 3 am
Strange sounds, chickens killed

Strange growls and shrieking sounds were heard coming from the woods near Glassport. This community, located close to the Monongahela River, is not far from the city of McKeesport in Allegheny County. The loud vocalizations were unlike anything that the locals had ever heard before. A WCUFOSG investigator went to the area and interviewed about a dozen people who had been experiencing strange events. An unusual footprint was found inside an old chicken coop.

At another nearby location, the investigator interviewed a man who had gone outside at about 3 am on this date to investigate the shrieking sounds, only to find that his chicken coop had been broken into, and that three chickens were lying dead within thirty feet of the coop. They showed no signs of mutilation and what killed them was not discernable. There was another chicken found behind the coop whose demise was more unusual, and which suggested that it might have been the victim of fowl play.

This chicken had been roosting in a small coop enclosed with a plywood door and a hook to keep it locked. The owner of the property found that the coop had been damaged, apparently in an attempt to remove the bird. The plywood had been torn up and the hook was unlatched. Examination of the remains of the bird indicated that it had been disemboweled. The property owner also found that a larger cage located near the smaller coop, and that weighed over fifty pounds, had been overturned. The investigator also found a few hair strands on a tree trunk near the smaller coop. The hair was located about thirty inches above the ground. The specimen was obtained from the scene for later analysis. (See section: Analytical Studies Of Possible Creature Related Physical Materials)

September 3, 1973
Whitney, 4:30 am
Creature stands next to mobile home, state police respond

Chester Yothers and his wife lived near Whitney, a small community located just outside of Latrobe and near the local airport. The Yothers and some friends were sitting outside on their porch talking about the news of the day. They had heard the reports about a Bigfoot creature having been recently seen in the area. Chester was laughing about it and making fun of the idea that such a creature could exist. Just a few hours later, he changed his mind.

It was about 4:30 am on September 3, when Chester and his wife were sound asleep in their mobile home. Chester was suddenly awakened by the sound of a bumping against the dwelling. The man's first thought was that someone was trying to break into his garage. Chester got out of bed and looked out the bedroom window which faces directly onto the patio.

Chester was shocked as he caught sight of a huge creature standing on his patio only several feet away. He stood there for about thirty seconds staring at the hairy monster, making sure that it was not his imagination. He then awakened his wife and told her that if she wanted to see that thing they called "Bigfoot", that it was standing on the patio. Mrs. Yothers looked out the window and saw the huge beast standing there- motionless. The Yothers only saw the creature from the back. The giant man-like creature was about nine feet tall, standing on two legs, and was very broad shouldered, about two and-a-half to three feet across. The body of the animal was covered with black or dark brown hair about two to three inches long. The arms of the creature were very long, and hung down past the knees. There was no visible neck. The creature stood erect, with it's arms crossed in front. It's right leg was extended, with the knee slightly flexed. Chester stated that the creature did not look like a gorilla or bear, that it was more man-like. The man said that from the moment he saw the creature, there was not the slightest doubt in his mind that it was not a human being.

The creature was taller than his mobile home, and he felt that it could easily look over the top of the structure. Chester and his wife smelled nothing unusual at the time. Chester and his wife also said that during the time they watched the creature, that it was very quiet outside. They did not even hear a cricket. The two people stood there in amazement for two or three minutes watching the creature, which still stood motionless. They then moved to another window and saw that the creature had remained still. By now, the couple was quite frightened. They were fearful of turning on any lights, so they made their way in the dark to the telephone to call the state police. Chester recalled that he bumped into the wall at about that time.

Chester was a retired coal miner. The frightened man could hardly talk. Chester stated, "I dialed the operator. I told her I wanted the state police quick. That big thing they call Bigfoot was right outside my door." The operator quickly connected him to the authorities. Chester told the state police dispatcher what they were observing and indicated to him how frightened they were. When the man hung up the phone and looked out, the creature was gone. Chester thought that when he bumped the wall, or the fact that he had to talk very loudly to the police on the phone in order to be heard may have caused the creature to leave.

About 5 am three state police cars arrived with a total of six troopers. Upon their arrival, Chester turned on a flood light which was located over the garage door. Chester had thought about turning on that bright light while the creature was there, but then decided not to, thinking that the creature could possibly turn over his mobile home and might possibly cause bodily harm.

When the officers arrived, they saw wet footprints on the patio, along with fresh mowed grass from the lawn. The fourteen inch long tracks could be seen going through the wet grass as well. The trail of footprints at one point ended abruptly, causing Chester to ask if the creatures could fly. One trooper went into the bedroom and looked out the window from which they had watched the creature. He verified to the others that it was possible to have observed a dark figure standing outside from that location under those lighting conditions.

I was awake and heard the radio call from one of the troopers at the scene who called the barracks. The investigating officer was giving a detailed report to the dispatcher describing the creature and the evidence found at the scene. The dispatcher was trying to cut off the transmission, telling the trooper to keep that information off the air. Shortly after, one of the investigating troopers contacted me about the incident. George Lutz and I arrived at the scene a few hours later at a time that was convenient to the Yothers.

Upon examining the dwelling and surrounding area, we found muddy spots against the structure where it appeared that someone or something had stepped from the rear lawn over a flower bed and onto the patio. Several of the spots appeared to have been made by something pressing against the house, and one spot was streaked as if made by something in motion. There were also red smear marks found on the home, and there was a bent section of siding near the top of the residence as well. These marks had not been seen before by the owners.

At a nearby neighbor's home, what appeared to be a three-toed footprint was found in a flower bed. That impression was not fresh, apparently having been there for a while. One detail that Chester had related was that the creature was looking away from he and his wife. The creature was staring at a nearby neighbor's porch where several children were sleeping outside. It never approached toward that location.

Chester and I talked frequently in the months after the creature encounter. He and his wife were a very nice couple, and there was no doubt that their personal Bigfoot experience had impacted their lives. As I recall, soon after the incident, the Yothers left their mobile home for a period of time after the initial sighting. Chester no longer had any doubt that such creatures did exist, and he later talked with the media about his sighting.

Artist conception of creature seen near Whitney
Used with permission of Robert McCurry

September 3, 1973
Whitney, 4:45 am
Neighbor sees tall form across from the Yothers' residence

Another resident in that general area at about 4:45 am that same morning, was awakened by some dogs who were barking loudly. This person smelled a strong sulfur odor and observed a tall form standing in a driveway across from the Yothers' mobile home. This person thought at first that she was looking at a tree, then realized that there was none in that location.

September 3, 1973
New Alexandria, 5 am
Strange sounds and smell

Outside of New Alexandria, at about 5 am, a family living near a coal mine was awake and preparing to leave for work. Soon after going outside, some family members noticed that the usual background sounds of nature suddenly became very quiet – even the crickets had stopped chirping. The dog also began to bark excitedly. It was not long after that a loud crying bellow, seemingly close to their property, broke the silence.

The mother, who was inside the house, ran down the stairs yelling out – asking what the sound was. One of the sons grabbed his rifle and went outside to see if he could see the source of the screams. The fellow said his hair was standing on end as he listened. He found his dog standing in place as if unable to move, trembling, and with its ears standing up.

The screams continued for about fifteen minutes and they seemed to move further off in the distance. One witness commented that he had read the newspaper accounts about the Bigfoot creatures and their accompanying screams but had found it hard to believe until now. He was now convinced that something strange was prowling around.

Later that afternoon in the same general area near the Loyalhanna Creek, a group of people were attending a picnic when the terrifying bellowing screams started again. Something large and, according to a witness, "loud as hell," was moving through the grass near the creek. They never saw what it was and apparently never pursued it. That same morning the witness mentioned that his brother, who had a police band monitor, had heard a police car being dispatched to a location where a UFO had reportedly landed in a field.

September 3, 1973
Indiana, Indiana County, 8:10 pm
Hairy creature seen near rural home
That evening at about 8:10, two people living in a rural area near Indiana, PA, observed a large hairy creature moving through a wooded area near their home.

September 3, 1973
Aultman, Indiana County, 9:15 pm
Creature seen in car headlights
About an hour later in the same general area where the creature had been seen near Indiana, some folks were about to visit their daughter's rural mobile home. As they pulled their car up to the structure, their headlights of the car shone on a tall creature about fifty feet away. The creature stood about eight to nine feet tall, appeared stooped, and had eyes that glowed red. The creature walked into the nearby woods and was not seen again by the witnesses. The people notified police about the strange intruder.

September 4, 1973
Homestead, Allegheny County, 12:10 am
Two creatures in shrubs

A report was received from Homestead, Allegheny County, at 12:10 am, near the Monongahela River that two witnesses were walking home when they saw two large and hairy creatures with big red eyes behind some bushes. According to the account, when the beasts started moving in their direction, the observers ran away.

September 4, 1973
Herminie, 9:30 pm
Creature near a house

A report was received from the state police concerning a Bigfoot sighting they received from a family who lived near Herminie. The creature was seen about 9:30 pm.

September 4, 1973
Derry Township, 9:30 pm
UFO beams light toward the ground

It was also about 9:30 pm when another strange incident was taking place back at Derry Township at the Superior Mobile Home Court. Several witnesses observed what they described as a very large torpedo-shaped object moving across the sky over the community. The object was estimated to be about five hundred feet above the ground and it emitted a bright beam of light toward the ground as it passed over.

September 4, 1973
Alverton, 10:03 pm
Smell and red eyed figure

About thirty minutes later near Alverton where some previous oddities had taken place, a woman was sitting on the porch when she noticed a sulfur smell, uncommon to the area. She asked two other people if they could detect the odor, and they confirmed it. Just about that time, the dogs became very agitated and barked wildly. In the distance, they saw a dark figure with red eyes walking toward them. Someone yelled to turn on the bright spotlight from the house toward that direction. A broad shouldered creature quickly turned around and moved away in the distance. The creature was estimated to be about ten feet tall. The smell of sulfur was now very strong in the vicinity. A Bigfoot creature had been prowling this area for some time, and the local farmers were not taking this lightly. They were keeping their guns nearby and loaded.

September 5, 1973
Ruffsdale, Evening
Three creatures observed near residence

A woman who lived near Ruffsdale called the state police to report this incident. She reportedly saw three creatures in the yard behind her home on that evening. There were two very large creatures along with a smaller one. When she saw them, two creatures were lying down, and the other creature was standing. State police called the WCUFOSG concerning the report.

September 6, 1973
Indiana, Indiana County, 11 pm
Creature Looking into mobile home

On September 6, in Indiana, PA, a woman and her children occupied a mobile home in a wooded area of Indiana County. About 11 pm, something was causing the dogs outside to become very upset. While peering out of the window to see what was causing the disturbance, she saw a Bigfoot creature looking back at her through the window. She turned out all of the lights, looked out again, and it appeared that the unwelcome prowler was gone.

September 6, 1973
SITU Responds to Greensburg

As a result of an August 31, Associated Press (AP) wire story concerning the creature sightings that we were investigating, Allen V. Noe, Acting Director of the Society for the Investigation of the Unexplained (SITU) based in Columbia, New Jersey, contacted me for more details about the Bigfoot sightings in the area. SITU was founded by the late Ivan T. Sanderson, a well known scientist and author. SITU accumulated information on unexplained incidents reported around the world. Among the topics which they followed were sightings of Bigfoot.

Their concern was that a proper scientific study be made if a creature was locally captured. SITU could provide some specialized scientific expertise, and through their contacts, at least two internationally known anthropologists could be called upon to determine the status of such a creature, whether human, subhuman, or animal. I felt that the input of SITU could be helpful with the continuing investigation. They also had the capability to have hair samples studied, which could help identify from what type of animal they originated from.

Allen Noe, his wife Polly, and member Robert E. Jones decided to drive to Greensburg on September 6, to look first hand into the strange incidents occurring here. Allen and his companions appeared very serious and professional, and they all had a knowledge of Bigfoot and other Fortean history. The SITU team stayed for a few days, then returned to New Jersey on September 10. During their stay, the trio had the opportunity to interview a number of first hand witnesses who had seen the creatures. They also responded with us to some incidents reported on the hotline.

During our conversations, I made Alan Noe aware that I had left physical traces possibly related to some of the Bigfoot cases with the Carnegie Museum, but I had never received any results of their findings. We decided to drive into Pittsburgh and we obtained this material. Later, various hair and feces samples were taken back to SITU headquarters in New Jersey for future analysis. Those samples were later sent for examination to Frederick Ulmer, formerly Curator of Mammals at the Philadelphia Zoo, who was retired at that time. Some other future Pennsylvania creature related samples were also forwarded by SITU to Professor George Agogino, of the Paleo-Indian Institute of the University of Eastern New Mexico.

As the accounts of the Pennsylvania Bigfoot sightings were making national and local news, various researchers began to descend on Greensburg and the communities where the creature sightings had been occurring. A reporter from the National Enquirer flew in to meet with us and to follow up on some of the local creature incidents. He spent some days here interviewing witnesses and investigators and gathering other information. He seemed impressed with the information which he had accumulated. I understood that he was leaving Greensburg, then flying out of the country to do another interview which concerned extraterrestrial visitations.

Bob Daley, an engineer from Hatfield, PA, and an investigator for North American Wildlife Research, arrived in Greensburg on September 2, to do his own investigation into the credibility of the creature reports in western Pennsylvania. Bob was a very serious individual and he seemed quite intrigued with the investigations that we were conducting. He had the opportunity to interview some first hand creature witnesses. Bob later joined the WCUFOSG.

September 9, 1973
Ligonier, 5 am
Strange sound, torn screen, depressed area nearby

Mrs. Tobias (pseudonym) was having another restless night. It seemed as though in recent days something was disturbing her normal, restful sleep pattern. It was around 5 am on September 9, when the woman walked outside on her porch to empty some coffee grounds when she heard something very unusual. What she heard was a heavy breathing sound or a loud sigh seeming to originate from between the cellar door and the porch. Mrs. Tobias is familiar with animals but had never heard a sound like this before.

The woman awakened her husband, who also heard the sound. It now seemed to be moving from the end of their property along the fence. The man then began to notice an odd smell which he described to a WCUFOSG investigator as smelling similar to burning sulfur. His wife was having sinus problems and could not smell anything. Sometime later, the Tobias's noticed that their German Shephard was beginning to act oddly. The dog ran to the living room window, and started to bark, but abruptly stopped in the middle of a bark. The dog then quickly moved behind a couch and hid.

Generally, if a stray animal or stranger comes near their property, the German Shephard and the other dogs chained outside responded loudly, but the canines were acting unusually. All of the dogs were quiet, except for one which would give an occasional utterance. Mr. Tobias also wondered why the family cats, which were outside of the house, were running around crazily.

On the living room screen door, the family had discovered three zig-zag indentations that could be seen from an angle. The mark was four inches wide and six to eight inches long, and to the family, looked like a paw print with long fingers where something had pressed against the screen. The shape of the mark could only be seen at night, when the outside lights were on and the inside lights were off. They showed the investigator a cat scratch on the screen to compare with the other one. The family said that it had a slight fluorescent appearance to it. The dog refused to go outside afterwards. Photos of the screen marking were taken by the investigator.

Later on the evening of the event, Mrs. Tobias went to her garden to pick some vegetables and discovered a flattened area of grass and weeds, which had not been there earlier in the day. Mr. Tobias looked over the area. The family had many deer in their woods and they were familiar with their habits. This depressed area was unusual.

September 11, 1973
Keystone State park, Derry Township, 5 pm
Creatures swimming in lake

A man visiting Keystone State Park in Derry Township saw something very strange in the lake. The witness reported to the state police that he saw two very large man-like creatures, but covered with hair, swimming in the water. The man stated that the arms and legs of the creatures were much longer than that of a human. The state police sent an officer to the scene and met with the witness. The officer obtained the UFO Hotline number from the barracks and had the man contact us.

September 11, 1973
Superior, 7:15 pm (UFO)

A woman who lived in the Superior Mobile Home Court in Derry Township reported observing a solid spherical object with square windows moving over the nearby tree tops. Near Derry at 8 pm, a large object described as looking like a radio tower in the sky reportedly approached close to a vehicle.

September 11, 1973
Superior, 10:15 pm
Creature observed near mobile home court

Several residents of the Superior Mobile Home Court in Derry Township reported observing a large hair-covered creature in the nearby woods which seemed to be circling around the dwellings. Later some odd footprints were found at a nearby old mine shaft.

September 11, 1973
Dillsburg, York County, 10:30 pm
Nurses observe bright colored lights in sky

According to the Sept 12, 1973, edition of the Gettysburg Times, about 10:30 pm near Dillsburg, several nurses observed bright colored lights in the sky which soon sped away.

September 11, 1973
West Newton, 11:10 pm
Large object spotted over tree tops

At about 11:10 pm, a witness from West Newton in Westmoreland County reported seeing a large round orange object over the tree tops.

September 12, 1973
Waterford, 12:30 am (UFO)

There was a report that a large, white elliptical-shaped object, which was in a vertical position in the sky, was emitting three smaller, orange objects. The smaller objects were going in and out of the main object. The objects were observed over the Derry Ridge.

September 12, 1973
Blairsville, Indiana County, 10:40 am
Bigfoot daylight observation walking through cornfield

It was a bright and sunny morning when three friends decided to take their daily walk. The location was between Blairsville and New Derry. The area is very rural farmland surrounded by woods and cornfields. The women were talking about everyday subjects and the last thing they were thinking about was Bigfoot. Suddenly, two of the ladies spontaneously yelled out, both looking ahead. The third woman saw what they were focused on at about the same time.

The women could not believe what they were seeing. It was a tall, slender ape-like creature making a path through the corn. One of the women said, "The figure was amazingly tall and slender. It was more brown than black (and hard to describe, but sort of gray.) It was walking upright with forward sloping shoulders and long arms." The creature, covered from head to toe with hair, also had very long slender legs. The long arms of the creature hung down below its knees. The face of the creature was not seen since it was moving away from the observers.

The creature made long eight-foot strides that took it from an unobstructed hayfield into the cornfield where they lost sight of it. As the creature entered the tall cornfield, the witnesses thought that it was interesting that the creature did not slow down and stop to separate the corn stalks as it moved through. "It just ploughed into it." The three women neither heard sounds, nor did they smell anything unusual at the time. One of the ladies commented, "I wish someone could prove us wrong. As of now, we are sure what we saw was not human."

I also learned that about ten days prior to the encounter with the creature, one of the witnesses who lived in the general area reported hearing strange yelping sounds at night, and also a chilling elongated wail. The woman had mentioned this to her husband at the time, but did not want to frighten her children. Her husband later learned that others in the area had also heard the sounds as well.

On the night of September 18, 1973, at about 10:20 pm in the same area, another witness reported seeing an odd sphere of bright light which flashed on and off, then suddenly vanished after about ten minutes.

September 13, 1973
Indiana, Indiana County, 8:45 pm
Man shot at creature. Possible physical evidence

On Thursday evening, September 13, 1973, two state troopers from the Indiana barracks had responded to a creature incident that had occurred in a rural location a few miles outside the town of Indiana. A resident stated to the officers that a large, hairy creature had visited his family home and had taken some apples. The creature walked across the road in front of the house and the man shot it. The creature continued into the woods and screamed. The officers warned the man not to shoot at the creature again.

We were notified by the Indiana state police barracks about the report. The information we received indicated that there were possible blood spots on the roadway. I contacted the witnesses and got directions to that location. I quickly traveled with a WCUFOSG investigating team to the location of the shooting. While we did not recommend shooting at these unknown beings, the report of possible physical evidence related to a creature could be very important in determining what the creatures were.

When we arrived at that location, a number of local neighbors were there to greet us. Many of them had their own personal accounts to relate. First, we met the family who lived in the house where the shooting had occurred.

We learned that at about 8:45 pm the mother was in the kitchen cooking when she heard a loud thumping sound. She looked up to see what she described as the back side of a giant, hairy man-like animal on her back porch. It jumped off the porch and hit the ground with another thump. The family had earlier picked a bushel of apples and then placed them in a bucket on the porch. The creature was seen eating a whole apple as it moved around the corner toward the front of the house. The creature apparently had an appetite for the fresh apples. The family had picked the apples at about 7:15 pm and had filled the container. Many of the apples were now missing. The family also noted that had it been a bear, it would likely have turned over the bucket.

The woman yelled to her teenaged grandson, Rick (pseudonym), to look outside. Rick also saw the creature and quickly ran to get his gun, a .35 caliber rifle. Momentarily, they heard a scratching sound outside at the side of the house. The young man turned the lights off so he could see better as he looked out the window. Rick pressed against the glass, and suddenly jumped back with a scream. The creature, which had been bent down, now had its hideous face also pressed against the window. The creature was about eight feet tall and covered with dark hair. The face was somewhat human like, but the nose appeared to be flat. The eyes were described as reddish-brown and the size of cow eyes.

Rick grabbed his gun and ran outside onto the front porch. He saw that the creature was now very close, standing in the yard by a tree in front of the house. The fellow assumed that when he screamed, he caused the creature to move from its location by the window. The animal was bi-pedal, but appeared to be somewhat stooped as it moved across the road toward a heavily wooded area. The creature was taking long strides, as it only took about three steps to cross the road. The creature was swinging its long hairy arms as it moved.

Rick did not want to shoot toward the direction of some local homes, so he waited until the creature was a clear shot. He also wanted to make sure of what he was shooting at. Rick stayed on the porch and fired two rounds at the hairy, dark hulk. He was aiming toward the back of the creature and felt that he had hit the beast. The creature seemed to move faster after it was shot at, but it appeared unharmed.

Once the animal moved into the woods, an ungodly scream rang out from that area. Only one very loud sound was heard, but it was enough to cause many neighbors to run outside to see what was going on. The creature had an apple in its hand, but dropped it as it crossed the roadway. Rick and the others walked over to the road. Lying on the road surface was the apple, which appeared to have been chewed, and several wet drops which appeared to be blood.

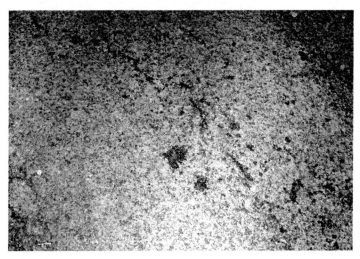

Substance on road after Bigfoot shooting near Indiana
© Stan Gordon

The state police told the residents that the apple had apparently been eaten by a bear. The police took the apple. Our team photographed the area and gathered the possible "blood droppings" from the road to have it analyzed. The family was sure that what they had seen was not a bear or any animal with which they were familiar. They were upset that the authorities were not taking them seriously. Through the auspices of SITU, the samples were sent to Professor George Agogino in New Mexico for study.

There were other folks there who appeared very serious and concerned and wanted to share some of the recent local Bigfoot encounters which they had heard about. On the previous Monday night (September 11, 1973), about twenty miles from the current location, a man near Brush Valley reportedly heard a series of strange sounds in the woods. First, he heard the sound like that of a crying baby. He went outside to investigate, then heard what sounded like a grunt, and then it began to emit a crying sound as if originating from a man. The witness became scared and went back inside his home.

One neighbor recounted another recent event that is said to have happened to a woman who lived near Marion Center. This young woman had a large German Shepherd dog which suddenly moved into a small crawl space and began to shake, apparently in fear of something. The lady realized that something was wrong and ran for her rifle. The woman lived by herself in a mobile home. She went outside and not far away saw a Bigfoot that she described as horrible looking. The creature's face was dark with a flat nose and large lips. She reportedly shot at the creature as it moved away.

Also in the area, one local woman described seeing a creature looking in her window. A local man related an event where a man was driving along in his car when suddenly, a creature began to run alongside of his car. It reportedly kept pace with the vehicle for a period of time as it moved along at about 40 mph.

Some years after the shooting event, myself and another investigator, Joe Kosczuk, returned to that remote location deep in the woodlands of Indiana County. We had gone back to the area since we had heard that other possible sightings had been occurring. It was a comfortable evening and all appeared normal. We had finished up our discussion with some witnesses and were walking around the location, when suddenly I began to experience an overwhelming feeling of dread.

I was stopped in my tracks. I had never experienced such a feeling before, nor any time since that night. It was a strange, overall encompassing inner feeling that sent cold chills through my body. It seemed as though something wanted us to leave that area immediately.

Joe also began to experience a similar feeling at just about the same moment. We left the area, but saw nothing un-usual. Some Bigfoot witnesses had on occasion described such a feeling of over powering fear before or during their observation of a Bigfoot creature.

September 14, 1973
Jeannette, 11:30 pm
Strange sounds and smell near mobile home
Several residents of the Silver Dolphin Mobile Home Court were sitting around exchanging stories when one woman went outside for a walk. The lady had not been feeling well and she suddenly began to vomit. Moments after the woman lost her stomach contents, a loud similar vomiting sound,

as though her actions were being mimicked, broke the silence from the nearby woods. A loud scream then bellowed through the area. Residents also noticed that an uncommon sulfur-like odor permeated the air at the same time.

Some of the residents found a large, flattened area in the woods behind the mobile homes. Near that area, some very large droppings were also seen. They knew that there were no horses nearby. Some corn was also found that had been husked and eaten in an unusual manner. These reports did not come in until some time after the occurrences. One resident recalled that a year before, some girls had come across some odd three-toed footprints up in the same woods.

September 15, 1973
Derry, 2:30 pm
Girl sees creature while riding pony

A young girl was taking an afternoon ride on her pony in the countryside outside of Derry. Her attention was drawn ahead of her. Down the road she observed what she estimated to be a six feet tall hair-covered Bigfoot creature walking in her direction. Even though the creature was some distance away, her pony suddenly stopped and would not move. The pony then turned around, and quickly galloped down the road. The girl rode to a local home where she used the phone to report to a friend what had happened.

September 16, 1973
Whitney, 4:35 am
Woman sees large figure standing near bushes

A woman was awakened at 4:35 am by her dog, that was barking loudly. The lady looked outside and observed a tall figure standing behind a group of bushes near the village of Whitney. When she went into another room to look from a different location, she saw that the intruder had gone. Later after looking over the area where the figure had been seen, several odd footprints were found on the bank by the woods.

September 16, 1973
Latrobe, evening
Pet deer killed, chickens missing, track found nearby

That same evening only a few miles away from Whitney, a strange series of events occurred on a small farm in the Westmoreland County countryside outside of Latrobe. As one of the owners stated in their written report, someone or something had entered their property and had slit the throat of their pet deer. The pen where the deer was kept had not been disturbed and the fastener was still in place.

Also about sixteen chickens had vanished, the only traces left were some feathers. The chickens were kept in a large coop and the door was kept open so that the fowl could move around. The chickens did not always stay in that housing, since they also liked to visit the nearby barn. One of the dogs that had been chained on the property also appeared to have a lame leg after that night.

The owners were perplexed by the events. They wondered why the intruder did not rob the family or steal something from the property. Why did the culprit seem to focus just on attacking the animals? A WCUFOSG investigating team went to the scene to speak with the family and to look over the property where the animal assaults had occurred. Near the chicken coop in an area where hay was strewn about, a three-toed footprint measuring thirteen inches long was found. The impression could not be cast, but photographs were taken.

September 18, 1973
Derry Township, 10:20 pm
Bell Farm creature 10 feet from woman
UFO reported minutes later

At the Bell Farm (pseudonym) in Derry Township where there had been strange ongoing events during the summer as reported by family members and visitors, more inexplicable incidents were about to unfold. At about 10:20 pm, Mrs. Bell was walking to the driveway where her husband's truck and her car were parked. She had her eyes to the ground, since a lot of apples had fallen and she did not want to slip on one. The woman was going to visit some acquaintances in Latrobe and was looking forward to a relaxing evening.

As the woman approached the parking area and was about ten feet from the truck when she noticed something out of place. Next to the truck was a tall, dark form which she thought was a tree. She soon realized that there were no tree in that exact location. Then she clearly saw it. Standing upright, at least eight or nine feet tall with very broad shoulders was a hairy man-like creature. The beast suddenly took one step in her direction, then raised up its long arms. The woman cried out loudly. In response, the creature bellowed out a similar sound, as if mimicking Mrs. Bell's loud cry. The frightened woman ran to the house and screamed louder. The creature also made a much louder scream as it moved off.

Other residents ran outside after hearing her screams. Mrs. Bell told them that she had seen the creature, that it did not appear to want to hurt her, only that it really frightened her. She thought the creature had run off through the field. Mrs. Bell did mention the strange calm around the farm property prior to her encounter with the mystery beast. This same eerie calm was noticed on the other occasions either when the creature had been seen or when the strange cries had been heard ringing through the woods. As Mrs. Bell described it, everything was still, and nothing was moving. She said there were no bird sounds and all the dogs from the farm were crowded up in a corner hiding back inside of their pens. The cows were huddling against a fence at a location that they did not generally frequent. Mrs. Bell's puppy, which generally walked with her, did not accompany her to the car that night.

About ten minutes after Mrs. Bell had seen the creature, her husband and another man went out looking for it in the fields. They did not see the creature, but they instead observed a UFO. What they saw was a large, red tubular-shaped object moving over the hillside behind the farm. The object illuminated the ground below in a red light as it moved out of sight. Referring to the luminous object mentioned, Mrs. Bell said, "I don't know if it has anything to do with this thing, 'the creature,' but every time we see that or hear that, that light is pretty close."

WCUFOSG investigator Barry Clark had spent a number of evenings staking out the Bell farm since a number of recurring mysterious events had taken place there. One evening in September, Barry actually experienced some first hand incidents that he would never forget. It was on that night that he heard the creature. Barry stated, "I actually got to hear that thing scream. It was an earth-shattering, scary scream. It started out as a very deep rattling, and then turned into an awful like howl and growl at the same time."

Barry recalled that one of the dogs at the farm was on the mean side. "That dog, just before the scream occurred, went underneath a mobile home and didn't come out. When the scream occurred, the dog buried itself so far under that mobile home that you couldn't get it out." The man who owned the property was so frightened by the creature visits that he went out and purchased an H&H safari rifle to protect his family.

Mr. Bell and his wife had reported that among the odd things that had been occurring around their farm was an odd, bright star-like object which would appear in the sky around 10 pm. This bright object looked quite large in the sky and would change colors, from a silver, to a blood red, and back to a silver color. Barry had previously investigated reports of a similar object reported by other local residents. They all seemed to be reporting the same object generally appearing in the Northwest sky, according to his compass readings.

On the same night as Barry heard the creature scream while still at the farm, he had a UFO sighting. The object was similar to the one seen by the Bells and others on previous occasions. The object was larger and brighter than the planet Venus when it was seen on a clear morning. It was changing from a blood red color, then to a silver color. Barry said that the trio stood there watching the object as it suddenly moved in seconds, with a jerky movement, from about a 45 degree to 90 degree position. Barry soon was in radio contact with another man, his wife, and another fellow located not far away from the farm, who were simultaneously watching the same bright object in the sky. Barry drove up to see them on a hilltop which provided a clear view of the surrounding sky and the mysterious aerial device.

As the four of them watched, there were five sudden brilliant flashes of light about one second apart from each other that lit the sky like a welder's arc. Each flash came down as a ring of light that circled the entire section of the sky that they were observing. With each flash, the ring section became larger, and became a deeper blood red. As each ring came down, it became larger on a tubular section of light. There was a dark section between each glowing ring area.

And then the observation got even stranger. The sky suddenly became full of small, bright silver lights that came toward the larger object, which was now solid red in color. As these smaller silver lights approached the larger object, they appeared to change to red. The sight gave the observers the impression of bees going into a hive. It was as if they each had to slow down to take their turn to enter it. The woman started crying and jumped into her car. The three men stood there in disbelief.

The object suddenly began to grow larger in size as it seemed to be dropping toward the ground. The four people left the area and arranged to meet down the road at a local diner. Barry requested that they not discuss the event among themselves, but to individually write down what they had experienced. The next day they met to compare notes. The accounts were all very similar.

The events of that night had a profound effect on Barry's life. First Barry heard the creature scream, and within a few hours watched an object in the sky for which he and the other observers had no explanation. Barry decided he had enough and decided to stop his pursuit of the Bigfoot and UFO cases in the area. Barry said he could not help but wonder if there was some association between the creature sightings in the area and the UFOs that were also being observed.

Previous Bigfoot encounter and other strange incidents at the Bell Farm

Mrs. Bell was an educated and intelligent woman. She was having a hard time dealing with the strange intrusions on her property. She said she did not believe in things from outer space, nor did she believe in monsters, at least not until after some first hand encounters. She and others had observed strange lights around the farm beginning around July. The most common UFO was described as looking like a red safety flare in shape. One evening, some of the horses had taken off into a field. Some men began a search for the animals where a strange light had been recently seen. While searching, they found a perfectly round burned area which they estimated to be about fifteen to twenty feet in diameter.

It was in August on a warm foggy night that Mrs. Bell had her first encounter with the unknown creature. She was driving on the country road near the Derry Township farm at about 7:30 pm when she saw a huge hair-covered creature exit a cornfield and walk across the road ahead. The woman said when she first saw it she kept blinking her eyes, since she thought that she was seeing things. The witness had the opportunity to obtain a good view of the creature. Her first thought was that it was a gorilla that had escaped from a zoo.

The creature, however, was walking erect, just like a man, upright on two legs. The creature was moving quickly as it crossed the roadway. The witness said that it only took two steps and it was across the road. With two more steps she said that the creature crossed over a chained area. As the woman drove down the road, she saw that the chain was swinging, so apparently the creature had brushed it as it moved down the path.

The Bigfoot, which was relatively close, did not move toward the vehicle. It did, however, look directly at the woman. According to Mrs. Bell, the creature was covered with brown hair, except on its chest. There was long hair on its head and forehead, but not on its face. The head of the creature seemed small and out of proportion to its very broad shoulders and its enormous chest. There was not much of a neck. Its very long arms hung down by its knees. It did not have long legs compared to its large body. The creature kept looking toward the woman as it moved off. There was no odor noticed in either of the two creature encounters.

When Mrs. Bell reached the house, she was very upset and went to bed. She could not sleep, was frightened, but was reluctant to tell anyone about what she had seen. She realized that she needed to talk with someone about what she had observed and finally told some neighbors and her husband. It was her husband who suggested that they report what was going on at the farm. Not only family, but also other visitors to the farm would also experience strange events around the property as well.

Mr. Bell had heard the creature breathing down by the barn. What he heard was not a normal human breathing sound, nor the sound of any of the farm animals with which he was familiar. The unusual non-human, loud heavy breathing sound was becoming very common. Many people over wide spread areas had reported the sound in association with local Bigfoot activity. I had heard it myself on more than one occasion while conducting investigations at the locations of these creature encounters. There had been repeated activity at the Bell farm during the summer.

One evening I had received a call from the family that the creature had just been down by their barn and they felt that it was likely around in the nearby woods or fields. I responded with George Lutz to the farm. When we got there, in the barnyard we discovered three-toed impressions and took photographs of them. The cows were acting very strangely as they crowded around the barn, attempting to gain entrance into the building. The other farm animals were very quiet. The dogs were not barking. It was a dark and very warm night and it was uncomfortably still and quiet.

George and I searched the area for other evidence along with family members. All of a sudden, breaking the silence from the cornfields quite a distance away were loud, heavy breathing sounds, as if one was gasping for air. From that same general position, we could hear something heavy moving fast through the fields away from us. George and I began to pursue the source of the sound through the dark fields ahead. We were never able to get close to whatever it was. We did, however, record on tape, the deep asthmatic-like sounds.

Mr. Bell also mentioned an interesting coincidence. It seems that both times the creature was seen by his wife, there had been some fuel spilled nearby. He speculated that the animal, for some reason, was attracted to the fuel spill. Barry Clark recalled that many of the mobile home locations, which had reported Bigfoot sightings, had mercury vapor lamps on poles nearby. He wondered if that was a significant coincidence. Barry also wondered why there were so many Bigfoot encounters near mobile homes.

September 20, 1973
Indications of government interest in Bigfoot reports
The creature encounters were still continuing. The public and media interest continued, as well. I had little sleep with the

phones still ringing off the hook all night long. For weeks I had been hurrying off to widespread locations at all hours of the day and night. As stories of the creature encounters continued to make the news, it was apparent that hoaxed events would increase.

These fabricated events generally dealt with footprint findings. Most of the time it was easy to determine what tracks appeared to be authentic, in comparison to those that had been created by various artificial means. There were some wild goose chases as well. But there were many sightings of these creatures which appeared to be legitimate. Some creature observations turned out to have an easy explanation.

In one instance, a reporter at The Latrobe Bulletin received a call from a frightened New Derry resident. The woman was riding down a highway and noticed what appeared to be a very large dead hairy creature on the side of the road. She assumed the creature had just been hit by a vehicle. The reporter grabbed his camera and hurried out to the area. I quickly arrived on the scene as well. The woman was correct. There was a very large dead creature lying in the bushes. Unfortunately, it was a dead dog.

On September 20, among the many phone calls that I received, one conversation would stand out. The man on the phone indicated that he worked for the U.S. government. He stated that they were aware of the reports of the Bigfoot sightings occurring in Westmoreland County and the surrounding areas, as well as the investigations that the WCUFOSG was conducting into those incidents.

The man suggested that the government was interested in learning more about these creatures. The caller indicated that if we happened upon a case where we had strong physical evidence that would prove that such creatures exist, that I was to contact a particular person at a government facility in Washington, D.C.

I was told to contact, "The Bureau of Sports Fisheries, Bird and Mammals Lab." I was also provided the mailing address, and phone number of the facility. Had we come across any actual dead bodies of such creatures, the Bigfoot mystery would likely have been solved. That, of course, did not occur. We found interesting circumstantial physical evidence in some of the cases, but we knew that this was not enough proof to solve the Bigfoot mystery once and for all.

September 20, 1973
Greensburg, Near state police headquarters, 1 pm
Boys find tracks in woods

Two local boys were walking through a wooded area near the Troop A State Police Headquarters in Greensburg. At about 1 pm the boys discovered a series of large unusual footprints and were concerned after hearing the talk about a Bigfoot creature being seen in the area. The two boys ran to the state police station and reported what they had found. The boys thought the police did not believe them, so they left the barracks and went home.

September 20, 1973
Alverton, 10:30 pm
Tall creature seen near a house

On September 20, a relative was staying over at a house in Alverton where there had been previous visits by a Bigfoot creature. This guest observed a tall creature standing by the kitchen window at about 10:30 pm The only feature that the witness could see was red eyes.

September 21, 1973
Latrobe, 2 am
Dog grabs Bigfoot by the heel, woman chases after the creature

It was around 2 am when nineteen year old Becky Collins (pseudonym) and her sister were awakened by the sound of a dog growling and chewing away at something. There was also a sound like metal being struck, described by the witness as a "tinny" sound. Becky lived in a modern housing development just on the outskirts of Latrobe. Becky's sister went back to sleep. The witness went to the bedroom window to look outside to see what was causing the commotion.

Becky could not believe what she was seeing. Just across the street about forty feet away was a mail box, and next to it was a creature that looked like a tall, hairy muscular man. Becky surmised that the tinny sound could have been this creature banging on the mailbox. What was even stranger was that a beagle dog was growling loudly while it had the right heel of the creature clenched tightly in its mouth.

Becky hurried down to the next level and went to the front door to get a better look. The creature stood about six and-a-half feet tall, was not broad shouldered, and it had very small hips. Its shoulders were bigger than its hips. The creature was very light on its feet. The entire body of the creature was covered with black hair, which was not very thick. The head was similar to that of a human male, but the neck was shorter and broader than most humans. There was hair covering the entire neck area, with no bare skin visible. She could not see its' face or eyes from her position.

The only areas of the body which seemed devoid of hair were the palms of the hands and around the elbows. The arms of the creature hung down well below the knees, much too long for a human. The creature twice swung its long arms at the dog as though trying to scare it off. Oddly, the creature never actually hit the dog.

The beast finally broke away from the grip of the dog and began to run down over a hill. I went to the location to interview Becky. She was very intelligent and sincere. She was very detailed in recalling what had taken place and was emotionally moved by the experience. Becky said she could never figure out why she reacted the way she did as this event was unfolding.

Becky told me she had no idea why she went out in the middle of the night in her nightgown to follow after the creature. When Becky saw the creature running away, she ran out the door and began to pursue it. The dog was barking and chasing after the hairy beast, but was having trouble trying to keep up with it.

One detail that the young woman pointed out was the agility of this creature, which took very large steps. It covered a lot of ground with each long stride, more than a human could. Becky explained how the creature, as large as it was, appeared very light on its feet. But when the feet of the beast touched the ground, the witness could feel the ground vibrating, and heard a booming sound with each step. The creature never swung its' oversized long arms as it moved. She followed the creature to the top of a hill and stopped at that point.

Watching as the creature moved downward to a location on the other side of the hill about seventy feet away, it was lost from sight as it moved through the weeds and brush. Becky could see the weeds moving. The dog continued to follow after it, but for whatever reason stopped barking. The beagle went into the weeds after it, but soon returned. The dog left the area and was not seen again. This dog's reaction to the close presence of this Bigfoot was very odd, since in most cases, dogs near these creatures have generally refused to move or bark.

After the dog left the area, Becky suddenly came back to reality. The sounds of movement had all stopped, and there was just the sound of silence. The woman realized that she was standing alone in the weeds and did not know the whereabouts of the creature. Suddenly Becky was overcome with fear, and ran back to her home where she would be safe.

September 21, 1973
Greensburg, 2 pm
Boys see creature near police barracks, troopers respond

On September 21, a group of boys were playing down in the woods behind the Greensburg state police headquarters around 2 pm that warm and sunny day. The woods are very thick and full of trees and brush, and extend for a considerable distance until they end near Donahue Road. The boys lived in the area and were familiar with the wooded terrain and the wildlife that inhabit that thicket. However, the gang of local lads was not familiar with what they were about to see.

As they moved through the dense brush, they suddenly caught sight of a strange creature ahead of them in the woods. They reported seeing the upper body and the head of a tan colored gorilla-like creature. It appeared that the creature was stooped down. The boys could see the head of the creature moving back and forth. One boy threw a stone at it. The boys all ran. At one point a sound like that of a baby crying rang through the woods.

The youngsters ran to the nearby state police headquarters to report that they had seen a monster. The boys were very shaken up. The officers took their accounts seriously. Two state troopers walked down behind the barracks with the boys to the area where they had seen the creature. Large footprints were seen on the ground. Near the area where the creature was seen, they found some patches of tan colored hair, similar to the color of the creature, on some tree branches and the ground.

The troopers took the hair, and told the boys they would have it sent to a lab to try to determine what animal it came from. The officers wrote up an incident report on the case, and included their opinion that the boys had seen something unusual in the woods. We never heard the results of those lab tests.

While the search was underway, some of the boys claimed to have seen the creature much further back in the woods. The WCUFOSG was notified about the incidents. The flurry of Bigfoot reports occurring in this area for many weeks was attracting much interest locally and nationally.

Allen V. Noe, treasurer and acting director of the Society for the Investigation of the Unexplained (SITU) from New Jersey, had returned to Greensburg to further investigate the ongoing Bigfoot reports and offered the assistance of its' scientific experts and analytical capabilities to the WCUFOSG. Noe accompanied another WCUFOSG investigator and myself to the wooded areas to search for evidence. We met three of the boys who had witnessed the events.

As we searched the area, several large footprints were found in the soft ground. The toe impressions were not clearly discernable in the grassy area. The footprints were measured at fourteen inches long and seven and-a-half inches wide across the toe. There was also some odd fecal matter which appeared to be filled with small rodent bones and teeth. This material was collected for analytical study as well. Some small patches of what looked like tan colored hair was also recovered.

September 21, 1973
Derry Township, 11:30 pm
Creature seen in field near Bell farm

A man was searching around in a field with his high beam light, down the road from where the Bell farm (pseudonym) is located when the beam hit a large, black, hairy creature standing between some pine trees. As the beam struck the creature, it raised its head, and the man could see its eyes, which were glowing with a red and orange color.

While much of the body was hidden from view most of the time, the creature was estimated to be about seven feet tall and appeared ape-like. The creature turned and ran up a hill, walking bent over and with its head in a downward position. The man went to the Bell farm to tell the owners what he had seen. The witness stated, "I would bet my life on what I saw. I saw something unusual, and I feel that it must have been Bigfoot."

September 22, 1973
Penn Hills, Allegheny County, Early evening
Boys hear movement in woods

A report came into the UFO Hotline from a Channel 11 TV reporter in Pittsburgh. Several local boys were riding their trail bikes in a nearby wooded area they visited frequently along Indiana Road in Penn Hills. This was a large, nearly one hundred acre wooded location full of berries, brush and trees in the vicinity of a stone quarry.

As the boys rode along, their attention was drawn to the sound of something large moving through the brush by the sound of limbs cracking and breaking. The boys became alarmed and hurried home. A short while later, the boys became curious and went back into the woods to look around and found a series of footprints that looked very strange. A heavy rain occurred during the night. They planned to return to the area the next day.

September 23, 1973
Penn Hills, Allegheny County
More ape-like tracks found deep in the woods

The next day, September 23, several people returned to the woods to look for more evidence. They went deeper into the tree covered area where they found a number of detailed five-toed tracks. A cast was made of one of the impressions. The dimensions of the casting were eleven inches long and five inches across the four-toed area. The print measured about seven inches across the entire toe area.

These tracks were most interesting and not like the other footprints which had been surfacing during our investigations into other alleged hairy creature reports. This print was like that of an ape. It would be unusual for an ape to be running loose in a wooded area near Pittsburgh.

SITU's Alan Noe and I made a quick trip down to Penn Hills, which is a Pittsburgh suburb where we met a number of the witnesses. We interviewed the boys and we went into the woods and searched for evidence. We had learned that one year earlier, one of the boys was taking a summer jaunt through the same woods and had observed a hairy creature up in the trees which appeared to have long arms and legs – and even a tail. The boy was ridiculed after telling his story to relatives and friends, so the subject was dropped.

September 23, 1973
Penn Hills, Allegheny County, Early evening
Monkey-like creature in tree

Early that same evening of September 23, another young boy was taking a daylight walk through the same wooded area where the ape-like tracks had been found. As he walked along, his attention was drawn to a commotion in some of the tall nearby trees. There, climbing in the trees was a monkey-like creature about four feet tall. The animal made a loud growl, then suddenly whipped around the branch of a tree. The boy caught a glimpse of its monkey-like face and he saw that the creature did have a tail. The unknown beast ran off after the encounter with the boy. This deepens the mystery even more, since apes do not have tails.

There were no animals missing from the Pittsburgh Zoo, and I was not aware of any circus that might have passed through the area reporting any escaped animals at the time of these encounters in 1972 or 1973.

September 23, 1973
Penn Township, 10 pm
Woman reports seeing creature in back yard

A woman was in her rural home when she looked out of a window toward the back of the house. The witness reported seeing a hairy Bigfoot creature walking through her back-yard and continuing into the nearby woods.

September 24, 1973
Greensburg, 2:30 pm
Boys see creature lying in woods

Two young boys were walking through the woods not far from the state police headquarters at Greensburg. The boys walked those woods frequently, but that would soon change as a result of the experience that was about to occur. The lads were walking behind another local facility at about 2:30 pm where apparently the maintenance staff had recently dumped a large pile of grass cuttings.

Lying upon that pile of old grass clippings was a very large gorilla-like creature with a pointed head that appeared to be sleeping. The boys panicked and ran to a local family to report what they had seen. A man and his son accompanied the boys back to that location, but the creature was gone. I spoke with one of the boy's parents. The boy had told them the story soon after the event. The parents said that their son was visually shaken up and scared. A WCUFOSG team went to the site. Bob McCurry drew a sketch of how the creature looked sleeping in the woods, while the witnesses looked on and explained the details of what they saw.

September 24, 1973
Greensburg, 5 pm
Newspaper boy sees creature on hill

Another local boy was delivering newspapers in the vicinity of the state police headquarters at Greensburg. From that location he could see toward the woods. In the distance on a hill, he caught sight of a tall, hairy Bigfoot-like creature, which was tan in color. The boy stated that the creature walked in a stooped manner, almost like it was drunk.

September 24, 1973
West Newton, 8:30 pm
Creature seen running through woods

A man was walking in his grandfather's field where a lot of beans had been planted. Recently, the beans had been vanishing in large numbers and the family was attributing it to the deer in the area. It was dark when the man heard a high pitched sound ahead of him in the nearby woods. He aimed his light in the direction of the sound and caught sight of the body of a large, hairy ape-like creature moving through the woods. The man ran home and told other relatives, who verified that he appeared quite frightened and the hair on his arms was standing up. When WCUFOSG investigators arrived on the scene an hour later, the man still appeared very shaken.

September 24, 1973
Penn Hills, Allegheny County, 9 pm
Hairy creature encounters trail bike

A local boy was riding his trail bike in the same wooded area where there had been previous recent sightings of a hairy creature. It was about 9 pm when this boy was riding around a bend near the oil well area, when his headlights struck the lower portion of a dark, hairy body standing near the edge of the woods. The witness became alarmed and immediately went back to his house.

The boy called a friend to tell him about his odd animal encounter. The two boys went back into the woods to investigate. Upon returning to the same area, both boys claim to have again seen the creature, but at a greater distance and deeper in the woods. They only got a glimpse of it as it moved away deeper into the trees. The boys mentioned that normally the woods were filled with normal nature and wildlife sounds, but when this strange animal was around, the woods were silent.

September, 1973
Greenock, Allegheny County
Clues along path

The community of Greenock lies down river from McKeesport. The WCUFOSG had received information that some alleged Bigfoot sightings had been occurring around that area. Several people came across what appeared to be a fresh path where something large had trampled down tall weeds and brush. The site gave the impression that something had run through the area. The weeds were broken off at about four to six inches off of the ground. Some unusual footprints were found not far from that location closer to the river bank.

Part 7: Drawn deeper into the unknown

The continuous encounters with these hairy creatures had been occurring for weeks. While many of the creature sightings suggested that we were dealing with an unknown zoological specimen, some of the cases had us scratching our heads. It was difficult enough to consider the possibility that there may indeed be a scientifically unclassified member of the animal kingdom roaming the forests and woods of Pennsylvania. But how did we deal with the creature cases that had other strange aspects to them? These accounts were originating from individuals who were just reporting what they experienced and wanted some answers as to what was going on.

It was our position to investigate all of the cases with an open mind and see where the evidence would lead us. We were soon to find that we were about to enter deeper into a real twilight world, where more strange aspects of these hairy creature events were about to unfold.

September 27, 1973
Beaver, PA, Beaver County
Bigfoot with luminous sphere, aerial object beams light into woods

It was about 9:30 pm on September 27, when two teenaged girls were standing outside waiting for a ride. One of the girls was visiting her friend who lived in a wooded area of Beaver County. The young ladies were in conversation when suddenly their attention was drawn to a sight that they would never forget. Coming across the road and running toward a wooded area was a seven to eight-foot-tall Bigfoot-like creature which was covered with white hair.

Seeing the albino, hairy creature was strange enough, but there was another detail which added to this mystery. The creature was carrying a luminescent sphere in one hand. The girls also mentioned that the eyes of the creature were brownish-red. They smelled nothing odd when the encounter occurred. The girls were quite shaken when they ran back into the house.

The witnesses told their story to the father of one of the girls, who incidentally owned the woods where the creature had been entered. WCUFOSG investigator Bob Boyde went to the scene to interview the girls and the father. It was learned that the property owner went down into the woods a short time after the creature had been seen. His daughter said he was down in the woods for over an hour. About the time that her father had entered that wooded area, an object moved across the sky, and was initially thought to have been an aircraft. This aerial object also projected a beam of light down into the same woods.

Artist conception of Beaver County Bigfoot and UFO event
Used with permission of Keith Bastianini

Those who knew the man said that he was acting unusually after the incident. When our investigator interviewed the man soon after the event, he denied that he went down into the woods after his daughter and friend's creature encounter. This man also stated that, "There are some things that shouldn't be discussed" and "that he did not want anyone tramping around in his woods."

It was later learned that this man appeared to become very interested in talking about the end of times and prophecies, and indicated that the end of the world was going to occur in six months. There is the possibility that this man experienced a lost hour of time while down in the woods. He refused to discuss his missing hour and stressed that he did not want anyone in his woods looking around.

September 29, 1973
Youngwood, evening
Strange animal, "Cross between monkey and a dog"

The Kaufman family (pseudonym), lived in a housing development outside of Youngwood. On the evening of September 29, Mrs. Kaufman heard what sounded like a baby crying. The sound was so close that she thought that someone had dropped off a crying child on her porch. When the woman turned on her porch light and looked outside, there was no baby, but instead there was a strange animal. The creature looked like a cross between a monkey and a dog.

The first physical trait that caught Mrs. Kaufman's attention were the big round red eyes of the animal which appeared luminous, as if the porch light was reflecting in its eyes. The mysterious animal had a body which was larger that a cocker spaniel and it had a big hump on its back. The creature was covered with fur, which Mrs. Kaufman described as beautiful, very shiny and of a brownish-black color. The animal, which had a small face, also had a tail about twelve inches long, which was quite wide, and interestingly had rings around it.

When the woman first caught sight of the beast, it was sitting on the porch with its front paws downward. She watched as the animal got up at times and moved around on the porch, then sat down. The woman indicated that she was sure that the animal was aware of her presence, but it did not seem to bother the animal at all. It was so close to her, that the woman indicated that she could have caught the animal.

Just days before, Mrs. Kaufman had called her mother to tell her that she had seen apparently the same odd creature, about twenty feet away in her front yard behind some trees. The first observation was in daylight, and when the creature was first seen, it was standing up on its two hind legs. By the time her mother arrived at her house, the animal had departed. Her mother made fun of her daughter, teasing her that she did not know her animals. Her daughter said that she had never seen such an animal before. Mrs. Kaufman considered calling the local police, but was afraid of being ridiculed. Here was another mysterious creature to add to the growing list of anomalies.

October 1973
Waterford, PA, (UFO)
We didn't learn of these incidents until sometime after they occurred. A UFO reportedly landed in a field and on a rural roadway. A WCUFOSG member was able to obtain photos showing a burnt area on the road and a disturbed area in a field.

October, 1973
Mifflinburg, Union County, 11 pm (UFO)
This witness was going to work and traveling east towards Mifflinburg when he observed four or five red lights in the

sky all in a single line. The lights moved slowly from the left side to the right side of the vehicle. The lights all glowed and pulsated rather then blinked, and seemed to be square in shape. After several minutes, the lights seemed to suddenly vanish.

October, 1973
Irwin, evening, (UFO)

A family observed a disc-shaped object with flashing red lights. The object hovered for a short time, then moved off in the distance.

October, 1973
The officials get involved

From the phone calls that the media, police, and my UFO Hotline were receiving, it was evident that the general public, especially in the areas where the creature sightings were most active, wanted to know more about the origin of these creatures. Some people were beginning to feel that the situation warranted getting the government involved to find out just what was going on. Apparently some citizens of the Keystone State began to call upon their local representatives to take an interest in these reports and determine what this matter was all about.

On October 1, there were some indications that government officials were going to take a look into the ongoing reports. A WCUFOSG regional investigator had learned that two members of the House of Representatives from his area were reportedly showing an interest in these events and were going to contact the state police concerning their findings. The WCUFOSG also received a phone call from a congressman's office in western Pennsylvania, indicating they wanted to learn more.

On this same date, I received a phone call from the office of another government official. The assistant on the phone called to say that they were receiving many inquiries about the Bigfoot reports in the southwest Pennsylvania areas. The man requested a meeting with me to discuss the current status of our investigation.

On October 2, two men from the office of Congressman John H. Dent visited my home. These gentlemen were very professional and courteous. They asked many questions and appeared to be open minded and curious about the very strange events that had been unfolding in the surrounding counties. I made them aware that some of the alleged creature encounters were indeed nothing more than misidentifications or hoaxes, but many of the cases appeared to be legitimate.

I showed the visitors some of the reports and evidence that had been collected. Also, I mentioned the phone call I had received on September 20 from the man who had given me the contact number in Washington. They seemed interested in this information as well. We kept in touch as the wave of sightings continued.

October 2, 1973
Beaver Run Dam, dusk
Hunter sees huge Bigfoot creature in woods

Ted Adams (pseudonym) had hunted in the woods of Pennsylvania for many years. Ted was bow hunting on October 2, 1973, about two miles from Beaver Run Dam near Mamont. This man encountered something in the woods that day, which for the first time in thirty years of hunting, had frightened him badly. He was scared enough by the experience that he contacted the state police, who then contacted me.

Ted had walked a good distance into the woods to where he had hunted before. He was looking for some squirrel, but there was little sign of any wildlife that was generally abundant in the area. He had been out for a while and since it was nearing dusk, he decided to return to his vehicle. On the trip back, he heard a sound he thought may have come from a squirrel. There was a small creek Ted had to cross near where he had parked his truck.

For whatever reason, Ted looked back toward the trail that he had just come from and was shocked. Standing in that area was a huge hair-covered creature, which Ted said looked like "an oversized gorilla." Ted said he hit his hands against his head making sure that he was not seeing things. The creature still stood there. As Ted watched, the beast walked onto the trail and then on the pipeline by the trail.

Ted crossed the creek very quickly and ran over to unlock his truck. He removed the arrow quiver from his back and jumped inside his vehicle. When he turned on his headlights to see in the distance, the hair on his body was beginning to stand up. The hairy creature was standing about seventy five to one hundred feet away and looking directly at him. Ted had enough. Starting his vehicle and was preparing to leave, he looked up again to find that the creature was gone. He took no further time searching for the creature. When Ted arrived home, he reluctantly told his wife about his strange encounter.

Composite sketch of the Pennsylvania Bigfoot
Used with permission of Charles Hanna

Ted sat back in his chair studying the high ceilings in his house. He was trying to determine how tall the creature actually was. His best estimate was that the huge gorilla-like creature stood at least eight feet tall. Ted said that the creature walked on two legs. In the dark lighting conditions, the body of the creature appeared to be covered with shaggy tan hair, with a gray hue to it. He smelled no unusual odors. Ted said he will never forget that hunting experience.

October 3, 1973
Irwin, 10 am, (UFO)

A woman reported seeing a luminous round object with two lights. The object was so bright, that the witness reported her eyes were watering after it left.

October 4, 1973
Middletown Township, Delaware County, 2:30 am
Two state troopers sight UFO

Two Pennsylvania state troopers were on routine patrol when their attention was drawn to a large light in the sky shining toward the ground. The troopers left their vehicle and observed the object, which was hovering about 1,200 feet off the ground. The object was described as heart-shaped and encircled by red lights. At the bottom of the object, a large, intense white light was shining toward the ground. According to one of the troopers, the object hovered for about ninety seconds, then fell downward like a feather.

As the object hovered, one trooper shined a spotlight at it. The object then moved toward the east at a high rate of speed. Also, the bright white light went out, leaving only the smaller red lights visible. Within a few seconds, the red lights went out, and a slight purring noise was heard as the object moved off in the distance. While the object hovered, no sound of an engine was detectable. The entire sighting lasted about two minutes.

October 4, 1973
Irwin, 10:30 pm (UFO)
The witness was inside his home when he noticed a bright light through the window. The man turned and looked up to observe a large, luminous white cigar-shaped object hovering in the sky. There were no lights on the object, which stayed in one location for about two to three minutes. The man called North Huntingdon Police, who told him to call me at the UFO Hotline number.

October 4-7, 1973
Derry Township, evening
Bigfoot repeats farm visits, family experiences paranormal events
Vince Jackson and his family (pseudonym) lived on a farm in Derry Township. Vince had lived in the area for many years. He had also been employed by the same company in Westmoreland County for a long time. Vince and other family members had been experiencing some strange events in October of 1973, as well as previously. Occasionally Vince would try to discuss these matters with some of his work associates, but often left the discussion feeling disgusted and mad, since he generally found himself the brunt of ridicule. One co-worker, however, was aware of our investigations and suggested Vince contact us.

A WCUFOSG team went to the Jackson farm to interview the witnesses soon after learning of the family's experiences. Vince, his wife and another relative sat down at their dinner table to discuss the strange happenings with us. The family was reluctant at first, since they expected that we would also probably laugh at them. They soon realized that we were serious about investigating these reports and they could share their experiences with us without being ridiculed. Apparently the "creature," which many other local residents had been reporting for weeks had been making a number of repeat visits to their property.

The mysterious trespasser seemed to be coming through later in the evenings around 10:30 pm during the four nights from October 4 -7. In fact, it seemed to travel the same path down through a field, then crossing through their property and then off through the woods. The family mentioned that the animals on the farm always seemed aware when it was nearby. Vince and his wife mentioned that their cat's ears would go straight up when the creature was getting close, and then it would run off and hide.

The dog would bark unusually loud when the creature was approaching their vicinity. Vince mentioned that on one occasion, his large dog actually pulled so hard on his chain that he turned his pen around as the creature got closer. The horses would stare in the direction where the beast would exit the property. Besides seeing the animal reactions, the family knew when the creature was approaching by the sound of it running. Its' heavy footsteps hitting the ground broke the silence.

They also reported that a strong odor, similar to burned chicken feathers, would penetrate the air around their home as well as inside the house when the creature was nearby. On one of the evenings, Vince could hear it approaching and he whispered to his wife to listen. They hoped to see the creature as it got into view so Vince turned on some outside lights to illuminate the area. That was a mistake, as they could hear the creature suddenly turn and move in the opposite direction.

One relative lived in a nearby mobile home. She had not seen the creature, but had heard it. On one occasion it sounded as though the beast was brushing up against the mobile home. The sound came from the back of the dwelling near the fuel tank. The woman could clearly hear a heavy breathing sound for a period of time.

She found it interesting that when her furnace suddenly kicked on, the breathing noise stopped, but then she heard the sound of something heavy running off. At the same time, she described a strong odor that filled her trailer. The woman said that it smelled very bad. She said the best way she could describe the odor was when you scald a chicken or a pig, or similar to rotten meat.

The woman had noticed this same strange odor several times in recent weeks, when on a warm night she had left her windows open. Vince mentioned that they could hear and smell the creature, but he could not understand why they could rarely see it. On occasion, they would see the erect, dark shape of something unknown in the distance. One time Vince ran after the creature with a camera to try to get a picture, but it had left the area by the time he reached that location. He thought that the creature may have been sleeping in that area, but could not find any such evidence.

The creature had also been visiting the farm earlier in the summer. There were a lot of apple trees on the property. The creature seemed to enjoy eating the apples. When it would be walking up by those fruit trees, the people could hear the thump of its footsteps and also that heavy breathing sound. One family member said that it sounded like it was talking at the times when it was eating. The animal also apparently enjoyed the family's corn crop as well. At one point the family kind of laughed about it eating too much corn after finding numerous ears that had been peeled back.

The family also said that there seemed to be two different smells associated with the creature. In the summer time when it was feeding on the crops, it seemed to have a smell which was more chemical-like, rather than the strong dead animal smell that they detected in later months.

The hairy beasts had also visited the Jackson farm in approximately the fall of 1970. At that time, both a taller, and smaller, hairy Bigfoot creature were seen at different times. The woman who saw the smaller animal said that it had glowing red eyes. That witness explained that the eyes looked like the reflectors that people place along their driveways. Vince had many other strange accounts to reveal and he did so very reluctantly.

Vince and his wife had in years past seen UFOs as well, as had many other residents who lived around Derry Township and the Chestnut Ridge. During one event, Mrs. Jackson and some other folks observed a large, round, spinning object with lights all around it that descended quite low. She was disappointed that she did not have a camera with her at the time. The object took off very quickly in the direction of Latrobe.

Mrs. Jackson also discussed another strange UFO encounter that occurred about 1971, when a small spherical object about the diameter of a big spotlight was observed moving across the sky and dropping toward the ground. The witness said her head felt very strange like she was hypnotized. She was being drawn to the object and was walking uncontrollably toward it, "like a magnet drawing me."

She was carrying a cigarette lighter in one hand, which soon became awkwardly tucked between both hands that took on a praying position as she approached the strange object. Another person saw the woman walking in the dazed state, and ran toward her yelling. At that point, the object ascended over the trees and out of sight.

Then there was another past event where Mrs. Jackson and another person were in a car when they observed a strange object rather low in the sky. They followed the object for a distance down a country road, when something else happened during the event that really frightened the two women. From out of nowhere, a car suddenly appeared right behind them. The car was right on their tail. It was a straight stretch and there were no side roads where the car could have entered.

They pulled into a driveway along the roadway, thinking that the driver of the car would believe that they had arrived home. They watched as the car pulled up the road a little further, turned around, and was facing their direction as though watching them. When the women thought it was safe, they sped out of the area.

Vince really did not want to talk about his personal ESP experiences that had happened to him over the years. He had premonitions of future events dealing with people that he knew, which commonly came true. As our investigations continued into creature and UFO cases and we interviewed witnesses and their families about their encounters, we began to find that some individuals claimed to have had a history of paranormal events or ESP abilities.

What did we see?

Since the Jacksons had reported what they believed was a Bigfoot creature coming through their property on a regular basis for several nights in a row, we decided to stake out the area. We had responded to many sighting locations during the past few weeks, but none us of had the opportunity to have a direct visual encounter with any of these elusive creatures. One of our team members had access to a set of military type night vision binoculars. These optics had the latest technology to be able to see in the darkness, and we had the use of them on this night.

Something very odd occurred that evening which I am rather reluctant to mention. It was a comfortable evening, and we were keeping our eyes and ears open for any out of the ordinary activity. Our eyes had become adjusted to the darkness of the night. The surroundings were quiet. Suddenly, the sound of heavy foot steps approaching the farm broke the silence. The heavy thuds hitting the ground became increasingly louder and were getting closer. Another investigator was using the night vision device and looking over the area.

I was focusing my eyes toward the direction of the foot steps, which now seemed to be very close, but I could not see anything. I was handed the binoculars. I only used it for a few seconds, but I could swear that while looking through the device, I saw two luminous eyes ahead of me, about seven feet or so above the ground moving past us, as we heard something like heavy footsteps running off past us. If they were eyes, I did not see what they were attached to. The green luminosity of what I saw appeared to be related to the technology of the night vision device. The other investigator and I began to question each other. The other researcher said that he saw what appeared to be some disc shaped objects meandering over the area, but he apparently did not see what I saw.

October 6, 1973
Flatwoods, Fayette County, 1:55 am
UFO Hovers Over Car

Three people were traveling on Route 201 heading toward the Belle Vernon area. They were between Flatwoods and Vanderbilt when the incident occurred. It was rather foggy, and since there are a lot of deer in that area, they were moving relatively slowly. Suddenly their attention was drawn to an object low in the sky, which they first thought was a small airplane moving over a field directly toward them. As the object came close, they noticed two short, triangular-shaped wings, each with a red light underneath. The back of the object was rounded out and was covered in red lights. The object stopped directly over the hood of the car, and was only about two feet above them.

At the same time, the car radio, which was playing, suddenly became filled with static. The driver was very frightened at the sight of the mysterious object and stopped the car. The two other passengers watched the object with amazement. The object stayed over the car for about ninety seconds. The lights from the object made it difficult to see the details of the UFO. The object seemed to turn slightly, showing the more rounded area with the red lights flickering around it. Under the object, a bright yellow-amber beam of light was emitted. What really frightened the observers was that there was absolutely no sound as the object hovered directly over them.

Suddenly the object began to rise upward just a few feet. The object turned at an angle, and seemed to float up and down for a few times, then rose higher in altitude. The object then glided off into the distance toward the direction of Uniontown.

The witnesses contacted the Belle Vernon State Police barracks upon arriving home. The state police contacted me at 4 am after sending officers to search the area where the UFO incident had taken place. The police had also called local airports to see if any aircrafts were missing and verified that there were no missing aircraft.

October 10, 1973
Saltsburg, Indiana County, 9 pm (UFO)

Two men were out driving on a back country road when one man observed a series of unusual lights in the sky and pointed it out to the other fellow. One exited the vehicle while the other hung his head out of the window and watched as the lights passed over the car. What they saw were four gold colored brilliant lights that were equally spaced, and were in somewhat of a triangular configuration. These lights were much brighter than standard aircraft navigational lighting. The lights did not blink and there was no sound associated with the sighting. As the light formation approached, it was moving relatively slowly, but when the lights passed overhead, they seemed to increase in speed, and rose higher into the sky before moving out of sight.

October 12, 1973
North Huntingdon, 3:20 am (UFO)

The witness had just left his night job. The radio station he was listening to had just given the time. The man was traveling east on Clay Pike approaching the intersection of Robbins Station Road and was about to turn left toward Route 30. He slowed down at the traffic signal, which was changing from yellow to red. Suddenly out of nowhere, a huge brilliant light appeared to the right of the signal light. The witness's first impression was that it looked like the sun was coming over the horizon. The luminous, round object approached to about one hundred to one hundred fifty feet over the traffic light. There was light emitting from the main object, which gave the witness the impression that it was searching the area for something.

The witness had lowered the sun visor on his side to help block the luminosity of the object, which lit up the entire inside of the car. The witness was actually concerned that he could become blind from looking at the object. While the object was nearby, the man noticed that his headlights were dimming and that there was a humming sound coming through the car radio. After about thirty seconds, the object made a turn and flew off into the sky. The witness was quite upset after the encounter and notified the North Huntingdon Township Police.

October 14 or 15, 1973
Whitney, evening, Glowing eyes
Two women who lived down the road from the Yother's, told Mr. Yothers that they had seen a pair of glowing red eyes looking down from a hill that overlooked the mine area.

(see September 3, 1973, Whitney report.)

October 14, 1973
Irwin, 8 pm (UFO)
There were several reports from the Irwin area of a brilliant round object hovering in the eastern sky for about a minute before moving across the sky toward the west. First reports were that the object was bright orange and appeared motionless in the sky along Route 30. Others calls came in from various area locations such as Harrison City. One witness

said the object at one point dropped lower in altitude, then just suddenly went out and was not seen again.

October 15, 1973
Catawissa, Columbia County, 5:40 am
UFO turns car around on roadway

On the morning of October 15, 1973, an unusually strange UFO encounter occurred in Columbia County. The witness, Edward Deutsch, was driving up Crooked Mountain between Catawissa and Ringtown at about 5:30 am when he had an encounter with a UFO that he would never forget.

WCUFOSG investigator Robert Daley spoke with the witness and learned more details about his sighting. Mr. Deutsch had been driving that same road to his job for many years, but never before had anything unusual occurred. As the man drove up toward the mountain top, he suddenly noticed flashing lights that reflected on the hood of his automobile. At about the same time he also noticed an odd, loud humming noise.

When the man looked upwards, he saw something mysterious. In the report that the witness provided to the WCUFOSG, Mr. Deutsch described seeing a round object, which was about the size of a truck tire and all white, except for the small red, green, and white blinking lights on it, which were going on and off. The object was "whirling around" about one hundred feet or so above his car. As the man continued to watch, he began to realize that the wheels of his vehicle were turning. Then the UFO rose upwards and quickly departed the area at high speed.

The man sat there perplexed. When he gained his composure, he soon realized that his car had been turned around in the opposite direction on the roadway. In the minutes after the car had been turned and the object had departed, Deutsch said that he felt scared. In the days that followed, as the witness traveled over that same route, the man continued to have an uneasy feeling.

The man had mentioned that just after the object departed, a hunter was also coming up the mountain. The man stopped and talked with Mr. Deutsch, who told him about what had just happened. According to Mr. Deutsch, the hunter told him he had also seen the object. The witness indicated that he had later tried to find out the name of the hunter, but was not able to locate him. This UFO account was described in a story by Gerald McKelvey, "The UFO Whirl: A Fearful Sight," The Philadelphia Inquirer, Philadelphia, PA, 21 October 1973.

Week of October 15, 1973
Apollo, 7 am (UFO)
I received a report from the Rainbow Control police dispatch center concerning a UFO incident. Four young girls were waiting for a school bus when reportedly a large, round object with lights appeared in the sky and began to descend in their direction. The girls became very frightened and ran off in different directions. The object was seen moving up over a hill and out of sight.

October 16, 1973
New Alexandria, 7:30 am (UFO)
Several witnesses reported observing two large, bright silver cigar-shaped objects, which were relatively low in the sky. The first object hovered a short time, then moved off. The second similar object zig-zagged across the sky.

October 16, 1973
Irwin, 8 pm (UFO)

The UFO Hotline received numerous calls from around the Irwin, North Huntingdon, Jeannette, and Trafford areas reporting strange lights and objects in the sky. Some reports concerned seven to eight yellow lights in a formation. There were also reports of a large, cigar-shaped object observed with many lights which stopped in the sky and then just looked like a cluster of stars before it faded away and just vanished. One family near Irwin who watched a cigar-shaped object stated that they heard an odd beeping sound coming through their radio and television while the object was observed.

October 16, 1973
Pocopson Township, Chester County, 8 pm (UFO)

The October 17, 1973, edition of the West Chester (PA) Daily Local News, reported that just after 8 pm several nurses observed six lights of various colors. The light sources, which were blinking, moved up and down in the evening sky. Other UFO reports came in from across the state that same evening.

October 17, 1973
New Castle, Lawrence County, 9 pm (UFO)

I received a call at 9:06 pm on the UFO Hotline from the New Castle State Police installation. They had a report that a young girl had been frightened when two large metallic oval-shaped objects hovered about one hundred feet above her. The objects were described as about thirty feet across in size and very luminous. The objects spun and made no sound. There were red, green, and white lights around the structure and a beacon at the top.

The police also said that within ten minutes of that report, another man called in from a different location reporting seeing a very similar object. That same evening at about 9:10 pm west of Greensburg, a bright orange light moved across the sky and faded out in the western sky. A few minutes later near West Newton, three yellow lights were reported which appeared to be attached to an object of undetermined shape. Other sightings were also reported this night from areas around Levittown, West Newton, and Wilkes Barre.

October 18, 1973
Natrona Heights, Allegheny County, 7:30 pm (UFO)
A husband and wife reported observing a bright light in the sky as they traveled along a road. The couple claimed that their car stalled out for no apparent reason as they watched it.

October 18, 1973
Glen Campbell, Indiana County, 7:45 pm (UFO)
Several people observed a strange object in the sky with red and blue lights. An orange light was emitted from the main object while under observation. The object reportedly dropped lower to the ground. It was noticed that the dogs in the area became quiet and television interference was occurring.

October 18, 1973
Jeannette, 7:45 pm (UFO)
Five local residents were taking a walk when they observed a yellow light in the sky. As it got closer, they saw an object which was glowing yellow all over and described it as oval shaped with a bubble at the top. The object was observed for a few minutes as it moved toward Harrison City.

October 18, 1973
Natrona Heights, Allegheny County, 7:55 pm UFO Photographed

The UFO Hotline began receiving reports of a glowing heart-shaped object hovering in the sky over the Natrona Heights area. A WCUFOSG investigator arrived at the scene and observed the object high in the sky. The investigator was able to take a black and white picture of the luminous object before it departed.

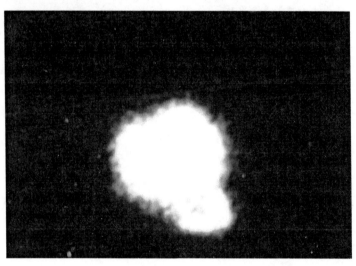

UFO Seen over Natrona Heights
Used with permission of the photographer

October 18, 1973
Wallaceton, Clearfield County, 11:10 pm (UFO)

A man and his family had just arrived home when a strange light was observed in the sky. They saw a bright blue light that moved steadily across the sky at a high rate of speed from southeast to northwest. The blue light, which flashed brightly, was observed for about thirty seconds. As the object passed over, a very loud sound was heard. The man also noticed that dogs around the area were barking more than usual. He was concerned enough about the strange light in the sky that he reported his observation to the Clearfield State Police installation, who referred him to my UFO Hotline.

October 19, 1973
Hempfield Township, 10:15 pm (UFO)

A woman was driving home from work on Route 136. As she reached the top of the hill above the bypass, an extremely brilliant white light shot across the sky right in front of her car. The light was moving south to north and was observed for just seconds. The lady stopped very quickly. Her car engine stalled and her headlights went out. She immediately attempted to start the car again, which she did with no problem. The headlights came on as well. The woman said that after the observation, her eyes began to water, and twenty four hours later, they were still irritated.

October 20, 1973
Jackson Township, York County, 8:10 pm
Police chief observes hovering UFO

The chief of the Jackson Township Police Department joined the ranks of UFO observers according to the story which appeared in the October 22, 1973, edition of the York (PA) Dispatch. The chief observed an object that was blimp-like in appearance and glowed. The object remained stationary over a barn for about thirty minutes before moving off into the sky.

October 20, 1973
Dawson, Fayette County, 10:30 pm (UFO)

A man reported that a football-shaped object passed over his car causing the car engine, headlights, and radio to go dead. There were reportedly numerous smaller orange lights seen in the sky in that area during the night.

October 21, 1973
Rillton, about 7 pm (UFO)

There was a sighting of two luminous objects moving across the sky that were making a purring sound. There were also similar reports during the evening from the nearby Irwin area.

October 21, 1973
Rockwood, Somerset County, 8:10 pm (UFO)

An adult and several children observed a circular object about the size of a large car that had lights all around it. The object followed the car closely and remained with them for several miles until they arrived at their home. The object then hovered about fifty to one hundred feet over the tree tops. The object made no sound and took off with a burst of speed when it departed. One of the children was very upset after seeing the strange object.

October 21, 1973
New Castle, Lawrence County, 8:23 pm (UFO)

I received a report from the New Castle State Police installation informing me that they had received a number of calls about three orange discs spinning through the sky over the city of New Castle. The objects were heading in the direction of Butler.

October 21, 1973
Norvelt, 9:15 pm (UFO)

Witnesses observed a slow moving object with a series of white, red and green lights move across the sky. The object changed direction, then began to go back to the position it first started from. Another similar object was hovering in another part of the sky. The first object then moved above the hovering object and moved closer together. Then the two lights moved off together until they could not be seen.

October 21, 1973
Washington, Washington County, 9:15 pm (UFO)

A call was received on my UFO hotline from the Washington State Police installation reporting that two troopers were observing three objects in the sky. One bright object was stationary and the two other objects had red and green lights on them.

October 22, 1973
Beaver Falls, Beaver County, 7:10 pm (UFO)

According to reports received from the Beaver Falls State Police installation, a local resident reported observing a wing-shaped object with lights all over it. The object was moving between 600-1,000 feet above the ground. The object had passed over the man's home three times.

October 22, 1973
Vandergrift, evening, (UFO)

A call was received from Rainbow Control police radio dispatch center, that they had received some calls about orange lights in the sky from several local communities.

October 23, 1973
Scottdale, 6:55 am (UFO)

The witness was walking near Southmoreland Junior High School when his attention was drawn to a bright object moving across the sky from the east. The object took a position over the tree tops about thirty yards from the witness. It continued to hover as the witness watched and tried to figure out what the object was. When the object first approached the area, it appeared as a white domed-shaped structure. It appeared to be completely round, and all white, glowing and pulsating. The witness could see a brightly illuminated fish tail-shaped appendage connected to the back of the object. It was also emitting a sound similar to a refrigerator running. After hovering a short time, the object made a right angle turn and accelerated into the sky.

October 23, 1973
Vandergrift, evening, (UFO)

The UFO Hotline was notified by the Rainbow Control police radio dispatch center, that they had two reports about strange orange lights in the sky in the Kiski area.

October 23, 1973
Saltsburg, Indiana County, 6:30 pm
Creature in cornfield, deer frightened

Two men were hunting along Route 981 near a flood dam. It was about 6:30 pm and the temperature was about sixty degrees. The men were about three hundred yards apart and were gazing at some deer in a cut cornfield. One of the hunters observed a tall figure step out of the tree line about two hundred yards away.

He at first thought that it was his buddy, but realized that this form was over six feet tall and weighed about three hundred pounds. At the moment that this tall human-like form stepped into the cornfield, the deer stopped eating and bolted away from the area. This hunter, who was well experienced, said that he had never seen a deer run like that before. At that point, the tall form had returned to the woods.

About fifteen seconds later, the second hunter heard something crashing through the crab apple trees about forty five yards below him. He said whatever it was, it was moving very fast and appeared to be covering an extensive area in a short time. Just prior to the tall form stepping out from the woods, both hunters heard in the distance a voice on a bull horn estimated to be about one-half mile away. They both heard the voice say something like, "If it doesn't come out of the woods, we will go in and shoot it." They also heard the sound of hounds at that time trailing something. I had checked with the local fire department to see if they had been out on a search mission with their dogs, but they had not.

October 23, 1973
Eighty-Four, Washington County, 7:30 pm
UFO runs car off road

Three witnesses were driving down a road near the community of Eighty-Four in Washington County when they noticed what they thought were two headlights of a car up on a hill side. What they assumed was the car began to move along the hill side slowly in their direction. They slowed their vehicle down to watch the lights, but now realized that this might be some type of aircraft which was now flying very low. As the people approached a curve in the road, the lighted object approached close to their car.

One passenger told the driver to stop so that they could try to identify what the object was. The driver had become concerned and decided to keep moving. The travelers noticed that there was a lot of static on the car radio while the object was being observed. The two lights at the front of the object were so bright that it was hard to look at the object. What they could see was a very large structured object that looked something like an airplane in the front section. From that point, the main body of the object was very long, and then was rounded in the rear section.

As the driver accelerated the car down the road, suddenly the object came straight at the car. "If I wouldn't have run off the road, it would have hit us," the driver stated in her report on the UFO incident. It seemed to those in the vehicle that this unknown object appeared as though it did want to run into them. The small child sitting in the car seat in the back seat of the car began to cry just before the car ran off the road. When the car came to a complete stop, the child screamed out loud. The car came dangerously close to a structure.

Also when the car stopped, the object turned directly in front of them, and a whooshing sound was heard. The headlights of their car began to dim. The object took off at a high rate of speed and was lost from sight. The driver had trouble starting her car after the object departed. The witnesses had never seen or experienced anything like that before. When they got home they called the state police. The two adult witnesses, for about a week after the encounter, felt nervous and jumpy, and experienced odd dreams about what had occurred.

October 24, 1973
Canonsburg, Washington County, 5:30 pm (UFO)

A man reported observing military jets chasing two bright round lights across the sky. During the next hour, there were reports from various locations reporting odd contrails in the sky that were not typical of aircraft.

October 24, 1973
Leechburg, 10:45 pm (UFO)

Police reported to the UFO Hotline that a man observed a round object with blue, red, and green lights that dropped straight down from the sky and approached close to the ground.

October 25, 1973
Numerous UFO sightings kept UFO hotline buzzing

The UFO Hotline was ringing early on the morning of October 25, 1973. At about 1:40 am several calls came in from the Jeannette area where witnesses reported observing three flashing blue, red and green lights in the sky that were in a straight line configuration. One of the lights descended, then reversed direction and ascended straight up into the sky.

At 2:25 am a report was received that police and local residents were observing luminous blue and green lights in the sky near Philipsburg in Centre County. There was a sighting of a red object with a tail moving swiftly across the sky at 6:30 am near Rillton. That evening, colored lights were seen near Lycippus at about 7 pm.

About thirty minutes later and not far away over in Mount Pleasant Township, several people observed a strange object in the sky with two lights on the sides, and two red lights in the front and back. At 7:50 pm over near Latrobe, more witnesses observed red, green and amber lights zigzagging through the sky. At 10:24 pm a report was received from the West Point area outside of Greensburg. A man reported seeing another odd aerial object with yellow lights at each end, along with a blue flashing light. The object was moving at a high rate of speed toward the northwest. While these UFO reports were of interest, the phone call that came in at 10:30 pm would take our Bigfoot and UFO investigations into another realm.

Part 8: Into Another Realm

October 25, 1973
Uniontown, PA, Fayette County, 9 pm
Landed UFO with two Bigfoot on farm

When the phone rang at 10:30 that Thursday night, I answered the call in my office. The man on the phone identified himself as a state trooper from the Uniontown barracks in Fayette County. The trooper gave me the details of a very unusual incident which he had just returned from investigating. He also told me that a key witness was also with him at the state police barracks at that time.

The law enforcement officer sounded very concerned, and even a little shook up, and suggested that we should send a team to that Fayette County location at once. It would take some time to organize an investigating team and gather our research gear. We also were not familiar with that area of Fayette County, so it would take us some additional time to find that location.

I had learned from the trooper that the incident took place at about 9 pm, in a rural community outside of Uniontown. I also spoke with the twenty two year old witness, Steve Palmer (pseudonym), who had experienced the strange events of that evening first hand. Steve sounded very shaken and was apparently having difficulty dealing with what had occurred. Both of these people sounded very sincere, and the details that I heard suggested that this case warranted an immediate response to the scene of the incident.

I made some calls and several WCUFOSG members responded to the alert. The team was made up of George E. Lutz, a former Air Force pilot and officer, Fred Pitt, (pseudonym) a photographer, David Smith, a physics teacher and the Westmoreland County Civil Defense (RADEF) Radiation Defense Officer, Dennis Smeltzer, a sociology major, and myself. We checked out our flashlights, two-way radios and other gear. We also checked out the batteries in our radiation survey meters and cassette tape recorders.

We made the state police and the witness aware that we would be heading toward that location, and plans were made to meet Steve at the local mall. When we arrived at the mall parking lot at about 12:45 am, Steve was there to greet us. A while later, his father, Mr. Palmer Sr. (pseudonym) accompanied him. The trooper was not able to meet with us that evening since he had to get up early the next morning for his scheduled work shift, and had to get some sleep. He was interviewed again at a later time. Steve was a big fellow, who stood over six feet tall and weighed two hundred fifty pounds, yet was soft spoken. He was still visibly shaken as he described what had taken place only hours before.

About 9 pm Steve and his wife were driving out to his father's farm to visit with the family. They were going down the dirt farm lane toward the farmhouse when their eyes were drawn to an unusual object low in the sky. What they saw was a large, round object, red in color, and at least as big as a barn. The strange spherical object appeared to be hovering about one hundred feet above the ground. When the couple reached the farm house, they realized that other family members were already watching the UFO from the porch.

A total of fifteen people from that rural community watched the large red sphere for a period of time. Steve jumped into his pickup truck and drove across the road to another neighbor's house, where he could get a different view of the strange object. Steve and some neighbors watched as the red object slowly began to descend toward the pasture on his father's farm.

Two young neighbor boys went back with Steve to the farmhouse – determined to investigate the strange light. Before proceeding toward the field where the object appeared to have landed, Steve went into the farmhouse and grabbed a 30.06 rifle along with some ammunition. The total ammo consisted of six rounds, of which two were only tracers.

The three fellows had been noticing that the dogs all around the area seemed unusually upset and were barking loudly. As the fellows climbed into Steve's truck, they could hear in the distance a loud odd whirring sound, somewhat similar to a lawnmower. Besides the whirring noises, there were also mournful baby crying sounds piercing through that normally quiet rural countryside.

Steve and the boys drove up the unpaved road toward the field where the object appeared to have come down. Steve parked his truck in a position where the headlights of the vehicle could light their path up the hill. As the trio of curiosity seekers began their journey, they noticed that the headlights were dimming rapidly as though the battery power was being drained.

The boys made it to the field where the farm animals grazed, and they all stood there in disbelief at the strange sight in front of them. About two hundred fifty feet away, was a huge, luminous object which appeared on the ground or just above it. The object was no longer round, nor red, but now appeared to be a bright white domed structure with a somewhat flat base. They now realized that loud whirring sound was coming from that object. The object was estimated to be about one hundred feet in diameter, and the light emanating from the device lit up the surrounding area. There was also an odd smell in the air, something like burning rubber.

The sight of the glowing object was frightening enough to the three observers, but then their attention was drawn to a fence line about seventy five feet away, the direction from which the wailing baby crying sounds were seemingly originating. Walking along the six-foot-high barbed wire fence, were two very tall, dark figures that were slowly moving toward the observers. As they watched, their first thought was that they were bears.

While rare, it would not be unprecedented to have bears around that area, but the witnesses soon realized that these creatures were much different. As they continued to watch, they realized that these creatures were very tall and were covered from head to toe with brownish-grayish hair, some of which was hanging from their bodies. The first of the two beasts was estimated to stand over eight feet tall wile the other creature about seven feet in height.

There was no neck apparent on these creatures, which walked upright, and their arms were very long, hanging down to around their feet. The physical trait that really drew the attention of the witnesses was the bright, glowing green eyes of the beasts which appeared to be about the size of a fifty cent piece.

The creatures seemed to be very rigid in their movements as they continued to walk along the fence line. The two beasts were wailing loudly as they proceeded onward. There appeared to be some pattern to the creature's movements as they took long strides while moving along the fence line. When the largest creature, which walked ahead, reached the next fence post, it would bellow forth with the crying sound, as if telling the other creature to move forward. The smaller creature appeared to have to take very long strides to keep up with the larger one. When the smaller creature arrived at that fence post, the lead creature would then move on to the next one.

The now frightened trio talked among themselves trying to rationalize what was taking place. The one ten year old became overwhelmed by what was happening and ran from the field. Steve loaded his weapon, encouraged by the other boy. Steve's first volley was a tracer bullet, which he fired over the two creatures.

When the second shot – also a tracer – was fired toward the beasts, there was a remarkable response from the larger being. The creature made a brief whine, then raised its right arm and reached toward the luminous tracer as if to grab it. But what occurred next in the field was most amazing. At exactly the same time that the creature grabbed for the tracer, the huge brilliant domed object suddenly vanished from sight.

The object did not lift from the ground and move off, it just simply vanished in front of the startled witnesses eyes. At that point, the two noticed a strange glowing area on the ground where the object had been located. The whirling noise also ceased and the surrounding area became very quiet. The two remaining witnesses watched as the hairy creatures turned and began to follow the barbed wire fence, moving in the direction of the wooded area.

As the creatures moved off, Steve shot at the beasts. He fired three rounds and felt certain that he had hit the larger creature at least once, but there was no sign that either creature was harmed. Steve recalled how the creatures turned their heads in his direction, giving him a good look at their luminous green eyes. Both fellows began to feel some eye irritation at about this time. Steve had been hunting for years and could not understand why the creatures had not been stopped.

The witnesses had enough and ran fast from the field to the pick up truck. They returned to the Palmer farmhouse, where they discussed what had occurred with the family. Next, they all went to a neighbor's where they called the state police to report what had happened. The investigating officer arrived at the farm at about 9:45 pm.

Steve joined an officer and in got into the patrol car and they proceeded toward the field where the events had taken place. The headlights of the patrol car were directed toward the location where the object had landed. The luminous ring was still visible. The trooper wanted to make sure that the bright area was not being caused by his car headlight beams, so he moved his vehicle. The glowing area remained.

The men also noticed that the animals in the field were keeping their distance from the glowing area. The glow extended to about one hundred fifty feet diameter, and extended up about twelve inches up from the ground. When the trooper shined his flashlight beam into the luminous area, he could barely see it. The officer also stated that if he had a newspaper and would have bent down in that location, he could probably have been able to read by the glow. The trooper also said that the temperature inside the glowing area seemed to be a little warmer than outside of it.

He did indicate, however, that it may just have been as a result of all of the excitement at the time. The trooper, seeing that Steve appeared to be upset and was perspiring, made a decision to return to the state police barracks. As they walked toward the vehicle, Steve said they both heard the sound of loud footsteps in the nearby woods that seemed to be moving in their direction. When they would move, they would hear the sound of something large moving with them. When they stopped, it would take a few more steps then stop.

According to Steve, this is what happened next. Steve loaded his last bullet into his gun. The men heard something ahead of them. As the trooper shined his flashlight, the beam struck what appeared to be the largest of the two hairy creatures about ten feet away. Steve said that he fired directly at the creature, which seemed momentarily to rock back and forth as though losing its balance.

It then charged toward them, hitting the fence that was between the men and the creature. The men hurried back to the patrol car and drove out of area. When the trooper and Steve arrived at the barracks, they were taken into separate rooms and interviewed independently by other troopers about the events of the evening. It was after their interviews that I was contacted by the trooper about the UFO landing and Bigfoot incident.

Artist conception of UFO and Bigfoot creatures in Fayette County
Used with permission of Keith Bastianini

At the mall, we checked Steve with our radiation meters, but only normal background levels were detected. We then proceeded to the Palmer farm and made our way up to the site of the incident. When we arrived in the area, the two young boys who had observed the UFO and creatures, as well as Steve and Mr. Palmer, were present. We asked the boys to stay behind in Steve's truck. Steve wanted to take a gun with him into the field, but we asked him to leave his weapon behind, and he complied. We worked our way up to the location where the UFO had been seen.

When we arrived there, the glowing area was no longer present. We immediately checked the radiation levels in the area, but only normal background readings were registering. We were observing the cows in the field, noting that they still kept their distance from the area where the UFO was observed. There was no other physical evidence observed at the spot where the object was seen.

More strange events unfold

George Lutz and I turned on our cassette tape recorders. It was about 1:45 am as our team was searching for evidence that some odd events began to unfold. Steve and his father were standing down by the truck when they saw something strange down at the farmhouse several hundred feet away. The men started yelling to us, and we hurried back to talk with them.

The men both explained that the farmhouse was surrounded in a bright white light for just a few seconds. The fellows said it lit up as bright as daylight, but in a few seconds the light simply vanished. George Lutz drove Mr. Palmer down to the farmhouse to investigate. They radioed back that everything looked okay, and they returned to the field.

It was around 2 am when our team, along with the two Palmers, walked toward the fence line where the creatures had been walking earlier. Our attention was drawn to a large bull located in another nearby field. It seemed rather odd that the bull did not seem to be paying any attention to us but rather it seemed more concerned with something else in another location ahead of us. At just about that same time, Steve's dog, which had also accompanied us, suddenly became disturbed by something. He began sniffing the ground, and moved off as though it was trailing something. The dog would move a distance, then stop at times, while focusing its attention toward the woods.

We were looking for tracks, broken branches, or any evidence of the strange visitors. As we moved along, Steve was describing where and what had taken place earlier. George Lutz was walking along with Steve and was asking him where the creature had crashed into the fence, thinking that we might find some hair samples.

Lutz noticed that Steve was rubbing his head and face, and seemed to be experiencing some difficulties. Lutz asked him the same question, but there was no response. He then asked Steve if he was alright and again there was no reply. Steve moved back and forth in a jerky manner, as though he was about to faint. Lutz yelled to Mr. Palmer that there was something wrong with Steve. Both Lutz and Mr. Palmer, one on each side, grabbed hold of Steve so he would not fall.

George Lutz and I kept our tape recorders running to document the details of what had occurred or might take place. Then the events of that evening got even stranger. As Lutz and Mr. Palmer continued to support Steve, he started to breathe deeply, and then bellowed out a loud growl, which sounded more like that of an animal. This very large fellow then threw his father and Lutz to the ground. At that point, Steve's dog began barking and went after him, as if to attack. Steve, who was now running around in the field in a frenzy, went after his dog. The dog ran away whimpering, which was picked up on both tape recorders.

Mr. Palmer was very upset by what he was seeing and yelled out to his son. Steve replied with another loud growl. We all watched as this sizeable man continued running around, swinging his arms and bellowing forth frightening, growling sounds. Suddenly, an extremely loud, inhuman-like scream emanated from Steve and stopped us in our tracks. Then he growled three more times.

Dennis Smeltzer suddenly yelled out that he felt as though he was about to faint, and he appeared pale. Both Fred Pitt and David Smith went over to assist Dennis. Then Fred Pitt began to feel as though he could not properly breathe. We were stunned as we watched Steve suddenly fall face down into the pasture. George Lutz and Mr. Palmer ran over to Steve. I went over to help the other fellows.

It was about this time that something else quite strange occurred during this experience with Steve, which began to affect all of us in the field. George Lutz and some of the others detected it first. Then I began to smell it as well. It was as though the air around us had become permeated with a very strong, sickening sulfur or rotten eggs smell. It was time to leave the field.

Steve was moving slowly on the ground and moaning. As he began to communicate, Steve appeared to be sensing something that we were not perceiving. He seemed to be warning us that something was still in the area and was telling us we were to proceed out of the field. It was no easy job to pull this large fellow up from the ground.

David Smith remembered thinking, "Thank God we made them keep their rifles away." Under the circumstances, getting Steve and the other witnesses to safety was the first priority. We did not know what we were dealing with, or what dangers might lie ahead. George Lutz and Mr. Palmer held onto Steve as they slowly walked from the field toward the vehicles. The rest of us followed them out of the area.

Steve kept complaining about the ankle pain that he was experiencing. When Steve fell, his eyeglasses also fell off. As he walked out of the field and was handed his glasses, Steve asked who they belonged to, and indicated that he could see just fine. George Lutz noticed that Steve's hands were being tightly held in a grasping position, like a cat clenching its paws. Lutz tried to physically open Steve's fingers, but he could not move them, or straighten them out.

Steve began to talk about what he had experienced during the time that he had been running around. While he did not recall his physical actions of what happened in the field, he related that he saw a man-like figure cloaked in a black robe, a black hat and carrying a sickle. That apparition conveyed to Steve that the world would end if mankind did not change it's ways. Steve later talked about seeing a vision of the world burning. Steve was not a religious person, so these comments were out of place for him. Mr. Palmer had never seen Steve act like that before.

The Palmers decided to go back to the farmhouse. The members of the investigating team were concerned, curious, and yes, we were all somewhat frightened. What we had observed was both amazing and eye opening. We were trying to sort out the events of that night which had shocked us into the reality that we were dealing with the unknown. The sounds, smell, human and animal reactions had not been fabricated – they were all real. The events had been simultaneously recorded on two tape recorders.

It was strange enough to have a UFO and Bigfoot creatures observed at the same time and location. But how about the odd behavior of Steve, and the animals, and the wave of sulphur stench that had apparently sickened some of the team? And then there were the premonitions of future world events. When we played back the frightening screams on the audio tapes of Steve's episode in the field, we were shocked back into reality as to what had taken place. The tapes were astounding.

We still had to consider what had actually occurred to Steve and we wondered how this event might continue to affect him. We knew that we needed a medical professional to assist us in this matter. An eminent New Jersey psychiatrist,

Dr. Berthold E. Schwarz, M.D., was contacted, since he had dealt with other individuals who had reportedly experienced other UFO and paranormal events.

Dr. Schwarz had an extensive medical background and was very interested in the Fayette County case. We discussed the many details of what had taken place and he decided to make a trip at his own expense to Pennsylvania to investigate the incident. Dr. Schwarz however, was unable to drive out until November 1.

1973 artist conception of the UFO and Bigfoot Incident
Used with permission of Robert McCurry

George Lutz and I soon returned to the location and were looking over the area where the events had taken place in the field. At the spot where the creature reportedly had struck the barbed wire fence, the wire was broken. No hair samples were located.

The state trooper who had investigated the event also returned to the scene to look over the area. I later talked with a skeptical newsman who told me how he went out into the field the next day with Steve. He was questioning the witness and had asked him to take him to the spot from where he shot at the creatures. The reporter felt that if Steve had fired from that position, then there would be some evidence, perhaps the empty bullet casings. The newsman looked to the ground and found the casings at his feet.

Lutz and I went to the farmhouse to ask Steve additional questions about his recent strange experiences. Steve still had no recall about his bizarre episode in the field, yet recalled all of the details of that evening concerning his observation of the UFO and creatures. We talked with Steve about his personal interests, his family, and his UFO and Bigfoot sighting. Steve had no previous interest in such strange matters, and in fact, never took such stories seriously. Steve did not know what to make of the encounter. Steve was intelligent and generally enjoyed reading about farming matters.

As our conversation continued in the dining area of the kitchen, George and I noticed that Steve was not responding to the last question. George had just asked the man if he knew why the creatures and the UFO were seen at the same time and location. George and I suddenly became alarmed, as Steve was beginning to rub his head, and his breathing became increasingly rapid, very reminiscent of what had taken place in the field that night just before he ran into the field screaming. Lutz and I started yelling out loud and that seemed to cause Steve's intense reaction to that question to subside. We decided to wait until Dr. Schwarz arrived before any additional questioning would be done.

After Dr. Schwarz arrived in Greensburg, we discussed all the details of the case that had surfaced to date. Dr. Schwarz was given access to our research files on the incident and he listened to the tape recordings of the episode in the field with Steve. Some of those whom Dr. Schwarz interviewed were Steve, his parents, the state trooper, the twin brothers and their family, and the WCUFOSG investigators.

Dr. Schwartz conducted a detailed investigation of the case. It appeared to him that Steve and the other parties involved were truthful. There were numerous witnesses involved, including the investigating state trooper, and the members of the WCUFOSG team. There were also the tape recordings that documented some aspects of the event as it was unfolding.

Dr. Schwartz had described to me his professional opinion, that Steve had undergone what is known in the medical field as a "fugue" state precipitated by the strange occurrences that had taken place in the pasture. The 2004 New edition of the Merriam-Webster Dictionary defines this term as "a disturbed state of consciousness characterized by acts that are not recalled upon recovery." During our interviews, Steve could recall all of the events in detail of what had taken place that evening, except for when he was in the fugue state as he ran amok in the field.

I kept in touch with Steve, and George Lutz and I would make a number of trips to the Uniontown area during the following years to meet with him. As the months and years went by, Steve began to experience some strange events in his life, which would fall under the paranormal category. Steve had not had such oddities occur to him prior to the UFO-Bigfoot incident in 1973. Steve shared some of these events with others who were close to him, but generally did not want to talk about his ESP experiences with others.

He could not believe that he was experiencing first hand some of the strange events that he used to laugh at others about.

Soon after his 1973 encounter, Steve began to experience dreams and have visions of future events. He talked about an airplane crash, which he foresaw and later heard on the news had actually happened. In another case, he saw what appeared to be the ghost of a deceased in-law whom he had never met.

He also began to experience some special connection with birds. He related one incident to us where he was with a friend and pointed out a blue jay in a tree. He told his buddy to watch, that the bird was going to fly toward him and land on his shoulder, which it apparently did. Steve did not want these strange new gifts.

Steve receives some mysterious visitors

It was during one of our follow up interviews with Steve many years after the initial incident that details of another mysterious event came to light. We had never attempted any hypnosis sessions with Steve, due to Dr. Schwarz's recommendations. But now, so many years later, George Lutz and I thought we would discuss this possibility with Steve and Dr. Schwartz. When we brought up the subject of having one of our professional consultants regress him to that night, Steve looked at us strangely, and asked us why we wanted to hypnotize him again. Lutz and I were puzzled and we asked him to explain what he was referring to.

Steve recalled that about two weeks after the 1973 incident, two men came to his home to talk with him about the UFO-Bigfoot incident. One man was dressed in Air Force blues. The other man who accompanied him was dressed in a suit. Steve remembered that he was tall and had dark hair. Steve always thought that these men were members of the WCUFOSG and were just following up with more interviews.

In fact, Steve thought the Air Force man had been Lutz dressed in his uniform. When we heard this, George and I knew that this situation was unusual. The Air Force had been officially out of the UFO investigating business since 1970. It definitely was not Lutz or any members of the WCUFOSG who had hypnotized Steve. Steve said these men wanted him to describe in detail all that he could recall about that night concerning the UFO and the creatures.

After he completed giving his account, they told Steve that he was not crazy. The men had another surprise for Steve. The Air Force officer removed from his briefcase a series of photos of UFOs. Then even more startling were the pictures of hairy Bigfoot creatures that had been taken nationwide. One particular photo Steve was shown was taken in Georgia. It was an image of a hairy beast climbing over some fencing while carrying a pig under one arm. The men wanted the witness to point out to them any of the photos which appeared similar to what he had seen.

The military officer then told Steve that they were interested in hypnotizing him, and he gave them his permission. After the session, the men thanked him and went on their way. They told him they would be in touch, but Steve never heard from them again. Whoever these men were was never discovered. This leads to the obvious question, does our government have an interest in both UFO and Bigfoot cases?

Strange events at another local farm on the same night

Another family who lived on a farm in the same general area where the UFO landing and a creature episode took place later contacted me and verified that they also experienced some strange events on that same night. In a statement they provided, the people claimed that they observed a strange light in the sky at about 9 pm in the direction of the Palmer farm. It was something odd that they had never seen in that location before. About an hour later at their farm, the cows started making strange sounds. Being concerned, the farmer grabbed his shotgun and drove down to the barn to investigate. He shined his headlights on the cows that were still making the odd sound, and they suddenly became quiet. He looked around that night, saw nothing and went back to the farmhouse. It was a few days later when they realized that the cows would not move to the upper pasture as they had always done on a daily basis.

The farmer went up to investigate to see what the problem was. As he walked toward a series of trees which ran along a fence line, he began to smell a strange, strong odor. As he moved ahead, the smell got stronger. He never found out what was giving off the smell. It was a few days later that the cows finally moved up toward the upper pasture. They thought it was strange that the events on their farm started on the same night as Steve's experience.

Over the years, Steve and I talked about how his life had changed since his mysterious encounter, and how he wished that these experiences had never happened to him. George and I always enjoyed our meetings with Steve. Sadly, Steve has passed away.

October 26, 1973
Dawson, Fayette County, 9:30 pm
UFO paces car

Just a few miles away from the location where the UFO and Bigfoot were seen in the field outside of Uniontown, another close encounter with a UFO was reported less than twenty four hours later. A man driving in his car saw a large, unknown object move overhead. As the object passed overhead, the car engine, headlights and radio all momentarily failed.

November 1, 1973
Uniontown, Fayette County, 8:15 pm (UFO)

I received a call from the Uniontown State Police to alert me that a man who had aviation experience had observed something strange in the sky from his residence. The witness observed a formation of five orange-white lights moving low across the sky.

November 1, 1973
UFO observed over Beaver County area

In the days to follow, a series of strange events would unfold in Beaver County, about seventy miles northwest of Uniontown. On the evening of November 1, 1973, a number of UFO sightings were reported from the Ohioville Township area, then later from other Beaver County locations by numerous people. The following events were investigated by Robert Boyde, a WCUFOSG investigator in the area.

One of the first observations at 6:37 pm was reported by a police officer on patrol. The officer saw two objects that he described as pie-shaped devices with red and white lights revolving clockwise. The officer estimated that the objects appeared in size to be about that of a pie plate. The UFOs were first observed moving from the northwest to the southeast. When the objects hovered above a power line, the officer shined his spotlight at them. The objects responded by moving from side to side, as if trying to keep away from the light source. The lights of the silent object were brighter than the stars in the sky, and they never dimmed while under observation. The objects then departed from the area.

About an hour later, three witnesses about seven miles to the east watched a strange object hover in the vicinity of the atomic power plant at Shippingport. The three young women observed the luminous object while traveling and stopped to call police.

The object reportedly hovered for about five minutes. During that time, what the witnesses saw was an indistinguishable shape with steady red, white and green lights. There was also a bright beam of light which was emitted from the bottom of the object.

Then around 8:30 pm in the Midland Heights area, another UFO sighting was reported. The object was moving east and was described as about forty feet in diameter and displaying bottom lights, which were green, red, and white. After seeing the object move off, several observers got into their vehicle and began to follow the strange object. They watched as the object climbed straight up into the sky and was soon lost from sight. This last observation of the object had taken place near a farm and it was apparent that the cattle were disturbed by the presence of the object.

According to our investigator, at about this same time, the Midland Police were searching the area looking for a strange creature which had also been reported. A local woman said that she had seen a hair-covered creature in the woods with large, round, luminous green eyes staring at her as her flashlight beam hit it.

There was another UFO incident also reported on this same day that we did not learn about until some time later. The witness was driving along Monaca Road in Monaca, also in Beaver County, when this took place. It was about 10 pm when the man observed a bright light ahead in the middle of a field. The white light was round and about thirty to forty feet in diameter. The light was stationary and about twenty feet above the ground. The witness watched the light for about fifteen seconds, when it suddenly rose straight up into the sky and was lost from sight.

The next day, the man was still curious about what he saw and returned to the location on a motorcycle. At the location where the light had hovered, the grass was discolored, changed to a yellow color. There was also an odd smell present. The man also stated that he had driven his motorcycle onto the yellowed grassy area and found it odd that his motorcycle had suddenly shut off. When he pushed the bike away from that area, it started again.

November 2, 1973
Grapeville, 1:20 am (UFO)
Two people observed a luminous, white cigar-shaped object in the sky, which was illuminating the clouds around it. The couple watched the object for about twenty minutes, when suddenly the object began to evaporate and then disappeared from sight.

November 2, 1973
Irwin, 3:30 am (UFO)
Just a few miles away from Grapeville, another witness was drawn to a window to look outside to see what was so

bright. When the woman looked out, she saw a strange object in the sky that was shaped like a light bulb. The object, which stopped and hovered, emitted a beam of light.

November 2, 1973
Penn, 4 am (UFO)

Another UFO sighting was reported from nearby Penn just thirty minutes later. When the baby started crying early on this day and the child's mother got up to feed the infant, the woman happened to look out the window and saw something very odd. She observed a bright white disc-shaped object with a domed structure and what appeared to be an antenna at the top. The object had pulsating white and orange-red lights. The object, which was tilted on its side, then changed to an upright position. It had beams of lights projecting out from its sides.

November 2, 1973
Midland, Beaver County
Three-toed tracks found nearby

Early Friday, a local resident came upon a trail of strange footprints, about eleven inches long and five inches wide and was three-toed. They were quite similar to the tracks found in other Pennsylvania locations as well. These tracks were found in the vicinity where the UFO was seen near the Midland area farm the night before. The next day, another strange discovery would be made not far away from this location.

November 2, 1973
Hutchinson, 6:30 pm (UFO)

From the rural community of Hutchinson, two red, spherical objects were seen dropping from the sky toward the ground.

A short time later, a beam of light was observed from that area going up into the sky.

November 2, 1973
Hempfield Township, early evening
Mini UFO floats in cars

This was a very interesting incident to which a WCUFOSG team responded to soon after the incident was reported. This took place on a rural road in Hempfield Township, several miles outside of Greensburg. There was a small group of people at a gathering who had their cars parked in an isolated, rural location. Some of the windows of the cars were lowered when this activity took place. A plum-sized round object, glowing green in color, was observed as it floated around on the inside of one of the vehicles.

A short time later, the same object proceeded to enter another car through a window and floated around inside of it for a short time as well. Moments later, a wide beam of light, wider than a normal flashlight beam, suddenly appeared a short distance away, which then shined upwards from the ground and then vanished. The witnesses became alarmed and called the state police. We later learned that one of the cars involved had one window shattered the day after the incident.

November 3, 1973
Ohioville, Beaver County
Possible UFO landing site found

Two local men decided to go hunting on Saturday morning. They came across something else much more interesting and notified authorities. What they found was a possible landing site of a UFO. Robert Boyde, a WCUFOSG investigator was called to the scene to investigate. The location of the odd impressions was on farmland at the edge of a pasture near where a wooded area began. The men had found a perfect circular area about forty two feet in diameter.

There was about a two foot area of the outer side of the ring which was extremely green in color. About twenty three feet from the circular area, the investigator discovered a series of holes in the ground, which he speculated were caused by landing supports from the object, used for balance in that sloped location. One group of holes was in a triangular configuration, while another was more curved. The depth of the holes was up to five inches deep.

November 3, 1973
New Castle, Lawrence County, 7 pm
State police among crowd watching UFO

I received a call at 7:38 pm from Pennsylvania State Police at New Castle, reporting that there were three state troopers watching a UFO hovering in the sky. From the information I received, at about 7 pm, a strange object was observed hovering about 1,000 yards above the ground. The glowing object, with red lights rotating around it, at times brightened and then dimmed. The UFO was apparently observed by dozens of local residents. After about an hour, the object took off at a high speed toward the southwest in the direction of Ohio.

November 4, 1973
Coopersburg, Lehigh County, early morning, (UFO)

The November 4, 1973, edition of the Allentown (PA) Call-Chronicle, reported that a police officer and newsmen had observed a UFO on this date. According to the story, an Upper Saucon Township police officer sighted the object while on patrol north of Coopersburg. Three Call-Chronicle reporters also observed "a bright, shiny object cross the sky that seemed to disintegrate."

November 4, 1973
Lenni, Delaware County, 9 pm (UFO)

A UFO sighting report was received from the Middletown State Police. A witness reported seeing a large, circular object with lights, which flashed from right to left around it. The object hovered for a short time towards the west, then moved off into the distance.

November 4, 1973
New Castle, Lawrence County, 9:05 pm (UFO)

A witness traveling down a road outside of town observed an object with lights around it, that was shaped something like a space capsule. The object hovered ahead of the witness about thirty five feet above the road before departing the area. A truck that was approaching that location also stopped.

November 9, 1973
Industry, Beaver County, 11:30 pm (UFO)

A report was received from the local police concerning this UFO incident. WCUFOSG investigator Robert Boyde followed up on this case. Three witnesses observed two strange lights from a location about three miles from the atomic power plant at Shippingport. The objects appeared to be hovering near a hillside about a mile away from the witnesses' home. The one brilliant object looked to be about five times as large as the planet Venus looks on a clear night to the naked eye. The other object was much smaller and hovered next to it.

The observers, who were watching from a window in their home, went outside to take a better look at the strange light sources. Moments later, the lights simply disappeared. A few minutes after returning into the house, they all heard a very strange sound that seemed to be approaching from the northwest, the direction from which the objects were last observed.

The sound seemed to follow a narrow path and gave some the feeling that the sound seemed to be closing in on their bodies. One man described the sound experience as like a thousand dogs howling, which seemed to come in waves, but never varied in it's pitch. Another local resident heard the sound, but did not experience the same physical effects. It was about this time that the police were contacted.

It was also learned that two girls in that same area were nearly hysterical in a car after trying to get away from the sound. Three days after the incident, some of the witnesses said that they had been feeling extremely tired and had been experiencing slight headaches. One of the girls who was upset after hearing the sound, said that she had an odd pain in her left side the night of the occurrence and experienced nightmares as well. There were also reports that animals were very disturbed around the neighborhood when the sound incident occurred.

November 10, 1973
Bristol Township, Bucks County, 4:45 am (UFO)

A Bristol Township police officer observed a strange aerial craft while on patrol, according to the November 13, 1973, edition of the Philadelphia, PA Evening Bulletin. The officer apparently at first thought that it was an aircraft or a helicopter. The officer proceeded in the direction of the hovering object which appeared to be about 1,000 feet in the sky. The officer reported that the object was very large and was shaped like a fat cigar. The officer was able to make out the details of the object from the moon light and craft's lights. When the patrolman stopped, he shined his spotlight at the object, which then illuminated at the bottom. After a short time, the lights shut off, and the object moved toward the east.

November 11, 1973
Superior, early evening
Three hairy creatures near mobile home court

This sighting occurred at the Superior Mobile Home Court in Derry Township where other residents had reported previous creature encounters. A woman was sitting at her kitchen table and was gazing out of the window when she observed something quite unusual. At first she thought she was seeing three bears. She soon realized that these creatures were quite large and walking upright and moving up a hill at a very fast pace as if being chased. The creatures were covered over their entire body with dark hair and were moving toward an old mine area.

November 12, 1973
Superior, 7:09 pm (UFO)

A resident of the Superior Mobile Home Court reported observing two orange round lights dropping from the sky over the woods in the direction of an old coal mine.

November 18, 1973
Latrobe, 1:03 am (UFO)

A man near Latrobe observed an orange-white light described as the size of a fifty-cent piece and brighter than the planet Venus moving steadily across the sky toward the east. Soon the light changed direction and began to move toward the northwest before traveling off in the distance.

November 18, 1973
Farragut, Lycoming County, 10:30 pm (UFO)

Two cigar-shaped objects were seen about five miles east of Farragut by about a dozen people, according to the November 19, 1973, edition of the Williamsport, PA Sun-Gazette. The objects were observed for about eight minutes in the clear sky. The objects, which made various movements while being observed, then moved south toward a mountain at a high rate of speed.

November 24, 1973
Jeannette, 2 am Growling sound outside of house

A woman was frightened after hearing a loud growling sound near her window, which is about fifteen feet off the ground.

November 24, 1973
Jeannette, 7 pm
Creature looks in window

A young child told her mother that she had seen a creature similar in description to a Bigfoot looking into a window. Her mother saw it a short time later.

November 24, 1973
Jeannette, 10:15 pm
Creature returns, glowing eyes seen in woods

The woman who had seen the creature with her child at 7 pm called again saying that the creature had returned to the area. Her neighbor had also seen it this time. An investigator was dispatched to the area. Just before he arrived, the people heard an odd grunting sound.

November 24, 1973
Greensburg, 11:25 pm
Glowing eyes, strange sounds

Along Route 30, east of Greensburg and in the vicinity of the Greengate Mall area, a man and his girl friend were standing outside of their residence when they heard a crying sound coming from the nearby woods. The man turned around and looked in the direction of the sound and saw two large, glowing red eyes staring at the couple. The prowler with the red eyes moved into the woods. The couple was quite shaken by their experience.

November 24 or 25, 1973
Jumonville Summit, Fayette County, 11:30 pm
Unusual incident

A husband and wife curious about reports that a Bigfoot had recently been seen by a large group of people near Jumonville Summit decided to drive to that location and look around. They thought that it would be a nice area for them to walk their German Shepherd. The couple had heard that the hairy creatures enjoyed eating fruits of various types, so they took a variety of such treats with them. There was an isolated cave in the area near where the creature had reportedly been seen.

They decided to toss some grapefruit over the bank toward the cave. It was not long after that this couple claims that they heard a growl, then a crying sound, and then the sound of something large moving nearby. They did not wait to see what it was and ran back to their car. For a while they drove in the vicinity, then drove back to the location that they had run from. It was soon after they arrived that their dog began to act unusually. The family pet began to growl and its hair was standing up. After seeing the reaction of the dog, the couple decided to leave the area for good.

November 30, 1973
Gradyville, Delaware County, 7:15 pm (UFO)

A report was received from the State Police at Media concerning a UFO sighting reported by several people. The object seen was described as a large disc with small red lights emitting from it.

November, 1973
Ohiopyle, Fayette County
Man fires on creature which suddenly vanishes

It was during an investigation of another strange occurrence in February of 1974, that we learned of this incident. The witness involved, Tom Marks (pseudonym), had this very strange experience in November of 1973. The location of the incident is a remote wooded area not far from Ohiopyle. Tom and his family lived in a mobile home. His mother-in-law, Mrs. Hamm (pseudonym), lived a short distance away.

Tom had heard stories about the alleged Bigfoot sightings around the area in October, but when he discussed this with his wife, he told her "that someone had a little bit too much to drink." Tom would never believe that such hairy monsters could exist until that one day when he was running one of his hunting dogs. It was around 10 pm when he and the dog were near the corner of the woods. There had been a pack of wild dogs roaming the area, so Tom always carried a loaded 22 revolver with him. Suddenly, in the distance ahead of him, Tom noticed a dark figure. Since this was Tom's property, he yelled out to the stranger and asked him what he wanted and told him to stop. The dark form did not respond. As Tom approached closer, the figure turned toward the witness. Tom could not believe what he was seeing, nor what was to occur next.

This was not a human, but instead, a tall, hair-covered ape-like creature. Tom fired six shots from his revolver at the creature from a distance of about seventy five feet. Upon firing and apparently hitting the creature, the beast suddenly just vanished. Tom could hear the sound of the creature running off through the woods ahead, but he could not see it. At times, the sound of footsteps would stop, then continue on into the distance.

Tom just could not accept what had just happened and had trouble believing what he had seen with his own eyes. He went back to his trailer to pick up his Krag 30.40 rifle. Tom had it in his mind "to get one of those things." The man stated that, "It was something that wasn't supposed to be." Tom had made up his mind to go back into the woods and kill his prey. Upon going deeper into the woods, once again he saw a hairy creature and shot at it.

This time, when the creature was hit, it let out a very loud scream, like the cry of a baby. Tom had enough and returned home. Mrs. Marks was inside of the mobile home and heard the cry as well. She told me that the sound was like someone in deep pain. The family did not know who to report this occurrence to, so they notified a humane officer, who responded.

Just days after this incident, a large female black cat mysteriously disappeared from its secure outdoor cage. The large cage was divided into two separate compartments. The female cat was located on the left, while two of its kittens were on the right side. The large cat had been locked in the night before, but the next morning it was gone. The compartment, however, was still locked, but no cat. The lock on the door had to be turned to open.

The strange thing was that there had been a fall of fresh snow. There were no tracks leading to or from the cage, not even that of the cat. It was just around the time of the cat disappearance when another odd incident also occurred at that location. A loud humming noise suddenly encompassed the area. Where it originated from was never determined. Some of the animals appeared to be disturbed by the sound. The dogs all began to bark and the cats stayed close to their owners. Later, the cats refused to go outside as they normally would do.

November, 1973
Jumonville Summit, Fayette County
Creature seems to vanish and reappear

There were more Bigfoot encounters reported at Jumonville Summit in early 1974. A research team went to that mountainous location to look over the area and to interview some witnesses. One very strange account involving a Bigfoot creature reportedly occurred around the parking area at the large stone marker. A number of people went chasing after a hairy creature thinking at first that someone had dressed up in a costume, then realizing that was not the case.

Later, when some of the people were parked, the creature was reported to have come up behind them and looked into the window of the car and scared the occupants. The creature reportedly ran just a short distance ahead behind the tall stone marker and was peering at them. Observers mentioned that, oddly, the creature would be on one side of them, then suddenly it would vanish from that location, and appear at another opposite location. Even stranger from the same location was one account where witnesses could only see certain sections of the creature's body. For example, at times only the upper section of the creature, such as the head and torso was visible as it moved off.

December 1, 1973
Altoona, Blair County, 3 am (UFO)
A man observed six bright round lights in a row moving over a mountain ridge. The objects were observed for about seven minutes and then they seemed to suddenly fade away.

December 3, 1973
Penn, 1 am UFO lights up area
A man was driving home from work and was near Penn when he observed what appeared to be an illuminated house in the distance up behind some trees. The man was perplexed by what he was seeing. To him, it did look like a round house in the sky, but he knew that was impossible. The man drove a short distance to his home, from where he could still see the odd structure and which now was getting even brighter. The object seemed to be getting larger and was moving closer to his location. He quickly ran into the house and awakened his wife.

When they went outside, the object seemed to have changed shape. The object was now somewhat crescent shaped, or "like an inverted slice of watermelon," as described by the man's wife. The object was very luminous and glowed an orange color. The woman said, "I couldn't believe my eyes." A short time later the family called my UFO Hotline while the object was still being observed.

As the couple continued to watch, the crescent-shaped UFO began to dissipate. Then the object appeared to horizontally separate, and just the bottom section remained visible. The object did not appear to move off. It just seemed to fade out and disappear. The object appeared to be huge and was described as the size of two full moons. The entire observation was about six minutes.

December 3, 1973
Derry, morning
Large footprints observed

Two men were hunting on a farm and were following some deer tracks. Their attention was drawn to another trail, which was comprised of the largest and strangest footprints they had ever come across in the woods. The men had heard stories of Bigfoot encounters in the area and had been very skeptical until now. The men, in fact, became somewhat startled, and decided to cut their hunting activities short.

December 16, 1973
North Huntingdon, 6 pm (UFO)

A man was inside his home resting when his daughter ran inside and told him to quickly come outside. When the man arrived outside, his wife was pointing to a strange, frosty, pink-colored object, which was at first stationary in the sky. The luminous object looked like a crimson ball Christmas tree ornament and was revolving. The family called some other people that they knew in the area to also look at the UFO. All of the people were able to observe the object from their location. In about four minutes, the object began to slowly move toward the Penn area. The object, as it moved off, just looked like a pulsating light, which soon stopped blinking and disappeared from sight.

December 26, 1973
Jeanette and other areas, 7:15 pm (UFO)

The CB radios were buzzing around the Jeanette, Irwin, Claridge, and Herminie areas as people were talking about two unusual circles of lights in the sky. The objects were blue-white in color and hovered over the area, with the smaller object positioned to the top left of the larger one. After about fifteen minutes, the larger object made a fast turn and moved toward Herminie. That object hovered over that area for several minutes and then faded out and disappeared. The smaller object soon vanished as well.

December 26, 1973
Uniontown, Fayette County, 7:50 pm (UFO)

I received a report from an announcer at radio station WMBS in Uniontown, located in Fayette County. The station was receiving a number of calls from area residents who were seeing a cluster of six to eight multi-colored lights in the sky.

December 27, 1973
North Huntingdon, 12:15 am (UFO)

A man and woman traveling along Route 30 noticed what they first thought was an aircraft high above the left side of their car. The object, whatever it was, appeared to be motionless. The man shined the beam of his flashlight, which he turned on and off at times, toward the object. When the light hit the device, it began to drop in altitude, and moved closer toward the direction of the observers. The strange object was now close enough to see its odd shape, which had both triangular and spherical features.

The bottom of the craft was flat and somewhat rounded. The entire object appeared to be of a metallic, silver color. There were a number of individual white and blue lights covering the structure of the object. The UFO came to within three hundred feet of the witnesses and hovered about eighty five feet above the ground.

The witnesses became alarmed and left the area in their car at a high rate of speed. The object appeared to follow in their direction for a short distance before it departed. The driver was shaken by the experience and called the North Huntingdon Police, who referred to caller to my UFO Hotline number.

Part 6: 1974

Bigfoot and UFO Sightings Continue

When the 1973 year ended, the reports of strange occurrences continued into the New Year. The 1974 year brought more Bigfoot encounters, and sightings of UFOs, and some other very strange incidents as well. It was apparent, however, that the volume of creature reports had declined considerably in comparison to what had been experienced during 1973. Sightings of UFOs continued on a regular basis. Some of the 1974 UFO reports which came to our attention will be discussed.

Early 1974
January 21, 1974
Indiana County, Allegheny County reports
On the evening of January 21 near Heshbon in Indiana County, a coal miner reportedly saw a Bigfoot near a mine. Another witness was said to have seen a similar creature about three weeks before.

Also on January 21, in Lincoln Borough, Allegheny County, another strange event was reported. An experienced hunter took three dogs into the woods. His dogs suddenly became very excited and started running off. The man then heard a loud breathing sound and thought that his dogs had brought down a deer. He soon realized that whatever was making the sound was moving around him. The hunter became concerned when only two of his dogs returned. The man did hear the sound of heavy stomping and loud breathing following close behind him. The man aimed his high beam flashlight into the woods but could not see anything.

January 27, 1974
Irwin, 2 am
UFO chases car on PA turnpike

I received reports that a very interesting UFO encounter had occurred on the Pennsylvania Turnpike near the Irwin exit. A number of witnesses independently observed something very unusual at about 2 am One woman was on her way home from work when she had a frightful experience. It was a cloudy night and there was a light rain at the time when she observed two small, round dots of light close together in the sky. The witness at first thought they were stars until the two lights together began to suddenly drop very quickly from the sky, leaving a bright streak in the sky.

The lights arrived at a position about the height of a telephone pole above the ground and then moved in the direction of the woman's car. The lights approached toward the left side of the vehicle and came as close as ninety to one hundred feet. The lights were attached to a very large, solid, curved, gray object. The woman tried to give an estimate of size of the object by indicating that it was about as tall as a bus and as wide as her house. There were also two red lights shaped almost like portholes on the side of the object, which blinked a couple of times.

As the object neared the car, suddenly the engine of the car began to sputter, as if it was going to shut down. The object stayed close to the vehicle and hovered for about a minute. The woman tried to get away from the UFO and she noticed that when she was able to get some distance from the object, her engine ran normally.

There were two wide, bright beams of light emitting from the front of the unknown aerial object. The beams were so bright that they were at times blinding the driver. As the woman watched the object, she realized that it was difficult to understand how its movements were so fast and smooth. The witness stated, "It was unbelievable. I have never seen anything like it." A truck driver approaching the area saw the two round lights, describing them as like headlights in the sky. When he stopped at the Irwin interchange, he said that two other people in separate cars had also reported seeing the same thing.

January 29, 1974
Derry Township, early evening
Trapper sees creature
On January 29, near Keystone Park in Derry Township, during the early evening, a hunter went to check his traps, which he did on a regular basis. On the way down the path toward the reservoir, the man observed a creature in the woods. The creature stood upright and was tall. It appeared very broad shouldered and ran off in a clumsy manner. It moved in the direction of the Bell farm. The trapper had noticed on the last few nights when he had been out that pine trees in the area had many broken limbs that had not been there before.

What Are We Dealing With?

For weeks we had been dealing with many strange reports from the general public. Numerous people had been frightened by encounters with strange objects in the sky or mysterious creatures on the ground. We had heard many other strange accounts ranging from paranormal incidents to mysterious visitors showing up and interviewing witnesses. Even with reports of shooting at the creatures with various types of firearms, there were neither bodies recovered nor any indisputable, solid, physical proof to support the existence of these unknown hairy beings.

There seemed to be no doubt, however, that strange encounters were indeed going on. We had heard that in weeks past, some creature witnesses had allegedly been interviewed by WCUFOSG investigators, supposedly including myself. We realized upon hearing some of these reports that we had no record of those incidents and had concerns that someone was impersonating us.

On February 6, 1974, another well documented incident occurred with many strange elements to it. This case strongly suggests that a flesh and blood origin for these unknown creatures may not explain some of the Bigfoot encounters on record.

February 6, 1974
Ohiopyle, Fayette County, 10 pm
Woman shoots creature, creature vanishes

The State Police Barracks at Uniontown received a call at 10:55 pm from Mrs. Marks (pseudonym), the daughter of Mrs. Hamm (pseudonym), concerning some strange occurrences that had just taken place a short time before. The location of the occurrence was a remote, rural location close to Ohiopyle.

The state police dispatcher took the information and contacted a trooper by radio to respond to the scene. Also the Officer In Charge (OIC) was notified of the occurrence. The dispatcher knew from Mrs. Marks' voice that something had frightened her, and he did not laugh at her strange account concerning what she described as the shooting of creatures from a spaceship.

It was during this period in history that the United States was experiencing a national truckers strike. Gas rationing was in effect and there was some shooting violence on the roadways. Due to this national emergency, the National Guard was backing up the state police in Pennsylvania.

Along with the trooper, one national guardsman also responded to the location. When the pair arrived on the scene, the strange activity had ceased. The trooper learned that a strange lighted object out in the woods had departed a short time before his arrival. They interviewed the witnesses and searched for evidence. The ground was frozen from the cold temperatures and no footprints could be found.

Another state trooper and two additional national guardsmen also arrived on the scene to assist. The primary state police investigating officer told me that both witnesses appeared to be reliable and one woman was visibly shaken. What convinced the investigators that something odd had taken place was the way the animals were reacting when they arrived.

Between Mrs. Hamm and the Marks family, there were a total of four dogs at that location, including beagles, a bird dog and an Eskimo Spitz. The investigating officer told me how all four dogs were physically shaking, hiding in their housing, and would not bark at all. One officer tried to physically move one of the dogs from inside of its cage and it would not respond at all.

Their horse was also unusually nervous at the time. That animal generally runs for its oats to eat when they are put out, but had to be physically taken to a barn for its meal. Even then, it would only take a bite of oats, and then run off, which was not its normal behavior. The horse was also frequenting a section of the barnyard that it would never normally visit.

The cats in the Marks' trailer were also acting frightened. The cats were continually following Mrs. Marks everywhere she went, and wanted to cuddle close to her, which also was not their normal behavior. Mrs. Marks also pointed out that her six-month-old baby was up all night crying. The child had never done this since it was born.

George Lutz and I arrived at the location of the incident early the next morning, since we could not get gas the night before. When we approached the area, the dogs were acting normal and barking loudly at our arrival. We met with the primary witness, fifty nine year old Mrs. Hamm, who lived in a small, rustic home. This woman had lived in the woods all of her life, was very familiar with animals, and feared few things. Mrs. Hamm took us around and showed us her animal pens, and then we went into her home, sat down at the kitchen table, and set up our tape recorders.

Mrs. Hamm then described the events of the previous evening. It was between 10 and 10:30 pm when she was in her house watching television. Suddenly, she heard the rattling of tin cans on her front porch. There had recently been a pack of wild dogs that came through the area and she assumed that they were in her garbage. Mrs. Hamm loaded her 16-gauge double barrel shotgun with one shell of 8 shot ammo. Her intent was not to shoot the dogs, but to scare them away.

Once the chamber was loaded, Mrs. Hamm switched on the porch light and stepped into the doorway. To her shock and disbelief, there were no dogs there. Just six feet in front of her stood a huge, hair-covered ape-like creature. When the light was switched on, the creature raised its arms over its head. Mrs. Hamm's first thought was that the beast was going to lunge at her. She fired her shotgun at the creature's mid-section. At that moment, the creature physically vanished in a flash of light. Mrs. Hamm said the flash was very bright and was like the flash if someone was taking a picture with a camera. When the creature was seen, there was no sound or smell detected.

I will never forget the words that Mrs. Hamm used to describe the appearance of the creature to me. She said, "It looked like a great big hairy ape." She never mentioned the term Bigfoot. Mrs. Hamm said the beast was over seven feet tall, stood erect on two legs, and was covered from head to toe with dark, gray hair. The entire episode only lasted seconds, so she did not notice other physical details.

After the shooting, she went back inside her home and sat down, quite shaken over what had occurred. The Marks family, including her son-in-law, daughter and grand children, lived about one hundred feet away in a mobile home. Tom Marks (pseudonym) called Mrs. Hamm on the phone to inquire about the gunshot they had heard. She told Tom what had happened.

SILENT INVASION

The man loaded his 22 revolver and made his way toward Mrs. Hamm's residence. As he approached, he saw a dark figure running down the road but he could not see any detail. But as he approached near the woods, he saw, "four or five shadows of hairy people."

As he continued closer to the house, the creatures began to approach him at a fast pace. He shined his flashlight toward them and became frightened at what he saw. He dropped his flashlight, but aimed his revolver toward the beings.

The creatures Tom saw were similar to what Mrs. Hamm had described. Over seven feet tall, covered with hair, but these creatures had eyes that glowed like fire, even in the total surrounding darkness. Tom noticed that the creatures had long arms and walked upright on two legs, but with an awkward movement. He also did not notice any sound or smell when he was near the creatures.

Tom was frightened and fired two shots at the hairy monsters, then ran off toward the house, not looking back to see what was happening. When he arrived at Mrs. Hamm's house, he hurried inside and loaded his revolver. Tom was persistent that he wanted to get one of the creatures. Although this was his second experience with them since the previous November, he still could not believe that such beasts could exist.

After loading his gun, Tom went back outside but did not see any creatures. However, he saw something else very strange. An unusual blinking, luminous object was above the trees deep in the woods. There were no light sources in that area to confuse these phenomena with. The light was shaped like a Christmas ornament, blinking a bright red color in a pattern somewhat similar to a police car emergency light. After seeing the UFO over the woods, he ran back to his trailer to get his deer rifle. He also told his wife to call someone for help. Mrs. Marks then called the state police.

Porch where vanishing creature incident occurred
© Stan Gordon

While George Lutz and I were on the scene investigating, a humane officer also arrived. We discussed the case and the three of us continued to search for evidence. We searched around the property as well as the woods where the mystery light had been seen. We did locate BB pellet type holes in a tree, which would have been directly in line with the location on the porch from which Mrs. Hamm had shot at the creature. We also learned from the officer that there had been a recent rash of mysterious animal attacks in that general area, and that four of those cases were not easily explainable.

During our interview with the witnesses at the scene, some other unusual details began to surface. It was just after midnight, after the state police and national guardsman had left the scene, when Mrs. Marks called her mother to see if she was calmed down. The phone rang for a long period with no answer. She dialed the number again, and let it ring many times again, but still Mrs. Hamm did not pick up. Tom was asked to go back to Mrs. Hamm's house to check on her. Tom, still un-nerved from the previous creature-UFO encounter, refused to walk the short distance, and instead drove over.

When he arrived, Mrs. Hamm was sitting down and awake. She wanted to know why he came to the house at that time of night. Mrs. Hamm told Tom that she had heard him slam the car door when he was getting in and when the car passed by her window the phone rang. Her daughter had been calling on her phone constantly until her husband got into the house. Mrs. Hamm said, "The phone just wasn't ringing or I would have heard it."

We also learned of other strange previous experiences. It was approximately two weeks before the February shooting incident, when Mrs. Hamm was awakened by a tremendous thump, as if something very heavy had hit her house. (Other people who had been reporting creature encounters also reported a similar loud bang.) A search around the area found nothing that could account for the noise.

About a week prior to this February event, Mrs. Hamm heard an odd noise outside of her house late one night. Upon opening the door to look outside, she turned on the porch light and saw a bright flash of light ahead in the yard. This flash was similar to what she saw when she shot at the creature. Mrs. Hamm reluctantly told George and I that during the past summer when she was sleeping at night, she would feel someone touch her shoulder, and she would wake up very startled since no one else was in the house. At times, she would feel a presence in the house, but nothing was seen. The strange experiences around the Marks-Hamm property seem to have started with Tom's November, 1973, creature encounter and came to an end with the February 1974 incident.

George Lutz searching for evidence near shooting scene
© Stan Gordon

February 7, 1974
Wooddale, Fayette County, 12:55 am (UFO)

It was only about three hours after the Ohiopyle incident and just about fifteen miles down the road when another person reported a low level UFO sighting. The man was driving his car between Wooddale and Laurelville when he observed a thirty foot in diameter disc-shaped object. The UFO was only about one hundred feet away from the car and was hovering about one hundred fifty feet above the ground. The object was solid in structure with a white light shining from the top. There were also red, green, and blue lights emitting from the bottom of the object.

As the witness looked on, he detected a humming sound coming from the object as well as an odd chemical smell that permeated the air. The witness became apprehensive and quickly drove to his home where he told a relative about what he had just encountered. The witness had always been skeptical about UFO stories and was reluctant to call the authorities, fearing that he would be ridiculed. Another family member called the state police to report the man's experience, who referred the caller to my UFO Hotline.

February 15, 1974
Greensburg, 10:30 pm (UFO)

While traveling along Route 130 between Greensburg and Jeannette, a witness observed a bright, red spherical object in the sky. The observer pulled off the road and watched as the solid, round red light began to move horizontally toward Greensburg. The object initially began to drop slowly, then suddenly, it rapidly dropped and descended straight down to a position much lower in the sky. The object was lost from sight after about three minutes of observation.

March 12, 1974
Hempfield, 10:11 p.m (UFO)

Several people near Greensburg observed a series of strange objects that followed across the sky on the same path within minutes. The objects appeared blue-white in color and were star-like. The objects moved from the southeast toward the west and followed about thirty seconds apart, one after the other. A total of four objects were observed during this sighting.

March 13, 1974
Armagh, Indiana County, 9:20 pm (UFO)

A family observed another formation of strange objects as they traveled along Route 22 near Armagh. The witnesses observed five large cone-shaped objects that moved slowly from the northwest toward the southeast. Most of the objects were bright white, but the object that traveled on the outside of the group was pinkish in color. The objects appeared to be solid and moved steadily and quietly as they crossed the sky.

March 23, 1974
Washington County, 12:55 am (UFO)

Information was received that two law enforcement officers who did not want to be identified had observed a UFO while on patrol in a wooded area. The officers reportedly observed a very large elongated-shaped object above the ground that they estimated to be about six times the length of their vehicle. The lights on the object were described as similar to the lights on an old Pullman railroad car. As the men watched, they observed a pulsating light being emitted from the silent object toward the ground. There were also steady green and red lights on the structure of the elongated UFO. At one point the men were said to have exited their vehicle to watch the object. The object then began to move off further into the valley and could no longer be seen.

April 13, 1974
New Stanton, 8:15 pm (UFO)

A woman who was traveling on Route 119 near the Chrysler plant at New Stanton observed a mysterious object motionless a few hundred feet off the ground. It was still light outside and the witness could see what looked like a solid, bright, silver, round object just hovering. From the left side or rear section of the object, it was emitting what looked like a smoke trail. There was also a light at the front of the object that was similar to a headlight. The object continued to hover as the car moved off. The object was observed for about ten minutes.

April 14, 1974
Yukon, 8 pm (UFO)

A professional family was returning home after a family gathering and was traveling east on I-70 and was just crossing a bridge when the husband and wife simultaneously caught sight of an object falling from the sky. The man's first impression was that an airplane was going down. The object was about one hundred feet above the tree line when it was first seen. The object or objects were falling straight down toward the ground.

What could be seen were four or five red, elliptical-shaped lights, which could have been connected to one larger structure or possibly individual objects. The lights vanished behind a hill and were not seen again. When the family reached a hill, they searched for signs of a fire or crash but found nothing. The state police were notified as soon as the family arrived at their home. The sighting occurred in the vicinity of the Westinghouse Waltz Mills nuclear facility. Pennsylvania State Police at Greensburg dispatched a car to the area, but nothing was found.

April 18, 1974
New Alexandria, 8 pm (UFO)

A state trooper reported to me that he had observed a formation of flashing lights in a horizontal formation over a group of trees. About ninety minutes later, the officer saw a similar series of mysterious lights in the same general area.

April 19, 1974, widespread reports from PA-OH-MD-WV, 8:15 pm Bolide-meteor.

This UFO sighting was explained as a bolide, or an extremely bright meteor. There were numerous reports that originated from a very widespread area and received news coverage. Police and my UFO Hotline received numerous calls describing a bright, round ball of white light about the size of a baseball, followed by a long black and blue smoke trail. The smoke trail remained visible in the sky for approximately one hour. The state police received many calls from people who thought they were seeing a burning aircraft.

April 19, 1974
between Radebaugh and Grapeville, 7:30 am
Creature observed

On April 19, 1974, two men were driving between Radebaugh and Grapeville at about 7:30 am on a level stretch of road near some pine trees when a seven to eight feet tall, dark, hair-covered creature was observed in a stooped position. The men had to go to work and continued on their way.

April 20, 1974
Delmont, 1:45 am (UFO)

Two people were traveling on Route 22 near Delmont, when a bright, orange light was observed over a hill. The light was observed for about twenty minutes as it brightened and dimmed. A short time later, the same or a similar orange light appeared behind their car and was level with the back window.

This silent light source was somewhat rounded in shape and glowed like the sun. The brilliant object began to follow the car and was so bright that the driver could hardly look at it in her rear view mirror. As another car approached them from down the road, the orange light faded in brightness and moved off to their right. When they arrived at home, they called the state police and the UFO Hotline.

April 28, 1974
Hempfield Township, 11:15 pm (UFO)

Several residents in the Fort Allen housing development observed a bright object in the sky moving slowly towards them from the direction of Latrobe. The object at first looked like a star, but it became increasingly larger and took on a brilliant orange color as it approached. While under observation, the object took on an elongated shape, similar to a flame, and continued to move quite slowly. After about eight minutes, the object disappeared.

May 4, 1974
near Ligonier
Strange activities at a summer camp

During the early morning hours of May 4, at a summer camp not far from Ligonier, two female counselors were hiking through the woods when they encountered a long series of large three-toed footprints. The strange tracks took a path around the camp and some continued into the actual campgrounds where the young campers slept. One print was seen just outside a tent where a counselor was staying. According to those who saw the tracks, there was an indication that the footprints had been made by more than one creature. The length of the tracks ranged from seven to fourteen inches in length.

There was about a five-foot stride between the tracks, which were observed over an extended area. Those counselors who observed the tracks were experienced in the woods and were very familiar with the tracks of the local wildlife and had never seen anything like this before. The night before, some campers had heard strange high pitched sounds coming from the woods at about five minute intervals.

Just prior to seeing the three-toed tracks, another odd print, like that of a huge cat was also observed in the same area. The officials of the camp were so concerned that they decided to call the Carnegie Museum in Pittsburgh on May 7, who referred the call to the WCUFOSG.

May 7, 1974
near Ligonier
Investigation at summer camp
On May 7, George Lutz and I went to the camp to interview witnesses and look over the tracks in the woods. It sure was bad timing. Just as we entered the woods, we were hit with a torrential rainstorm, which quickly flooded over the area. We hurried back to the camp, where the camp officials gave us some towels. Unfortunately, any evidence was washed away.

May 10, 1974
near Ligonier
Camper reports strange experience
On May 10, at the same camp near Ligonier, one of the young female campers reported a strange experience to a counselor. During that night, the nine year-old reported looking out a window of a building where a number of the children were sleeping. She said that she saw a chimpanzee walking around in the campgrounds. This young camper had no knowledge of the strange tracks recently found around that campground. Other campers also reported a strange, rotten smell near a creek in the vicinity where the tracks

had been seen. Others claim to have heard something heavy walking around the camp that same night.

Week of May 14, 1974
Herminie, 11:30 pm
Gorilla-like creature

During the week of May 14, information was received from a man that his relative, who did not want to be involved, was driving near Herminie when a dark, gorilla-like creature walked across the road in front of his car. The witness had previously laughed when hearing about the Bigfoot reports in the area and returned to the location of the sighting the next day. The man and some friends reportedly found the brush smashed down along the road where the creature had walked.

About May 20, 1974
Near Delmont
Large creature observed

A man reported that his sister had heard an odd noise coming from the woods from behind her home near Delmont about May 20. She observed a large creature, which at first she thought was a bear. As she watched the strange animal, she realized that it was more ape-like in appearance. The creature walked off into the woods and continued until it was out of sight.

May 23, 1974
Sewickley, Allegheny County, 6 pm
Being in the metallic outfit

On May 23, near Sewickley in Allegheny County, another strange incident came to our attention. About 6 pm a teenaged boy was riding his motorcycle through a wooded area not far from his home. The boy commonly rode in this wooded area after school. As he rounded a bend, in the distance ahead, he observed a figure standing sideways. The figure was described as a tall man-like figure, about seven feet tall and thin. The odd thing was that the being was dressed in a shiny metallic outfit that appeared that it was made of stainless steel and was wrinkled all over except for the head, where it was skintight.

The head was described as football-shaped. After seeing the odd creature, the boy accelerated the engine several times, which seemed to attract the creature's attention, since it changed position and half squatted. It then turned, took three steps up a hill, and moved into the woods.

There was an unconfirmed report that on May 27, police in Beaver County had reportedly chased a Bigfoot into a wooded area.

May 30, 1974
Burnsville, Washington County, 9:30 pm (UFO)
A number of witnesses observed up to two balls of fire approaching from the West Virginia line. The luminous spheres appeared to stop motionless, then dropped lower toward the ground in the distance.

May 1974
Clearfield County, 9 pm
Light from UFO strikes witnesses
It was a period of time after this event had occurred that we were informed of its occurrence. About 9 pm two young men went outside for a walk to enjoy the clear, star filled night. They were looking skyward when they observed an orange ball of light approaching from the southwest. At first

they thought it was a satellite, but then as the object quickly dropped from the sky and moved in their direction, that theory quickly changed. The boys became startled as the object hovered only about fifty to one hundred feet above the ground, and only a short distance away in front of them.

The spherical object was similar to a ball of fire, yet it was not that bright. As the boys stared in amazement at the hovering UFO, another frightening experience was about to occur. A bright blue light suddenly shot forth from the bottom section of the object and struck both of the boys. The next thing the boys remember was the orange sphere accelerating straight up into the sky. In a matter of seconds, the object was out of sight. The boys regained their senses and ran into the house where they told one of the boy's mother about what had happened.

May 1974
Ulster, Bradford County, (UFO)

It was about 11:30 pm as the witness was driving along a dark country road when she saw a strange object in the sky. The sky was dark and there was a drizzling rain when the odd sight caused her to slam on the brakes. The woman pulled off to the side of the road to watch the large object, which was completely round and was moving slowly on a continuous path over some hills toward her left. The object then passed directly over the observer and crossed over the nearby Susquehanna River and then moved out of sight. The object was estimated to be the size of two car lengths, and blinked on and off with a bright, fiery red light. This first observation lasted about one to two minutes.

A short time later, the witness saw the object again after she had traveled a little further down the road. This time the object appeared directly overhead, about one hundred feet up. The object soon moved off toward the hills and was not seen again. This witness also reported being visited by a rather odd man who questioned her about the UFO she had observed. The man told her that he was doing volunteer work for the Air Force. The man had an odd voice which the lady described as, "strange and squeaky, high-pitched for a man". The odd fellow also seemed to have some type of speech impediment. The visitor stood about five feet tall and was small framed, with short, brown hair. The stranger had some UFO photos with him and he asked the woman if they were similar to what she had seen. The man left after about a two-hour discussion concerning UFOs.

We received information that at about dusk on June 3, two men walking across a bridge near Latrobe smelled a strange sulfur odor. They looked over the bridge and noticed large footprints on the ground and also observed a dark hair-covered creature.

June 14, 1974
Upper Darby, Delaware County, 9:10 pm (UFO)

The next UFO sighting activity reported to our UFO Hotline was followed up by WCUFOSG member Bob Daley. The local police had received three calls from area residents about strange activity in the sky. The initial call was from a young man who reported seeing an unusual glow in the sky. The next call was from a man in the area who described seeing what he said looked like a spear-shaped object.

A woman then reported that she and some friends were sitting outside when they watched a cigar-shaped object passing over only about fifty to sixty feet away and about telephone pole height off the ground. The object made no sound and had the witnesses not looked upwards, they would not have known that it was there. The elliptical object was of a silver-white color and had a V-shaped front section. The object seemed to accelerate somewhat as it moved off in the distance.

July 1974
Creature observations

Another second hand report of an incident in July of 1974 near Hutchinson involved two young men who were out in the woods target shooting when they saw a Bigfoot. The boys reportedly followed it for a short distance, and then decided to flee the area.

Back in Derry Township, a man told a close friend that about July 4, he saw a creature that he described as a baby Bigfoot climbing over a fence near his home. The man was reluctant to report what he had seen.

July 16, 1974
Greensburg
Something heavy moves into the woods

On July 16, about 10:30 pm, outside of Greensburg in a rural area near the Greengate Mall, a family reported hearing something very large and heavy run past their home and continue up into the woods. A friend of the family reportedly saw a Bigfoot carrying something under its arms in that area only a few days before.

July 20, 1974
Pittsburgh, Allegheny County, 12:55 pm (UFO)

A call was received on the UFO Hotline concerning a daylight observation of a solid, silver cigar-shaped object observed from the South Hills suburb of Pittsburgh. The object was described by the witness as looking like "a hot dog". The witness said the object was moving across the sky toward the south, that it suddenly stopped, then it descended slightly in elevation, then rapidly picked up speed and moved across the sky and out of sight. The entire observation lasted about ten seconds.

July 24, 1974
Laughlintown, 9:35 pm (UFO)
Four glowing, round, orange objects that were described as bright as the sun were seen moving across the sky from west to east. The bright spheres were flying in a perfect horizontal formation, and a slight hum was heard as they passed over and moved off in the distance.

August 14, 1974
Butler, Butler County, 9:35 pm (UFO)
A UFO sighting had initially been called into the Butler Police. The investigating officer indicated that the people reporting the observation were good, reliable people. A WCUFOSG member conducted an investigation as well. The police had responded to the sighting location, but nothing was observed upon their arrival. The police report indicated that fifteen residents had observed three objects in the Broad Street School area. Witnesses reported a somewhat V-shaped object, similar to a flame from a candle burning, which was stationary in the sky.

The object was larger and brighter than a star. The lights did not blink, but seemed to flicker, and there was a hazy circle surrounding the object. The object was seen for about five to ten minutes before it disappeared, then reappeared brighter in a different location. Two more similar objects were then observed moving at a high rate of speed across the sky toward the east. These objects seemed to have been more spherical in shape. One witness reported her television flickering oddly just after the sighting. The dogs in the area seemed highly disturbed at the time of the observations.

August 17, 1974
Jeannette
White gorilla-like creature spotted

Two teenaged boys who were camping off Millersdale Road outside of Jeannette on August 17, reported a strange experience. It was around 1:30 am while the boys were hiking down a trail when they observed a seven-foot-tall, white gorilla-like creature. The witnesses said the creature was very broad shouldered and had long arms. The boys were about one hundred feet from the creature and stopped to watch it. The creature, while progressing in its forward path, would at times step backwards, and then continue on.

What really baffled the two boys was that when they would shine their flashlight on the creature, it would suddenly just seem to vanish. When the light beam was moved away from the creature, it would reappear. This took place twice while the creature was under observation. After about two to three minutes of watching the creature, the boys ran home to safety. The boys also mentioned that a dog housed at nearby farm that was known to always bark at the slightest noise never made a sound during the time that the creature was seen.

Another detail that surfaced during the interview was that reportedly within days after the boys' encounter, another possible creature encounter reportedly occurred in that same area. Some local youngsters at a nearby farm noticed that the barn door was open. When they looked inside, they noticed what appeared to be a shadow of a "giant man" inside and they all ran off. Some nearby dogs were groaning and growling and were unusually upset. Another local family reported that something had frightened their horses that same day.

August 21, 1974
Youngwood, 9:35 pm (UFO)

There were a number of widespread UFO sightings reported on this same evening. Two bright, yellow-orange lights were observed from Youngwood moving horizontally across the sky from east to west. The lights appeared very low, about two hundred feet above the ground, and were silent. Both the state and local police were called and proceeded into the area. The 911 dispatch center called the UFO Hotline reporting three additional UFO sightings. The 911 center also contacted officials at a local fair, since there was the possibility that residents were seeing a searchlight display from that location. It was learned that the searchlight was not operating at that time.

Just minutes later, another witness near Latrobe reported a bright, orange-yellow light that seemed to spin in the sky. The light would become very bright, then fade out, and reappear again. The object was estimated at about 1,100 feet altitude, and moved very slowly while under observation for over ten minutes.

Other UFO reports came in describing a bright, white light hovering over various communities. Some of these sightings were likely the planet Jupiter, which was very bright that night.

September 5, 1974
Evans City, Butler County, 9:30 pm (UFO)

A call was received from Pennsylvania State Police at Butler concerning a UFO sighting reported to their station. The object appeared as a bright star-like object, with a steady light that moved slowly but steadily across the sky. Suddenly, as the witness watched, the object quickly accelerated it's speed and curved toward the northwest and moved out of sight.

About September 9, 1974
Delmont, evening
A strange report

This report came in from a credible source, but unfortunately those involved did not want to be interviewed. On or about this date, it was learned that two boys in a rural area outside of Delmont were playing in a field when suddenly a bright beam of light projected down from the sky near them. The two young fellows became frightened and ran home. Upon going back to the field the next morning, they reportedly found a dead dog that had been mutilated. The animal appeared to have claw marks on it and large footprints were seen around the carcass.

September 17, 1974
Adamsburg, 9 pm (UFO)

A family called to report that they had watched for fifteen minutes two reddish-green, bright star-like objects over the Adamsburg area. The objects kept circling over the area and were chasing each other across the sky. The witnesses commented on how the lights were able to change directions very rapidly. A call was received from the newsroom at the Greensburg Tribune-Review to inform us that they had also received a UFO report from the Mount Pleasant Township area.

September 19, 1974
Brenizer, 10 pm
Strange sounds

A woman who lives in a wooded area in Derry Township reported being alarmed by a sound similar to that of a baby screaming coming from the woods during the night. She had also heard the same sound the night before. She noticed that her dog appeared very nervous when the sounds were heard.

September 24, 1974
Midland, Beaver County, 9 pm
UFO chases truck

This UFO sighting came to our attention from the Center For UFO Studies (CUFOS) and was investigated by a WCUFOSG investigator. The initial report was made to the Midland Police Department when several people came running into their station yelling that they had been followed by a UFO. It was learned that five or six diamond-shaped objects were first observed in the sky.

During that time, a smaller, similar object appeared to come from within one of the larger ones. One of the objects shot straight up into the sky at that time. A short time later, one of the passengers in the truck noticed that a large object was behind their truck and was approaching from behind and was only about eight to ten feet above the ground. The five passengers watched as the car-sized, diamond-shaped object followed them for about three to four minutes.

The solid object had a total of four lights, one at each corner of the diamond shape. The lights were all white in color, except for the one red light at the rear of the object. There also seemed to be a white glow around the outer edge of the body of the object. The object, which made no sound, pursued the vehicle until another truck appeared that was traveling toward them. At that time, the diamond-shaped UFO tilted on its side, then shot straight up into the sky and moved out of sight. Both trucks stopped at that time. The driver of the other vehicle confirmed at the scene to the other witnesses that he had also seen the object.

At about 10 pm, a man looking through his telescope from the South Hill section of Pittsburgh in Allegheny County, watched a white, oval-shaped object with a red and blue tail move across the sky. The observation was so odd that the man called the Buhl Planetarium, who referred the call to us.

At 10:25 pm another UFO sighting was reported from the Youngwood area where a family had observed a bright white object which seemed pointed at the ends. The object was silent and moved quite slowly across the sky at an altitude of about fifteen hundred feet and was seen for over three minutes.

Not only were the public reporting strange oddities, but also even some WCUFOSG members had experienced some rather strange occurrences at times. On the evening of September 24, 1974, one investigator who had just left a meeting discussing the current incidents was pondering the details as to whether some of these events could possibly be real. At that same time, an odd event occurred. Suddenly, the hood of his car lifted straight up and blocked his view, nearly causing him to wreck. An examination of the hood found no malfunctions.

September 26, 1974
Towanda, Bradford County, 9:35 pm (UFO)

A UFO sighting report came to our attention from the Pennsylvania State Police at Towanda. A woman was driving near Luthers Mills when she noticed an object hovering in the sky. The shape of the object, which hovered for a few minutes, could not be determined, but it had a number of yellow-white lights at the top and at the rear section. While the object remained motionless, a soft sound was detected, but as the object suddenly took off, a high-pitched, piercing sound could be heard. The entire sighting lasted about fifteen minutes.

September 30, 1974
Arona, 12:15 am (UFO)

Two people were traveling in a car near Arona when they saw a solid, round light about three to four feet in diameter emerging from a hollow. The light approached to within ten feet of the car before moving off. There was a Kodak camera in the car and several photographs were taken of the object. The pictures show a very small, round object, which can be seen very faintly.

October 3, 1974
Oley, Berks County, 1:48 am (UFO)

A man near the Oley stone quarry reported seeing a strange object with a possible row of windows and lights coming down in the quarry area. The police sent a car out to that location, but the object had departed before they arrived. The operator at the Berks County Police Radio Communications Center who took the call from the witness said the man was very shaken.

WCUFOSG member Bob Daley, who looked into the report, spoke with the local police officer who also investigated and learned that the witness was a very competent person whom he had known for quite a while. The police officer said that the man who saw the object was so nervous after the encounter that he could barely speak. The police also noted the unusual absence of ducks and geese at the quarry pond after the reported UFO sighting.

The witness had just eaten a snack and was taking a walk when he noticed a bright light in the sky ahead. The stationary light began to move from his right to left, then suddenly made a left turn and began to move directly toward the startled man. What could now be seen was a silver, circular object, with red, blue, and white flashing lights, and possibly windows around it. The silent object came to about fifty feet above the ground.

An intense beam of light was emitted from the left side of the object. The object had been observed for about five minutes when the beam of light suddenly went out. Then about fifteen seconds later, the colored lights just seemed to disappear and the object was not seen again. The man noticed that the fowl had been scared away from the pond while the object was nearby. The man immediately called the police to report what he had seen.

October 27, 1974
McKees Rocks, Allegheny County, 7:15 pm (UFO)

Two people called Buhl Planetarium to tell them that they had spotted a strange, round object in the sky, which was larger than their car. The object made a whirling sound and had a number of evenly spaced portholes. The object also displayed numerous red, white and yellow blinking lights. The object kept darting back and forth and changing directions. The planetarium had the witnesses call the UFO Hotline.

October 28, 1974
Connellsville, Fayette County, 7:02 pm (UFO)

A young girl went to a window in the house after seeing a bright flash of light, and then saw a white sphere moving in front of her window. The ball of light then moved past another window in the house and was seen by her sister. At the time of the observation, they also heard an odd sound, "like someone throwing stones at tin cans".

November 23, 1974
off Avenue B Street, Latrobe, 9 pm
Boy sees man-like creature

On November 23, 1974, off Avenue B in Latrobe, a boy was riding his bicycle through a field at 9 pm when he saw a very tall, dark colored, man-like creature. The kids frequented this area since it is a good location for seeing deer. The youngster hurried off to a friend's house to tell them about what he saw. Four boys returned to the location where the creature had been seen and the creature was still there standing next to a pole.

When the witnesses aimed their flashlights toward the beast, they could see its large body and two large, pinkish-red glowing eyes, which glowed very bright. The eyes of this creature glowed much brighter when hit with their lights than the deer that they had seen at times. When the lights hit the creature, it took two large steps and ran off into the woods. The observers saw the creature peeking out from the trees toward them on several occasions. They heard a screaming sound and what sounded like trees cracking. One of the boys' mothers thought they should call the police.

The local police were notified and made a quick sweep of the area.

November 23, 1974
Jumonville, Fayette County
Dark figure approaches car

On the same day, November 23, back at Jumonville, Fayette County, another strange incident also occurred. It was about 11 pm while several young adults were walking around at that location that their attention was drawn to their car. One of their friends had a foot injury and had remained in the car, and he was screaming for help. When they arrived at the vehicle, the frightened man told them that a tall, dark figure had approached nearby. At first he thought that it was a tree, but then realized that this object was moving and running quickly. He also saw two large, white shiny eyes. The group went over to where he saw the dark form and found several large, odd footprints.

November 26, 1974
Jeannette, 7:30 pm, Hovering UFO

The woman driver was traveling on the Oakford Park Road near the pumping station when she observed a large, round object with very bright lights circling the area. The object had three red and one green beams of light that projected toward the ground, and hovered over the area for about five minutes. The object then departed the area at a fast speed. The witness complained of a headache after the sighting.

December 29, 1974
Gibsonia area, Allegheny County
Strange tracks

At the end of 1974, there was a report from the Gibsonia area in Allegheny County. On December 29, strange footprints were found in a grass and moss-covered area. These tracks appeared to be four-toed and the heel area sunk four inches deep into the ground. In the months to follow, more Bigfoot activity would be reported by numerous residents around the Gibsonia area.

December 30, 1974
Mount Lebanon, Allegheny County
Last UFO sighting in 1974

The final UFO sighting I received for 1974, concerned an observation on December 30, from the Mount Lebanon sub-urb of Pittsburgh. At 11:23 pm a witness reported seeing a yellow object with curved sides moving around in the sky for several minutes before moving off.

SILENT INVASION

Part 9
Recurring Strange Accounts

Overview of Paranormal Activity

The term "paranormal" was defined in Webster's Seventh New Collegiate Dictionary as "not scientifically explainable." There were numerous occurrences that took place during this series of events which appeared to fall within this definition. We were dealing with what appeared to be the reality that strange, hairy anthropoidal beings were wandering through the woods of Pennsylvania.

It would actually have been simpler if the information at hand suggested that we were dealing with an undiscovered primate. And then we had to deal with the on-going UFO sightings, some of which could not be easily dismissed with a clear explanation. And why in some cases did the appearances of the strange objects in the sky, at times, seem to coincide with the creature appearances?

In the 1974 MUFON Symposium Proceedings, with some reservations, I published some of my findings that were uncovered about this bizarre series of events. Since that paper was written, some of my thoughts about these mysterious happenings have changed somewhat. I still have no

explanation for why this extended visit by strange creatures and odd aerial devices occurred during this time period. It was difficult to deal with the reality that some of
the Bigfoot and UFO encounters appeared to be real. Even
stranger were the recurring reports from the public of other
"paranormal activity," or at the very least, various other
odd occurrences which seemed to be associated with this
anomalous outbreak.

Some of the oddities that occurred during this time were cases where investigators came across series of large, unknown
footprints, which suddenly just vanished, even though the
ground conditions were suitable for additional tracks. In
some cases the footprints seemed to have just suddenly appeared, having started at a point where there should have
been previous tracks in that particular series.

In some instances, it was odd to find only a single footprint at some isolated locations. There should have been
additional tracks found in that same area, since the ground
conditions were conducive for other tracks. We occasionally
heard people describing an odd "metallic sound," like metal
ripping, tearing, or scraping, which seemed related to the
appearance of a Bigfoot creature.

In some cases, witnesses reported that the Bigfoot creatures
seemed to have the ability to move almost instantaneously
from one location to another. To the observers, it was as
if the creatures could disappear, then re-appear at another
location close by in the blink of an eye. Then there were the
reports where only a partial section of a creature's anatomy
could be seen.

During one incident at Jumonville, only a section of the body
of the creature could be seen as it moved off. At times,

only the head and torso were visible, and at other times, only the lower body could be seen. There were a number of cases where people who encountered the creatures felt concerned for their safety and fired their guns at the creatures. Various types of firearms were used from pistols to shotguns. In some cases, the shootings of the creatures took place at relatively close range. Some reports indicated that the creatures responded after being fired upon by falling to the ground, then getting back up and moving off away from the shooter. In most cases, the creatures walked off as if not harmed at all.

There was the one well documented case where the creature was fired upon at point blank range with a shotgun, and the creature reportedly dematerialized in a flash of light. In one 1973 Ohiopyle incident, the creature was fired upon and apparently hit, then vanished in front of the shooter's eyes. The startled man could hear it running off, but could not see the creature.

Yet in other cases that came to our attention in future years, witnesses who were about to fire on a creature mentioned that they experienced an over powering feeling that they were not to shoot at the hairy beast. Some of these observers were experienced hunters and they could not explain why they could not draw their weapon at the creature. Some folks talked about an overwhelming fear, or just the feeling that they had to get out of the area immediately.

It was very commonly reported that in the locations where the creatures would be seen, the normal sounds and appearances of the local wildlife were absent. The birds, rabbits, squirrels, and deer, seemed to have temporarily abandoned the area. Quite often, even the cricket and frog sounds would stop when the creature was nearby.

SILENT INVASION

As investigators questioned the creature witnesses, and as we followed up with some of these people even years after the occurrence, we began to find some interesting details which most of those involved were very reluctant to discuss. There were a few individuals who seemed to experience some psychic experiences after their encounters. Some began to experience premonitions of future events, while others experienced what seemed to be visions of a religious nature concerning what they thought concerned the end of the world. Some folks began to experience ghostly visits or apparitions in their homes, which in most cases had not previously occurred. In some cases, other odd experiences reportedly took place including where individuals had an initial UFO or Bigfoot (or other strange animal) encounter, and later during their lives had further interactions with the paranormal, or UFOs, or even various other Crypto-zoological critters.

Some creature witnesses, and in some cases, UFO witnesses, had a difficult time dealing with the reality of their first hand mysterious encounters. Many of these people had laughed at the stories of Bigfoot or UFOs and never took those accounts seriously. In some cases, these people now found themselves questioning their own sanity.

There was one quite scary close encounter with UFOs in July of 1973, which was experienced by a woman who held a responsible position with a manufacturing company. It was about midnight as the witness and her child were traveling in their vehicle down Three Mile Hill between Acme and Laurelville when this mysterious happening took place. They had just passed the first turn off to Bear Rocks when suddenly, two fast moving solid objects with lights approached their vehicle- one from the left- and one from the right. The objects appeared to position themselves above the car and followed it down the road.

The objects were larger than the car and described as flat and round. They appeared solid and metallic and there were numerous white lights around the outside perimeter of the objects. The witnesses could see the objects while looking at it from a point underneath them. There were three red lights located in equal positions on the solid surface and a white light in the bottom center. There was no sound heard from the object, but the woman stated that her eyes hurt from the brightness of the lights that were emitted from the objects.

The woman became very frightened when she suddenly realized that she could neither control the steering of the car, nor would the brakes work. All of a sudden the brake pedal went clear to the floor. Also, the car radio, headlights, and engine all suddenly quit as well. For about two miles, the car was not under the control of the terrified driver, but rather seemed to be under the power of the strange objects overhead.

The driver and passenger found it hard to believe that somehow the car arrived safely to the bottom of the hill. Once the car had stopped, the round objects flew off in the distance and suddenly, the woman had control of the vehicle again. After she quit shaking, she checked the steering and the brakes, which now seemed to work again. In the years to come, this woman also had close encounters with Bigfoot and even a black panther in a remote wooded area.

August 1973
Allegheny County
A case of missing time

A woman whom I interviewed in person on several occasions had contacted me about a strange incident that had happened to her son in August of 1973, during the wave of anomalous activity. According to the boy's mother, her son and some friends decided to go looking for Bigfoot after hearing reports that a creature had been seen near some old mine shafts in a rural area of Allegheny County. The boys had departed for their hunt early and the mother was alarmed since it was very late and her son had not returned home.

Finally about 1 am her son arrived back home. The woman detected something was amiss. The young man seemed to be in a dazed condition. But what really shook up the woman was when she asked her son where he had been for so long. The boy replied that he had only been gone for a short while. He actually seemed confused when he was told what time it was. Her son then told her about the odd experiences that had occurred. It seems that the boys were exploring around the mine entrances when they began to hear loud, growling sounds.

Upon hearing those noises, the group became frightened and they ran back to their vehicles. The first car had already departed the location with most of the boys. The woman's son and his friend had not yet left the location when they noticed a heavy fog moving into the area. Near the front of their car and just above it, a strange spiraling mist, which seemed to be turning into some type of physical form, was suspended in the air.

Then suddenly, a very thin beam of light was emitted from the spiraling form and hit her son in the face. The mother told her son that he should report the incident. Her son was fearful, saying that, "he felt that the people in the flying saucers were watching him." He went on to say that if he told anyone what had happened, he would be harmed. The woman also noted that the shirt her son was wearing when he arrived home was completely soaked.

When the woman had the opportunity to talk with her son's friend, who was with him that night during the strange experience, he refused to talk about it. The mother also made me aware that a couple of weeks following the event with the two boys, that both boys were in separate car accidents on the same night. This woman was close to her son, and she felt that since that episode had occurred, he had undergone a change of personality. She was convinced that something else had also occurred to him during the incident that night which he had not told her about.

Many of the creature sightings took place in rural areas around mobile homes, or mobile home communities, on farms, or at houses. Other Bigfoot encounters took place in more populated areas, but generally bordered by nearby woods or mountains. Those who had been visited by these unwelcome, monstrous guests commonly reported that something was pounding or scratching on the sides of their dwellings. The creatures seemed interested in aluminum siding structures. The geographic areas where the hairy bipeds were being seen were commonly in the vicinity of old mine shafts, caves, lakes, railroad tracks, creeks, cemeteries, fuel storage locations, and various energy sources.

While most of the creature incidents occurred from dusk through the night hours, some of the creature observations occurred in daylight. There seemed to be a lot of activity on humid, foggy nights. The creatures appeared curious about human activity and approached very close to occupied homes at times. In one case, a Bigfoot seemed fascinated with a young child that was crying. In another instance, a creature stood and stared at a group of young children sleeping outside on a porch.

We had other reports where very young children that were inside the houses where a creature was prowling outside, were unusually upset and crying at the same time. Some parents commented that the children had never acted so upset before that incident. Were the children able to sense the presence of the creature?

An Interesting Coincidence-UFO Sightings and Bigfoot

As reports of creature sightings and UFO encounters came to our attention, my research associates and I noticed some interesting details. It appeared that in some instances, UFO sighting activity reported in some locations seemed to coincide with the appearance of the hairy giants.

As we continued to monitor the ongoing activity, we noticed that in some cases, a UFO sighting would be reported in a certain area, then within hours to days later, a creature sighting would also be reported in that same general area. We also saw that in some cases, a UFO would be observed minutes before, or minutes after, a creature encounter in the same vicinity.

Creature Features

The descriptions of the Bigfoot creatures observed in Pennsylvania during the 1973-1974 timeframe, and since that time period, have been similar. Witnesses commonly reported seeing a hair-covered, generally man-like or sometimes more apelike creature, which walked on two legs and stood between six to over nine feet tall. In many reports, the arms of the creature were very long, and hung down below the knees.

The broad shoulders of the beast were quite apparent. The head was generally described as small and somewhat pointed or cone shaped, and rarely was any neck observed. In some instances where the creatures were seen at a very close range, witnesses reported what appeared to be fang-like teeth. There were few cases where ears were reportedly seen, and the nose of the creatures would be described at times, but the feature most commonly discussed was it's eyes.

It was the nocturnal observations of the mysterious beasts with eyes that glowed that really made the hair raise on some observers. Reports of luminous or glowing eyes were often reported, but not in all cases. The glowing eye colors were commonly described as red or reddish-orange, and in some cases green was reported as well. In some of these cases, there were no reflective light sources in the area that would contribute to this odd physical trait. One witness mentioned that the creatures he saw had "fire red eyes that glowed in total darkness."

The hair was commonly of a dark color. However, we had some sightings of creatures covered with white hair as well. Then there was that awful smell that often accompanied the appearance of a Bigfoot. Those who caught a whiff of that unpleasant odor said that it smelled similar to rotten eggs, sulfur, or something that had been dead for a long time, or even rotten meat or food. It was down right nauseating according to several accounts.

Some people actually became ill for a short time after breathing the annoying odor. Dogs sometimes would not go back to their normal eating habits for days after having been near a smelly creature. In one case, the rank smell of a creature remained in the house for a few days after it had made its unwelcome visit to that residence.

Visitors from a Crypto-zoological Zoo?

While many of the creature observations reported during the 1973-1974 wave were of the six to nine feet tall range, broad shouldered and hair covered variety, there were some other hairy beasts observed with similar, yet different physical details. One hairy biped observed at close range for a period of time looked like an extremely muscular man that was covered with very thick, dark hair. This creature also displayed very long arms and ran with superior agility. The witness said that it could easily out run a deer.

There were other sightings of smaller, hairy bipeds sometimes seen in the company of larger ones. Then there were the pongid or ape-like tracks found in the woods in Allegheny County where sightings of a monkey-like creature were being reported. Also during the wave of activity, there were those even stranger reports of other odd animals or creatures that did not fall into the Bigfoot category at all. It was as if a zoo full of unknown beasts had been released on the good citizens of Pennsylvania.

Creature Cries!

According to some folks, just the sounds associated with the appearance of a Bigfoot creature were a frightening experience in itself. Those who described the vocalizations of the creatures told us about loud, growling sounds, while others mentioned a sound similar to a witches' laugh. The sounds most commonly reported, however, were described as similar to a woman in pain screaming or a baby crying. Other strange audible vocalizations from the creatures were described as asthma-like, similar to very heavy breathing sounds, and others were like a high-pitched bird whistle.

The creatures also seemed to be able to mimic the sounds of both humans and animals. In one case where a frightened woman squealed out loudly after seeing a Bigfoot standing nearby, the creature responded by making a similar squealing sound. The screaming sounds reported were frightening, but the volume of the sound in some cases was described as incredible and ear shattering, and many times sent chills through the bravest of the locals.

Analytical Studies Of Possible Creature Related Physical Materials

There were a number of hair, feces, and other samples gathered during our investigations of the creature sightings during this wave of encounters. As mentioned, samples were provided to the Society For The Investigation Of The Unexplained, (SITU) to be studied by their professional consultants.

In the Vol. 7, No. 4, October, 1974 edition of PURSUIT, the journal of SITU, the results were revealed. SITU published the full report of Frederick A. Ulmer, Jr., formerly with the Philadelphia Zoological Gardens, of his hair and feces analysis of what he called the Western Pennsylvania monster. Ulmer stated in the introduction of the report, "I regret that it is not more conclusive, but these things are not easy to work with and present no end to knotty problems."

The report from Ulmer stated:

"Hair Sample #1-24 Aug. 1973-Monongahela, Penna.-Tentatively identified as human hair.

Hair Sample #2-3 Sept. 1973-Glassport, Penna- Positively identitifed as human hair.

Hair Sample #3-26 Aug. 1973-Latrobe, Penna-Found near mineshaft. This bunch of hairs intrigued me to no end and I spent much time on them. Results - They are the hair of a cow, probably Holstein. Not much luck on immuno-techniques.

Hair Sample #4-21 Sept. 1973-(near state police barracks.) Greensburg - This matted mass of light colored hairs had a strong fecal odor about it and I am certain that it was part of some feces. I positively identified it as cat and suspect that it was a domestic cat, for the pigment was too light for a bobcat. A serum protein test was tried on cat anti-serum but there was no reaction. A positive reaction would have made it cat beyond the shadow of a doubt. However, I still feel that it is cat and the cellular structure strongly resembles that of a domestic cat.

Feces Sample #3 - This highly comminuted {pulverized, powdery} sample contained a claw bone and some meta-tarsal bones that I tentatively identified as coming from a chicken or a pheasant. There were also a great many chitin-ous remains of unidentified insects. The stool suggested that of a skunk or a raccoon.

Other Fecal Samples were inconclusive.

A report given to me by SITU, and dated May 3, 1974, from Dr. George A. Agogino, Professor of Anthropology at Eastern New Mexico University to SITU, described the results of tests conducted on what appeared to be possible blood samples.

The WCUFOSG team had recovered those samples from a road in Indiana County, after a creature had been fired upon on September 13, 1973. The creature had been seen eating apples prior to the shooting incident.

Professor Agogino wrote, "Tests on the samples which you sent to me showed that the substance was not blood. It appeared to be saliva and apple juice. Possibly from a bear or another animal who had been stealing apples and slobbered on the road. No other explanation seems valid."

SILENT INVASION

Part 10: Some Final Thoughts

I mentioned in my 1974 MUFON paper, that from 1973 through February 18, 1974, 118 creature related incidents were recorded. Many of those cases are discussed in the book. While much of the creature activity was reported in southwestern Pennsylvania, various other locations were also reporting activity. The counties with the most creature activity were Westmoreland, Fayette and Indiana, all of which border the Chestnut Ridge. The Chestnut Ridge area continues to be an active area for ongoing Bigfoot reports and other phenomena.

During my many years of research into these mysterious events, I have been involved with the investigation of hundreds of Bigfoot encounters and thousands of UFO observations reported from across the woods, valleys, and mountains of Pennsylvania. I am personally convinced that some of these Bigfoot encounters appear to be genuine and that many of the eyewitnesses truthfully described to the best of their abilities what the creatures looked like and what they experienced. For what reason would hunters, police officers, housewives, children, and people from all walks of life make up stories about encountering mysterious, giant, hairy creatures?

What did these people have to gain, since in most cases their identities were never made public and most refrained from seeking any publicity whatsoever? Reflecting back to the 1973-1974 incidents, what convinced me that these creature events were authentic was the fact that myself or other investigators on numerous occasions were on the scene of a creature encounter within minutes to hours after it had occurred. We witnessed the human factor. People were commonly very emotionally upset after seeing a Bigfoot creature. They generally asked several questions, such as what the creature was, where it came from, would it hurt them, and would it return again?

But most convincing were the odd animal reactions in the area, especially with the dogs, when the creatures were nearby. The unusual animal reactions were a recurring detail in many cases, and could not have been fabricated. Then, in some cases, there was the physical evidence such as footprints and broken branches and flattened trails that supported the details of what had taken place. There were also the strange creature sounds that had been recorded on tape. In many cases, the witnesses were frightened enough to call the police authorities and make an official report.

I can recall at least two cases where family members had a close creature encounter and were so terrified by the incident that they packed up some clothes and left their homes for a period of time before returning. In one case, a Bigfoot that had been visiting their property had frightened two men who lived in the country. I was there that evening soon after a creature visit as the men stood there with their guns and both were quite visibly shaken. Those men made my team and the state police, who had just arrived, wait until they went back into their house to pack some belongings.

They promptly locked up the house and stayed elsewhere that night.

During 1973-1974, as these strange creatures infringed on the Pennsylvania countryside, I spent many days and nights along with other WCUFOSG investigators searching the woods and mountains for evidence of these creatures. We saw much evidence of other wildlife that frequented those locations, but no conclusive physical proof that would support the reality that Bigfoot creatures also inhabited the area. No bodies, no bones.

Since the 1973-1974 creature wave, I have interviewed hundreds of individuals of all age groups and backgrounds who swear that they have encountered Bigfoot-like creatures around the state. Over the years we staked out areas, especially along the Chestnut Ridge, where there had been frequent sightings of the creatures reported by various witnesses. Except for some of the events that were mentioned in this book, I never had the opportunity to get close to a creature. I have never personally seen a Bigfoot or a UFO.

Many Bigfoot skeptics have asked, "where are the bodies"? I also have to ask the same question. Why have no bodies or skeletal remains of a Bigfoot been found by hunters who frequent the woods of Pennsylvania? That same question has to be asked about multitudes of similar Bigfoot-like creature sightings reported throughout the United States, Canada, and many other countries. If some of these creature accounts are authentic (which is my opinion), why is there no definitive physical evidence of their existence?

Another question often asked concerning the Bigfoot creatures seen in Pennsylvania during the 1970's wave is "are they the same creatures reported from other national or worldwide locations"? When I wrote an article on those happenings in the 1974 MUFON Symposium Proceedings, I stated that I didn't believe the creatures that were being seen at the time were the same as the typical Bigfoot creatures observed elsewhere. After thinking this over for many years, today I can't give a definite yes or no answer to this question. The hairy bipeds seen here in the Keystone state were in many cases physically comparable in many respects to those Bigfoot creatures reported around the country and some other parts of the world. There were, however, some non-typical description variations in some of the reports. I surely don't exclude the possibility that there may be other species of similar looking Bigfoot type creatures roaming the woods and forests of the world.

As reluctant as I am to say this, based on other nationwide reports that have come to my attention, if some of these creatures can disappear and have the ability to change physical form, then how can we be sure what we are dealing with? I surely don't have the answers, but will keep an open mind to all possibilities until the Bigfoot mystery is solved.

Some Bigfoot researchers will point out that the three toed footprints commonly found in Pennsylvania during 1973 and 1974, were not the typical five toed tracks often reported with other Bigfoot encounters nationwide and elsewhere. The more common five toed footprints have also been found in Pennsylvania for many years. In other parts of the country, both five, four and three toed footprints have been reported. The question remains, however, why after so many years and great numbers of Bigfoot observations, have no bodies or bones been discovered?

Looking back at the 1973-1974 incidents, there were indeed some strange details that surfaced in connection with some the creature reports. Many of those cases were investigated and documented soon after they occurred. If these events were true, then we must consider the possibility that some of these Bigfoot creatures appear to be even stranger than just an unknown physical flesh and blood animal.

It may be that in regards to some of these creature encounters, we are dealing with a phenomenon that appears to be outside of current scientific verification. While we spent many hours of the day and night pursuing these incidents during the surge of reports in 1973-1974, and saw various physical evidence which supported some eyewitness claims, no unknown creature bodies turned up, even after shooting incidents. There was just no definitive evidence recovered which would have answered the question as to what these creatures were.

The information that we uncovered during the 1970's creature encounters suggested in some cases that we might be dealing with an entity that has a physical and non-physical component to its existence. For example, a Bigfoot observed from a short distance away appeared to be a solid physical animal, yet when shot at, sometimes just visibly vanished in front of the observer's disbelieving eyes.

And what about the UFO sightings that could not be explained? As we have discovered over the years, some of these objects range in size from inches in diameter (as observed at very close range), to hundreds of feet in length. Some of these objects appear to be solid, constructed craft, while others are just light sources. Some of them seem to be intelligently guided and controlled devices from the many first hand cases I have investigated. The question remains, however, what are these unknown aerial objects?

Since I have not had the opportunity to have a personal UFO encounter, I have to base my opinion on the thousands of UFO reports I investigated in Pennsylvania for so many years. I have also monitored worldwide UFO reports on a regular basis and have examined information received from many researchers and investigators from around the globe.

My opinion concerning the explanation of the UFO sightings that remain in the unidentified category is that there are likely a number of different origins involved. Some of those anomalous lights may well be some type of unknown natural phenomena. I also have been in touch with some key investigators in past years who were very involved with the investigation of various alleged UFO crashes which reportedly occurred in this country and abroad. There are a number of incidents on record where mysterious objects have reportedly crashed to earth and have been recovered by the military of various countries. The two better known cases in the United States are the incidents near Roswell, New Mexico, and Kecksburg, Pennsylvania.

While some of those fallen objects of unknown origin were likely just the recovery of earth launched space vehicle debris, we should not exclude the possibility that some of these events might have been spacecraft that originated from beyond our planet. I have spoken with various individuals who claimed to have knowledge of spacecraft that were recovered and which did not originate from the earth.

Some of those I interviewed claimed to have seen small non-human beings as well. It is very possible that at least some of the UFO sightings reported may well be extraterrestrial visitors. Yet no actual spacecraft that originated from outside of the earth has surfaced for public scrutiny, and no remains of a Bigfoot have been found or have been identified scientifically.

Back in the 1950's and 1960's, when I watched "Science Fiction Theater," "The Outer Limits," the "Twilight Zone" and "One Step Beyond," so many of those television episodes were filled with fascinating ideas and technological equipment which at that time was beyond the current capability. But now many years later, we have seen some of those early ideas become fact.

Years ago there was much laughter among scientists about time travel and other realities, but now these subjects are being discussed much more seriously. One similarity exists been UFOs and Bigfoot (and various other mysterious creatures) in that there is only a limited amount of physical evidence to support the existence of either phenomena.

In some Bigfoot cases, we have strange footprints, ground disturbances, odd animal reactions, rotten smells, recordings of weird sounds, patterns of their activity, and an occasional photograph or video. There are UFO cases that have physical ground trace evidence, electromagnetic and animal disturbances, radar contacts, and video and photographic recordings.

In past years, I have investigated close UFO encounters where what appeared to be solid objects changed from one physical shape into another, or suddenly just vanished from sight. I have had incidents where certain individuals in a group could only see a large object in the sky, yet others among them could not visualize it. Is it possible that some people have the abilities to perceive beyond the normal visual and audio ranges of most individuals and are more likely to experience certain anomalistic events? Are some people who have a history of ESP experiences more likely to encounter UFOs or even a Bigfoot or other strange creatures?

Consider the cases of the vanishing Bigfoot encounters and the incidents where footprints just mysteriously stopped. Could some of these UFOs be time or, for a better term, inter-dimensional travelers? Are some of the Bigfoot creatures actually beings from another reality that somehow, on occasion, are able to drop in on us? Is it possible that there are certain geographical areas that contain some necessary properties that provide a gateway for these entities to enter and depart from our physical world when the conditions are right? What if the horrific smell sometimes reported with the creature observations is a clue to these beings ability to appear and disappear, rather then an association with poor hygiene.

When I started investigating Bigfoot accounts in Pennsylvania in the late 1960's, I really never gave any other serious consideration to their origin, other than that they were an undiscovered member of the animal kingdom. As time went on and we began to investigate the reports that came to our attention from the public concerning these unknown creature sightings, along with strange objects in the sky, and a variety of other paranormal events, it became apparent that there may well be more to the Bigfoot and UFO mystery than we had ever considered.

Let me be very clear. I do not have the answers to what direct relationship exists between the sightings of Bigfoot and UFOs, if indeed one exists at all. Most Bigfoot sightings do not include the observation of UFOs during the same event. The same goes with UFO close encounter reports. Very rarely is a Bigfoot sighting mentioned in conjunction with a low level UFO observation.

The point is, there are well documented cases from around the world where UFOs, Bigfoot, and other strange events have all taken place as part of an event, but they are indeed not that commonly reported. These types of encounters, however, may occur more frequently than any of us realize. I know for a fact that many Bigfoot and UFO researchers since the 1970's, and even today, refuse to publish or discuss such cases with their fellow researchers.

Many have told me that they do not want to be ridiculed by their research associates. There are some serious Bigfoot researchers who consider any mention of a UFO sighting associated with a hairy biped report to be unreliable, and therefore do not take such accounts seriously. There are certainly some UFO investigators who are firmly convinced that many UFOs are of extraterrestrial origin and that Bigfoot just does not fit in with their theories as to what these visitors should look like. UFO researchers also have commonly dismissed cases where Bigfoot and UFOs were observed together. Those investigators who have published such accounts deserve credit for having the fortitude to present to their readers such information.

I knew when these strange incidents began to come to my attention, that many of my colleagues would surely find such accounts hard to swallow. I also realized that, as an investigator, my position was to conduct an examination and inquiry of these incidents, compile the information, and share it with others in the UFO and Bigfoot community. Now so many years later, I still do not have the answers as to why these events occurred, and what it really meant, but I have no doubt that many of these cases and the witnesses involved, appeared to be legitimate.

I also do not have the explanations for these anomalous encounters, but I am certain that some unknown hair-covered bipedal creatures will continue to roam the forests and woods of Pennsylvania, and other areas, and that Unidentified Flying Objects will still be reported in the skies over the Keystone state and around the world.

It is quite likely that as the human race accelerates it's knowledge of science, and as more advanced analytical equipment is designed, we will have the capabilities to detect and seek out the unknown forces that, at times, interact with our normal lives. I can only ask you to keep an open mind about ideas which today might seem laughable to some, but may be understood by future generations enlightened by these advances.

Appendix

Articles and References of 1973-1974 PA Bigfoot and UFO Events

"UFO's (?) Sighted In This Area," News-Dispatch, Jeannette, PA, 26 January 1973

"UFO's Sighted in Norwin Area," Standard-Observer, Irwin, PA 26, January 1973

"Study Group Reports UFO's," The Latrobe Bulletin, Latrobe, PA 26, January 1973

"UFO's Spotted By Residents Of Pocono Area," (AP Story) Reading Eagle, Reading, PA 2, March 1973

"UFO's Over Milton?," The Standard, Milton, PA, 16, March 1973

"UFO seen by Sunbury Policemen," The Morning Press, Bloomsburg, PA , 21, March 1973

"Objects Soar Observers Say," The Daily News, Bangor, PA , 21, March 1973

"Gallagher. "Family Spots Manned UFO in Field," The Reading Eagle, Reading, PA, 28, March 1973

"Kutztown Joins UFO Sighter List," The Easton Express, Easton, PA, 3, April 1973

"Three sight UFO," The Pennsylvania Mirror, State College, PA, 25 April 1973

"Creature sightings reported in area," Standard-Observer, Irwin, PA, 14 August 1973

"Bigfoot In District?" News-Dispatch, Jeannette, PA,. 14 August 1973

"Monster Tracks" The Latrobe Bulletin, Latrobe, PA, 15 August 1973

"More Creature Sightings Here," Standard-Observer, Irwin, PA, 15 August 1973

"No Trace of Bigfoot," News-Dispatch, Jeannette, PA, 15 August 1973

"Creature report-Fouke monster or hoax," Standard-Observer, Irwin, PA, 16 August 1973

"Eyewitnesses sight creature in district," Standard-Observer, Irwin, PA, 17 August 1973

SILENT INVASION

"Constanzo, Bill. "Bill Costanzo's Column," The Latrobe Bulletin, Latrobe, PA, 18 August 1973

The Buffalo Mills creature case of August 19, 1973: Sources: The INFO Journal and The Eighth Tower by John A. Keel, Saturday Review Press, 1975, first reported in the Jeannette, PA News-Dispatch, August 14, 1973 edition.

"Bigfoot Sightings Claimed," News Dispatch, Jeannette, PA, 20 August 1973

"Bigfoot Is Still Roaming County," The Latrobe Bulletin, Latrobe, PA, 20 August 1973

"Bigfoot Sightings Persist," The Latrobe Bulletin, Latrobe, PA , 22 August 1973

"New Prints of Bigfoot Discovered," The Latrobe Bulletin, Latrobe PA, 23 August 1973

"Bigfoot Mystery In Blairsville Area," Indiana Evening Gazette, Indiana, PA, 23 August 1973

"Footprints Reported," News-Dispatch, Jeannette, PA, 24 August 1973

"Bigfoot Shows Up Near Yukon, Derry," The Latrobe Bulletin, Latrobe, PA, 24 August 1973

"Bigfoot We Love You....Don't Run," The Latrobe Bulletin, Latrobe, PA, 25 August 1973

"Westmoreland Monster Hunt Tracking Big Game," Pittsburgh Press, Pittsburgh, PA, 26 August 1973

"Bigfoot Around," The Latrobe Bulletin, Latrobe, PA, 27 August 1973

"Four Juveniles Face Charges," Daily News, McKeesport, PA, 27 August 1973

"Don't Use Guns To Hunt Bigfoot," The Latrobe Bulletin, Latrobe, PA, 29 August 1973

"Bigfoot Probed Minus Publicity," The Latrobe Bulletin, Latrobe, PA, 30 August 1973

"Myth or Not, Creature Worries Police," (AP wire story) The Titusville Herald, Titusville, PA, 1 September 1973

"New Jersey Team Investigates Bigfoot Reports In This Area," News-Dispatch, Jeannette, PA, 11 September 1973

"Bigfoot" Kangaroo On The Lam From A Local Butcher," The Westmoreland Weekly, Jeannette, PA? 12 September 1973

"Nurses Report Sighting UFO," Gettysburg Times, Gettysburg, PA, 12 September 1973

"Big Foot or whatever...it's loose in Penn Hills," The Progress, Penn Hills, PA, 25 September 1973?

"Santus, Sharon. "Creature Unnerves Residents," Contact, Indiana, PA, 3 October 1973

"It's Hibernation For Bigfoot," The Latrobe Bulletin, Latrobe, PA, 4 October 1973

"Bigfoot Probably Is Gone," Standard-Observer, Irwin, PA, 4 October 1973

"Pocopson Nurses Catch UFO Fever," West Chester Daily Local News, West Chester, PA, 17 October 1973

McKelvey, Gerald. "The UFO Whirl: A Fearful Sight," The Philadelphia Inquirer, Philadelphia, PA, 21 October 1973

Wohnsiedler, Jinny. "Police Chief Joins UFO-Sighting List," The York Dispatch, York, PA, 22 October 1973

"ABSMAL Affairs In Pennsylvania And Elsewhere." PURSUIT, Vol. 6, No. 4, October, 1973

"Policeman, 3 Newsmen Spot UFO," Allentown Call-Chronicle, Allentown, PA, 4 November 1973

"UFO Land Ho Or Ho Ho Ho," Beaver County Times, Beaver Falls, PA, 6 November 1973

Lovejoy, A. William. "Bristol Twp. Police Spot 2 Saucers," The Evening Bulletin, Philadelphia, PA, 13 November 1973

"UFO's Reported Sighted Last Night In Farragut Area," Williamsport Sun-Gazette, Williamsport, PA, 19 November 1973

"And Still The Reports Roll In, by Allen V. Noe," PURSUIT, Vol. 7 No. 1,P. 17, January, 1974

"Voice Print Analysis, By Robert E. Jones," PURSUIT, Vol. 7 No.1, P. 14, January, 1974

"UFO's, In Relation To Creature Sightings In Pennsylvania," By Stan Gordon, MUFON Symposium Proceedings-1974, P. 132, 22, June, 1974

"Pennsylvania ABSMery." PURSUIT, Vol. 7, No. 4, P. 94, October, 1974

"Pennsylvania ABSMery, A Report, by Robert E. Jones," PURSUIT, Vol. 8, No.1, P.19, January, 1975

Chronological list of reports with time, place and brief description

Date	Location & Event
January 1, 1973	Delmont, 9 pm, star-like object takes off
January 16. 1973	Greensburg, orange object moves across the sky
January 17, 1973	Westmoreland County, spherical pink-orange object
January 25, 1973	Westmoreland and Allegheny Counties, lights in formation, etc.
February 10, 1973	Manor, 2 am Strange object hovers near railroad tracks
February 11, 1973	West Point, 1:30 am Red spherical object reported in sky
March 1, 1973	Reading, Berks County, evening. Strange flashing lights over Sailors Lake
March 2, 1973	Hunker, 11:45 pm Luminous domed object near ground
March 8, 1973	Delmont, about 8:30 pm Star-like object moves across sky
March 8, 1973	Hamburg, Berks County, 10:30 pm Capsule-shaped object low in sky
March 11, 1973	Delmont, 2:45 am Cylindrical shaped objects reported
March 11, 1973	Jeannette, 11:50 pm Lights seen over radio tower
March 13, 1973	Murrysville, 7:45 am Transparent object observed in sky
March 15, 1973	Stahlstown, 7:20 pm Elongated object seen 500 feet off the ground
March 15, 1973	Milton, Northumberland County, 8 pm Odor, then strange objects reported
March 16, 1973	Mifflinburg, Union County, 5:30 am Domed-shaped objects hovering motionless
March 20, 1973	Bangor, Northampton County, 7:30 pm Objects reported to Blue Mountain Control Center

Date	Location & Event
March 20, 1973	Sunbury, Northumberland County, evening. Police officers sight object over housing project
March 20, 1973	Greensburg, 9:07 pm Cigar-shaped object reported in sky
March 28, 1973	Robesonia, Berks County, 1:30 am Couple reports object on ground
April 2, 1973	Kutztown, Berks County, 10 pm 25 people, police report motionless object
April 3, 1973	Greensburg, 7:30 pm Amber colored lights reported in sky
April 15, 1973	Between Penn and Manor, 8:30 pm Multiple witnesses report low flying object
April 24, 1973	Spring Mills, Centre County, 7:45 pm Oval shaped object approached observers
April 29, 1973	Belle Vernon, 10 pm Huge white ball observed 50 feet off ground
May 5, 1973	Erie, Erie County, 9:10 pm BB-shaped object crosses sky
May 11, 1973	Greensburg, 10 pm Disc-shaped object hovers 100 feet over lake
June 13, 1973	Irwin, 1 pm Blimp-shaped object hovers 500 feet off ground
June 26, 1973	Between Greensburg and Latrobe, 10:10 pm Spherical object moves across sky
June 27, 1973	Apollo, Armstrong County, 12:15 am Domed-shaped object emits red-green flames
June 28, 1973	North Charleroi, Washington County, 12:15 am Fishermen engulfed in bright light
July 2, 1973	Irwin, 10:30 pm Officer and wife watch object in the sky
July 5, 1973	Bethel Park, Allegheny County, Dusk. Bright red ball in sky seen by witnesses
July 6, 1973	Erie, Erie County, 1:39 am Officer sees lights drop into lake
July 8, 1973	Fayette City, Fayette County, 2 am Witness observes ball in sky

SILENT INVASION

Date	Location & Event
July 14, 1973	Between Greensburg and Latrobe, 12:26 am Man watches dome-shaped object in sky
July 18, 1973	Jeannette, 8:50 pm Man photographs BB-shaped object in sky
July 18, 1973	Latrobe, 10:15 pm Football-shaped object seen low in sky
July 21, 1973	Turtle Creek, Allegheny County, 10 pm Single object in sky separates into three objects
July 23, 1973	Pittsburgh, Allegheny County, 7:30 pm Man observes transparent spherical object in sky
July 29, 1973	Irwin, 9:30 pm Two women watch while yard illuminated by object
July, 31, 1973	The Prowler With Glowing Eyes
May or June	Encounter with a Bigfoot in the Greengate area
August 7, 1973:	A strange three-toed discovery
August 7, 1973	Beaver County, Creature with glowing eyes looks into mobile home
August 4, 1973	Harrison City, 9:25 pm Hour glass-shaped object seen over power line
August 4, 1973	New Alexandria, 10:27 pm Spherical object with fiery debris hovers over garage
August 10, 1973	Greensburg Country Club golf course, 9 pm Circular object spotted with illuminated windows
August 14, 1973	near New Stanton, 4:30 am Police officer observes glowing eyes
August 14, 1973	Greensburg, 1 pm Creature seen near fishing pond
August 14, 1973	Greensburg, 1:45 pm Another daylight creature observation near Radebaugh
August 14, 1973	Monroeville, Allegheny County, 9:25 pm Disc-shaped object low in the sky
August. 15, 1973	Hutchinson, evening. Huge strange footprints in Hutchinson

Date	Location & Event
August 15, 1973	Hutchinson, midnight. Something strange in the cornfield
August 16, 1973	Derry Township, evening. Creature lying in field
August	Derry Township. Creature pursued near Newcomer Plant
August 17, 1973	Kingston/Route 30, evening. Creature carrying deer
August 18, 1973	Wegeley, 3:18 am Huge creature in yard
August 18, 1973	Slickville. Creature near a mine shaft
August 19, 1973	Derry Township, 2 am Creature in field
August 19, 1973	Herminie, 6:50 am Woman chased by creature
August 19, 1973	Buffalo Mills, Bedford County, 8 pm Creature walks down street
August 20, 1973	Donahue, 12:01 am Creature seen by railroad tracks
August 20, 1973	Saint Vincent Cemetery, Latrobe, 9:20 pm Creature near car, engine stalls
August 20, 1973	Keystone area, Derry Township, 10 pm Witness passed five feet from creature
August 20, 1973	near Irwin. Numerous Bigfoot tracks discovered
August 20, 1973	Derry, Creature hit by car reportedly vanishes into thin air
August 21, 1973	Greensburg, About 12 am Three creatures on golf course
August 21, 1973	Latrobe, 12:15 am Red eyes looking in high window
August 21, 1973	Kingston/Latrobe, am Creature prowling near mobile home
August 21, 1973	Derry, 2:30 am Woman has face-to-face creature encounter
August 21, 1973	Greensburg, 5:30 pm Girl sees creature near housing development

SILENT INVASION

Date	Location & Event
August 21, 1973	Trafford, 9:30 pm (UFO) August 21, 1973
August 22, 1973	Trafford, 12 am (UFO)
August 22, 1973	West Newton-Strange sounds, dogs disturbed, odd smell
August 23, 1973	9:10 pm Apollo, Armstrong County, (UFO)
August 23, 1973	Yukon, Creature pursues car down the road
August 23, 1973	Penn, Family sees creature near their home
	Local Businesses Utilize Creature Reports
August 23, 1973	Latrobe radio station receives tape of creature sound
August 24, 1973	Monongahela, Washington County, Early morning, Creature on roof of house
August 24, 1973	Herminie, 9:55 pm Bigfoot in backyard-dog frightened
August 24, 1973	Superior, 11:30 pm Bigfoot pulls out electrical line from mobile home
August 24, 1973	Claridge, 11:30 pm Bigfoot Encounter
August 24, 1973	Derry, 11:45 pm Creature lying in field?
August 25, 1973	Hillside, 8 pm Boy on mini-bike five feet from creature
August 26, 1973	Luxor, 5 pm Creature chases family from woods
August 26, 1973	Derry, 11:30 pm Creature observed near ball field
August 27, 1973	Superior, 6:50 am White creature seen near mobile home community
August 27, 1973	Blairsville, Indiana County, 8:20 pm Strange activity at mobile home
August 27, 1973	Kingston, 10 pm Man shot at creature
August 27, 1973	Donohoe, 10:20 pm Creature on bridge
August 27, 1973	Irwin, 10:30 pm Red eyes looking in window
August 28, 1973	Beech Hills, 3 am Woman looks into the face of a creature

Date	Location & Event
August 28, 1973	West Mifflin, Allegheny County, 3 pm Creature walking in backyard
August 28, 1973	Superior, 7:30 pm Mystery man confiscates and destroys evidence
August 29, 1973	McChesneytown, Evening, Creature seen near residence
August 29, 1973	Greensburg, Evening, Boomerang shaped UFO seen-Bigfoot shot at in same area
August 30, 1973	Superior, 6:30 am Creature seen near mobile home court
August 30, 1973	Greensburg, Radebaugh Road, 6:45 pm Creature seen near railroad tracks
August 31, 1973	A strange coincidence. Witnesses from two cases, observe creature again the same day
Late August 1973	near Cooperstown, Bigfoot lifts trailer
September 1, 1973	Penn Township, Early morning, Did Bigfoot depart from a landed UFO?
September 1, 1973	Youngstown, 6:35 pm Creature approaches baby at cemetery
September 1, 1973	Latrobe, 7:35 pm Did a creature follow the mother and baby to a distant farm?
September, 1973	Stroudsburg, Monroe County, 11 pm (UFO)
September, 1973	Greensburg, 8:30 pm (UFO)
September 2, 1973	Adamsburg, 4 am Creature scares couple in mobile home park
September 2, 1973	Indiana, Indiana County, 5:30 am Creature standing near a garage
September 2, 1973	Alverton, 10 pm Red eyes and strange footprints
September 3, 1973	Erie area, Erie County, Early Morning (UFO)
September 3, 1973	Alverton, 2 am Tall figure observed, footprint found
September 3, 1973	Glassport, Allegheny County, 3 am Strange sounds, chickens killed
September 3, 1973	Whitney, 4:30 am Creature stands next to mobile home-state police respond

SILENT INVASION

Date	Location & Event
September 3, 1973	Whitney, 4:45 am Neighbor sees tall form across from the Yothers' residence
September 3, 1973	New Alexandria, 5 am Strange sounds and smell
September 3, 1973	Indiana, Indiana County, 8:10 pm Hairy creature seen near rural home
September 3, 1973	Aultman, Indiana County, 9:15 pm Creature seen in headlights of car
September 4, 1973	Homestead, Allegheny County, 12:10 am Two creatures in shrubs
September 4, 1973	Herminie, 9:30 pm Creature near a house
September 4, 1973	Derry Township, 9:30 pm UFO beams light towards the ground
September 4, 1973	Alverton, 10:03 pm Smell and red eyed figure
September 5, 1973	Ruffsdale, Evening, Three creatures observed near residence
September 6, 1973	Indiana, Indiana County, 11 pm Creature looking into mobile home
September 6, 1973	SITU Responds to Greensburg
September 9, 1973	Ligonier, 5 am Strange sound, torn screen, depressed area nearby
September 11, 1973	Keystone State park, Derry Township, 5 pm Creatures swimming in lake
September 11, 1973	Superior, 7:15 pm (UFO)
September 11, 1973	Superior, 10:15 pm Creature observed near mobile home court
September 11, 1973	Dillsburg, York County, about 10:30 pm, nurses report sighting UFO
September 12, 1973	Waterford, 12:30 am (UFO)
September 12, 1973	Blairsville, Indiana County, 10:40 am Bigfoot daylight observation walking through cornfield
September 13, 1973	Indiana, Indiana County, 8:45 pm Man shot at creature. Possible physical evidence
September 14, 1973	Jeannette, 11:30 pm Strange sounds and smell near mobile home

Date	Location & Event
September 15, 1973	Derry, 2:30 pm Girl sees creature while riding pony
September 16, 1973	Whitney, 4:35 am Woman sees large figure standing near bushes
September 16, 1973	Latrobe, evening, Pet deer killed, chickens missing, track found nearby
September 18, 1973	Derry Township, 10:20 pm Bell farm creature 10 feet from woman, UFO reported minutes later
September 20, 1973	Indications of government interest in Bigfoot reports
September 20, 1973	Greensburg, Near state police headquarters, 1 pm Boys find tracks in woods
September 20, 1973	Alverton, 10:30 pm Tall creature seen near a house
September 21, 1973	Latrobe, 2 am Dog grabs Bigfoot by the heel, woman chases after the creature
September 21, 1973	Greensburg, 2 pm Boys see creature near police barracks, troopers respond
September 21, 1973	Derry Township, 11:30 pm Creature seen in field near Bell farm
September 22, 1973	Penn Hills, Allegheny County, Early evening, Boys hear movement in woods
September 23, 1973	Penn Hills, Allegheny County, More ape-like tracks found deep in the woods
September 23, 1973	Penn Hills, Allegheny County, Early evening – Monkey-like creature in tree
September 23, 1973	Penn Township, 10 pm Woman reports seeing creature in back yard
September 24, 1973	Greensburg, 2:30 pm Boys see creature lying in woods
September 24, 1973	Greensburg, 5 pm Newspaper boy sees creature on hill
September 24, 1973	West Newton, 8:30 pm Creature seen running through woods
September 24, 1973	Penn Hills, PA, Allegheny County, 9 pm Hairy creature encounters trail bike

SILENT INVASION

Date	Location & Event
September, 1973	Greenock, Allegheny County, Clues along path
September 27, 1973	Beaver, PA, Beaver County, Bigfoot with luminous sphere, aerial object beams light into woods
September 29, 1973	Youngwood, PA, Strange animal, "Cross between monkey and dog"
October 1973	Waterford, PA, (UFO),
October, 1973	Mifflinburg, Union County,11 pm (UFO)
October, 1973	Irwin, evening, (UFO)
October, 1973	The Official's Get Involved
October 2, 1973	Beaver Run Dam, dusk, Hunter sees huge Bigfoot creature in woods
October 3, 1973	Irwin, 10 am, (UFO)
October 4, 1973	Middletown Township, Delaware County, 2:30 am, Two state troopers sight UFO
October 4, 1973	Irwin, 10:30 pm (UFO)
October 4-7, 1973	Derry Township, evening, Bigfoot repeats farm visits, family experiences paranormal events
October 6, 1973	Flatwoods, Fayette County, 1:55 am UFO Hovers Over Car
October 10, 1973	Saltsburg, Indiana County 9 pm (UFO)
October 12, 1973	North Huntingdon, 3:20 am (UFO)
October 14 or 15, 1973	Whitney, evening, Glowing eyes
October 14, 1973	Irwin, 8 pm (UFO)
October 15, 1973	Catawissa, Columbia County, 5:40 am UFO turns car around on roadway
Week of October 15, 1973	Apollo, 7 am (UFO)
October 16, 1973	New Alexandria, 7:30 am (UFO)
October 16, 1973	Irwin, 8 pm (UFO)
October 16, 1973	Pocopson Township, Chester County, 8 pm (UFO)

Date	Location & Event
October 17, 1973	New Castle, Lawrence County, 9 pm (UFO)
October 18, 1973	Natrona Heights, Allegheny County, 7:30 pm (UFO)
October 18, 1973	Glen Campbell, Indiana County, 7:45 pm (UFO)
October 18, 1973	Jeannette, 7:45 pm (UFO)
October 18, 1973	Natrona Heights, Allegheny County, 7:55 pm UFO Photographed
October 18, 1973	Wallaceton, Clearfield County, 11:10 pm (UFO)
October 19, 1973	Hempfield Township, 10:15 pm (UFO)
October 20, 1973	Jackson Township, York County, 8:10 pm Police chief observes hovering UFO
October 20, 1973	Dawson, Fayette County, 10:30 pm (UFO)
October 21, 1973	Rillton, about 7 pm (UFO)
October 21, 1973	Rockwood, Somerset County, 8:10 pm (UFO)
October 21, 1973	New Castle, Lawrence County, 8:23 pm (UFO)
October 21, 1973	Norvelt, 9:15 pm (UFO)
October 21, 1973	Washington, Washington County, 9:15 pm (UFO)
October 22, 1973	Beaver Falls, Beaver County, 7:10 pm (UFO)
October 22, 1973	Vandergrift, evening, (UFO)
October 23, 1973	Scottdale, 6:55 am (UFO)
October 23, 1973	Vandergrift, evening, (UFO)
October 23, 1973	Saltsburg, PA, Indiana County, 6:30 pm Creature in cornfield, deer frightened
October 23, 1973	Eighty-Four, Washington County, 7:30 pm UFO runs car off road
October 24, 1973	Cannonsburg, Washington County, 5:30 pm (UFO)
October 24, 1973	Leechburg, 10:45 pm (UFO)
October 25, 1973	Various locations and Centre County, Numerous UFO sightings kept UFO hotline buzzing

SILENT INVASION

Date	Location & Event
October 25, 1973	Uniontown, PA, Fayette County, 9 pm Landed UFO with two Bigfoot on farm
October 26, 1973	Dawson, Fayette County, 9:30 pm UFO paces car
November 1, 1973	Uniontown, Fayette County, 8:15 pm (UFO)
November 1, 1973	UFO observed over Beaver County area
November 2, 1973	Grapeville, 1:20 am (UFO)
November 2, 1973	Irwin, 3:30 am (UFO)
November 2, 1973	Penn, 4 am (UFO)
November 2, 1973	Midland, Beaver County, Three-toed tracks found nearby
November 2, 1973	Hutchinson, 6:30 pm (UFO)
November 2, 1973	Hempfield Township, early evening, Mini UFO floats in Cars
November 3, 1973	Ohioville, Beaver County, Possible UFO landing site found
November 3, 1973	New Castle, Lawrence County, 7 pm State police among crowd watching UFO
November 4, 1973	Coopersburg, Lehigh County, early morning, (UFO)
November 4, 1973	Lenni, Delaware County, 9 pm (UFO)
November 4, 1973	New Castle, Lawrence County, 9:05 pm (UFO)
November 9, 1973	(UFO), Industry, Beaver County, 11:30 pm (UFO)
November 10, 1973	Bristol Township, Bucks County, 4:45 am (UFO)
November 11, 1973	Superior, early evening, Three hairy creatures near mobile home court
November 12, 1973	Superior, 7:09 pm (UFO)
November 18, 1973	Latrobe, 1:03 am (UFO)
November 18, 1973	Farragut, Lycomming County, 10:30 pm (UFO)
November 24, 1973	Jeannette, 2 am Growling sound outside of house

Date	Location & Event
November 24, 1973	Jeannette, 7 pm Creature looks in window
November 24, 1973	Jeannette, 10:15 pm Creature returns, glowing eyes seen in woods
November 24, 1973	Greensburg, 11:25 pm Glowing eyes, strange sounds
November 24 or 25, 1973	Jumonville Summit, Fayette County, 11:30 pm Unusual incident
November 30, 1973	Gradyville, Delaware County, 7:15 pm (UFO)
November, 1973	Ohiopyle, Fayette County, Man fires on creature which suddenly vanishes
November, 1973	Jumonville, Fayette County, Creature seems to vanish and reappear
December 1, 1973	Altoona, Blair County, 3 am (UFO)
December 3, 1973	Penn, 1 am UFO lights up area
December 3, 1973	Derry, morning, Large footprints observed
December 16, 1973	North Huntingdon, 6 pm (UFO)
December 26, 1973	Jeanette and other areas, 7:15 pm (UFO)
December 26, 1973	Uniontown, Fayette County, 7:50 pm (UFO)
December 27, 1973	North Huntingdon, 12:15 am (UFO)
January 21, 1974	Indiana County, Allegheny County reports
January 27, 1974	Irwin, 2 am UFO chases car on PA turnpike
February 6, 1974	Ohiopyle, Fayette County, 10 pm Woman shoots creature, creature vanishes
February 7, 1974	Wooddale, Fayette County, 12:55 am (UFO)
February 15, 1974	Greensburg, 10:30 pm (UFO)
March 12, 1974	Hempfield, 10:11 p.m (UFO)
March 13, 1974	Armagh, Indiana County, 9:20 pm (UFO)
March 23, 1974	Washington County, 12:55 am (UFO)
April 13, 1974	New Stanton, 8:15 pm (UFO)
April 14, 1974	Yukon, 8 pm (UFO)
April 18, 1974	New Alexandria, 8 pm (UFO)
April 19, 1974	widespread reports from PA-OH-MD-WV, 8:15 pm Bolide-meteor

SILENT INVASION

Date	Location & Event
April 19, 1974	between Radebaugh and Grapeville, 7:30 am Creature observed
April 20, 1974	Delmont, 1:45 am (UFO)
April 28, 1974	Hempfield Township, 11:15 pm (UFO)
May 4, 1974	near Ligonier, Strange activities at a summer camp
May 7, 1974	near Ligonier, Return investigation to summer camp
May 10, 1974	near Ligonier, Camper reports strange experience
Week of May 14, 1974	Herminie, 11:30 pm Gorilla-like creature
About May 20, 1974	Near Delmont, Large creature observed
May 23, 1974	Sewickley, Allegheny County, 6 pm Being in the metallic outfit
May 30, 1974	Burnsville, Washington County, 9:30 pm (UFO)
May 1974	Clearfield County, 9 pm Light from UFO strikes witnesses
May 1974	Ulster, Bradford County, (UFO)
June 14, 1974	Upper Darby, Delaware County, 9:10 pm (UFO)
July 16, 1974	Greensburg, Something heavy moves into the woods
July 20, 1974	Pittsburgh, Allegheny County, 12:55 pm (UFO)
July 24, 1974	Laughlintown, 9:35 pm (UFO)
August 14, 1974	Butler, Butler County, 9:35 pm (UFO)
August 17, 1974	Jeannette, White gorilla-like creature spotted
August 21, 1974	Youngwood, 9:35 pm (UFO)
September 5, 1974	Evans City, Butler County, 9:30 pm (UFO)
About September 9, 1974	Delmont, evening, A strange report
September 17, 1974	Adamsburg, 9 pm (UFO)
September 19, 1974	Brenizer, 10 pm Strange sounds

Date	Location & Event
September 24, 1974	Midland, Beaver County, 9 pm UFO chases truck
September 26, 1974	Towanda, Bradford County, 9:35 pm (UFO)
September 30, 1974	Arona, 12:15 am (UFO)
October 3, 1974	Oley, Berks County, 1:48 am (UFO)
October 27, 1974	McKees Rocks, Allegheny County, 7:15 pm (UFO)
October 28, 1974	Connellsville, Fayette County, 7:02 pm (UFO)
November 23, 1974	off Avenue B Street, Latrobe, 9 pm Boy sees man-like creature
November 23, 1974	Jumonville, Fayette County, Dark figure approaches car
November 26, 1974	Jeannette, 7:30 pm, Hovering UFO
December 29, 1974	Gibsonia area, Allegheny County, Strange tracks
December 30, 1974	Mount Lebanon, Allegheny County, Last UFO sighting in 1974

Stan Gordon

Stan Gordon is an internationally recognized UFO and Bigfoot researcher. He is the primary investigator of the December 9, 1965, UFO crash-recovery incident near Kecksburg, PA. and producer of the 1998 award winning video documentary, *Kecksburg The Untold Story*. He is the author of the book, *Really Mysterious Pennsylvania*.

He has appeared on network television documentaries, including the Sci-Fi Channel, Discovery Channel, and History Channel. He has been featured on many television shows, including *Unsolved Mysteries*, *Sightings*, *Inside Edition*, *A Current Affair*, *Fox News Channel* and *Creepy Canada*. Gordon has been featured in numerous newspaper stories and magazine articles, some of which include the *Pittsburgh Press*, *The Philadelphia Inquirer*, and *The Denver Post*. He has been a guest on many national and international radio shows, including the popular *Coast to Coast*.

In 1969, Gordon established a UFO Hotline where the public could report sightings to him to investigate. In 1970, Gordon founded the Westmoreland County UFO Study Group (WCUFOSG), the first of three volunteer research groups which he would establish to investigate UFO sightings or other strange occurrences reported in the Keystone state.

Since November 1993, Gordon continues to investigate and document strange incidents reported from across Pennsylvania as an independent researcher. Over the years, Gordon has been involved with the investigation of thousands of mysterious incidents from across Pennsylvania.

Gordon is a former PA State Director for the Mutual UFO Network (MUFON), and was its first recipient in 1987 of the MUFON "Meritorious Achievement in a UFO Investigation Award". He also lectures nationally on the UFO and Bigfoot subject. Gordon has written numerous articles about these strange incidents and many books and publications have included his research as well.

Stan Gordon was trained as an electronics technician who specialized in radio communications. He has worked in the advanced consumer electronics sales field for over forty years. Since 1965, Gordon has been conducting on-scene investigations of strange encounters in Pennsylvania. Many of his news items and reports are available at his website, www.stangordon.info.

He resides in Greensburg, PA.

Roger Marsh

Roger Marsh is a content producer who works as a writer, playwright, Web producer and independent filmmaker as Tremont Avenue Productions. Roger is Director of Communications for both the Mutual UFO Network (MUFON) and Stan Gordon's UFO Anomalies Zone. He is a UFO and paranormal writer with Examiner.com and InCahoots.TV. He is the co-editor, with Philip Haddad, of *Ron Paul Speaks* (Lyons Press, 2008). He is the co-author of *Julie Taymor: Art on Stage and Screen*, (Wright Group/McGraw-Hill, Spring 2005.) As an acquisitions editor for major book publishers, hundreds of his book projects have been distributed both domestically and internationally, including *UFO Encounters and Beyond*, *Ghost Towns of the American West*, *The Holocaust Chronicle*, and *The New York Times* bestseller, *Ross Perot: What Does He Stand For?*

Roger wrote and directed the independent film, *Mars Attacks Mt. Pleasant* (2008); and *Haunted R&R Station* (2007). Ten of his plays have been produced – all works of comedy, including his serial dramedy, *Dime Novel Radio Theater*. Roger lives in Chicago with his wife, Joyce, and daughter, Laine.

Contact Information

Stan is interested in receiving reports of UFOs, Bigfoot, and other strange events in Pennsylvania, as well as information concerning the 1965 Kecksburg UFO case. He can be reached through the following channels:

Mailing Address:
Stan Gordon
PO Box 936
Greensburg, PA 15601

Phone
724-838-7768

E-mail
Paufo@comcast.net
sightings@stangordon.info

Website
www.stangordon.info

To order a copy of Stan's award-winning video documentary about the 1965 Kecksburg UFO crash on DVD titled, *Kecksburg: The Untold Story*, or his book, *Really Mysterious Pennsylvania*, order through his website, or call by phone.

RESEARCH RESOURCES
(Web Sites/Contact Info)

Stan Gordon's UFO Anomalies Zone : www.stangordon.info

Report UFO, Bigfoot and other strange incidents: sightings@
stangordon.info, paufo@comcast.net

BORU—Dan Hageman: www.boru-ufo.com

Center for UFO Studies: www.cufos.org

Coalition for Freedom of Information: www.freedomofinfo.org

CUE—Brian and Terrie Seech: www.center-for-unexplained-
events.350.com

Inexplicata—Scott Corrales: www.inexplicata.blogspot.com

Jim Brown's Destinations: www.jimsdestinations.com

John Ventre: www.johnventre.com

Keith Bastianini: www.heavensshadow.com

Kecksburg VFD: www.kecksburgvfd.com

MUFON: www.mufon.com

National UFO Reporting Center: www.nuforc.org

Paranormal Society of PA: www.paranormalpa.net

Patty Wilson: pineycreekpress@yahoo.com

Pennsylvania MUFON: www.mufonpa.com

Pennsylvania Bigfoot Society: www.pabigfootsociety.com

Location Index

Milton. 47
Monongahela 74, 112, 308
Monroe County. 148
Monroeville 82
Mon Valley 74
Mountain View. 55, 141
Mount Lebanon 295
Mount Pleasant. 225, 289
MUFON. 16, 59, 297, 311, 314, 342
Murrysville. 46

N

Natrona Heights 217, 218
New Alexandria 78, 138, 158, 215, 276
New Castle 216, 220, 250, 251
New Sewickley 73
New Stanton. 79, 275
Northampton County 48
North Huntingdon . . 212, 216, 260, 261
Northumberland County   48
Norvelt 106, 221

O

Ohiopyle. 256, 266, 299
Ohioville. 245, 249
Oley 291

P

Penn Hills. 31, 189, 190, 191, 193
Pennsylvania Dutch . 143
Philipsburg. 225
Pittsburgh. 40, 64
Pleasant Unity 41
Plum. 76
Pocopson Township . 216

R

Radebaugh 77, 79, 81, 134, 137, 277
Reading 44
Rillton 220, 225
Robesonia. 49
Rockwood. 220
Ruffsdale 161

S

Saint Vincent Cemetery   94
Saltsburg 212, 222
Scottdale. 222
Sewickley 280
Slickville. 90
Somerset County. . . . 139, 220
Spring Mills 53
Stahlstown 46

CPSIA information can be obtained at www.ICGtesting.com
Printed in the USA
LVOW102250280613

340822LV00008B/113/P